When the Bough Breaks

By Aphrodite Matsakis, Ph.D.

NEW HARBINGER PUBLICATIONS, INC.

Publisher's Note

This publication is designed to provide accurate and authoritative information in regard to the subject matter covered. It is sold with the understanding that the publisher is not engaged in rendering psychological, financial, legal, or other professional services. If expert assistance or counseling is needed, the services of a competent professional should be sought.

Copyright © 1991 by Aphrodite Matsakis
New Harbinger Publications, Inc.
5674 Shattuck Avenue
Oakland, CA 94609

Library of Congress Catalog Card Number: 90-63758

Printed on recycled paper

Cover design by Sheri Liebscher

Printed in the United States of America

1st Printing April, 1991 5,000 copies
2nd Printing January, 1992 5,000 copies

Table of Contents

Dedication

Ernest Hemingway once wrote, "Life breaks everyone and afterwards, many are strong in the broken places."

This book is dedicated to someone whose life exemplifies the truth of these words: my darling daughter, Theodora, who endured so much, yet emerged so beautiful, inside and out, so full of life and compassion for others, and so full of the joy of life.

Foreword

Over the last ten years, mental health researchers and child protection professionals have conclusively documented the widespread prevalence of child sexual abuse and the psychological risks it poses to both child victims and adult survivors. Extensive media coverage has conveyed this new information about child sexual abuse to the general public, including its prevalence, patterns of occurrence, and possible aftereffects. As a consequence, it is now recognized that sexual molestation is neither the rarity nor the aberration it once was believed to be; rather, its frequencey has been obscured by its taboo nature, the secrecy which surrounded it, and a misunderstanding of its dynamics. Children who complained of or reported abuse were often disbelieved or blamed, responses which served to reinforce the feelings of shame, guilt, confusion, and powerlessness originally engendered by the abuse.

Yet even today, with all of this newly acquired knowledge about sexual abuse, little information is available to the public about how to deal with a report of molestation and how to effectively assist a child who makes such a report. In particular, this information has not been made available to parents of children who report abuse, especially abuse perpetrated by another member of the family, a friend, or an acquaintance. Dr. Aphrodite Matsakis has written *When the Bough Breaks* to fill in this knowledge gap by educating parents. She emphasizes the importance of a compassionate and supportive response by a parent to an abused child. Such a response has the potential to prevent the "second injury" which commonly accompanies victimization. The second injury occurs when someone from whom the victim expects protection and empathy responds in a non-helpful and nonempathetic fashion. In contrast, a compassionate response, especially from a parent, has the potential to counterbalance the initial corrosive impact of the abuse. It also serves to prevent longer-term aftereffects and problems.

Dr. Matsakis recognizes that a parent is personally affected by the child's experience and report of sexual abuse (especially when the abuse is incestuous and issues of family betrayal and divided loyalty come into play, or when the parent was abused in childhood). In fact, the parent can be affected to such a degree that he or she can become vicariously traumatized or the victim of what has been labelled "secondary victimization." The parent has the complicated task of contending with his or her own reactions while tending to the physical and emotional needs of the child and maintaining the rest of the family.

This book supports the parent in two ways: by outlining and responding to the typical feelings a parent has in reaction to the disclosure of abuse (thus modeling the parent's response to the child) and by providing concrete information about child sexual abuse and its patterns, the signs and symptoms of abuse exhibited by a child, initial and longer-term aftereffects, ways to help, outside sources of help, and ways to evaluate the helpers and their effectiveness (thus assisting the parent to be informed and empowered in responding to the child). Several case examples are included in the text which realistically depict abuse scenarios in various types of families while illustrating how different values and parenting styles assist or hinder the child's recovery.

Dr. Matsakis is very straightforward in her description of the post-traumatic responses that are characteristic of abuse (or the post-abuse syndrome). She describes how serious and harrowing abuse effects can be, even in a very young child, and how and why such aftereffects develop. A detailed explanation of the healing process is presented, including what emotions are typical to the various phases of the process. Parents are offered concrete and pragmatic information about how to approach the child and how to offer effective assistance. The discussion of therapy covers locating, assessing, and working with a therapist and evaluating the child's therapeutic progress. This book further informs parents about the more severe consequences of abuse, such as acute depression, substance abuse, eating disorders, self-harm, and suicidality, and what resources are available for these various problems (specialized therapy or treatment programs, medication, short- or long-term hospitalization, and so on).

A parent has a special role in soothing an injured child and in re-establishing the child's security and well-being. This is especially true in the case of sexual abuse (and even more so in the case of incest) when the child's sense of safety in the world, trust in others, and positive sense of self have been shaken. As a clinician who specializes in working with adults who were sexually abused as children, I have had occasion to observe firsthand the damage done by an insensitive, blaming, or ill-informed response. The adult survivor's feelings of betrayal, grief, and mistrust are intensified and the damage of the abuse is compounded especially when the poor response is from a parent.

In defense of parents of the previous generation, few if any resources were available to educate and assist them. They did the best they could in the absence of information and in an atmosphere marked by taboo and silence. But the overall response was deficient, negative consequences were intensified rather than healed, and the toll taken by the abuse has escalated tragically.

When the Bough Breaks provides this previously missing information and thus offers the means of breaking the vicious psychological cycle of child sexual abuse. This crucial information makes the child's emotions and the healing process comprehensible to the parent while empowering him or her to competently support the child. I am grateful to Dr. Matsakis for her compassionate concern for both child and parent and for providing this valuable resource.

Christine A. Courtois, Ph.D.
Author, Healing the Incest Wound: Adult Survivors in Treatment
Psychologist, Independent Practice,
Washington, D.C.
Clinical Consultant
Abuse and Dissociative Disorders
Recovery Program
HCA Dominion Hospital
Falls Church, VA

Preface

I have known many losses in my life—the premature death of a child, an unhappy marriage and traumatic divorce, and financial ruin. But nothing devastated me more than learning that my eldest daughter had been sexually abused when she was ten.

Just recently I met the ten-year-old daughter of a friend. This little girl had trust in her eyes, smiled a lot, and was playing happily with some toys. I burst into tears, remembering my own daughter at ten. Her eyes were full of sadness, worry, and fear. She stopping playing at ten and hardly ever smiled or laughed. Instead, she sat on the living room couch for hours staring into space, unable to tell anyone how she felt. Her only other emotion seemed to be anger. Even when she was angry, she couldn't identify the source of her rage. She had a wall around her heart and trusted no one, not even me.

I didn't know what was troubling her until, at age sixteen, she told me about the abuse. She had kept it a secret from everyone for over six years. Perhaps she had repressed the memory entirely. Like many sexual abuse survivors, my daughter spent years taking out her anger at her abuser on herself in the form of self-hatred and depression. She dressed as if in mourning and seemed to take no pleasure from life. At times, she inflicted pain on herself in the form of mutilation. She was even suicidal.

Two hospitalizations, numerous therapists, and thousands of dollars (and prayers) later, my daughter is now beginning to love herself. She no longer wants to die, and laughs almost every day. Yet there were several years when the doctors and mental health professionals were not certain whether or not she would make it.

I wasn't sure if I would make it either. The strain of worrying about her, trying to find the appropriate care, and dealing with the multitude of responsibilities that attend having a hospitalized loved one taxed all my strengths.

The hardest part was making decisions about my daughter's care. Not only her psychological well-being, but her actual life was at stake. As a mental health professional, I spend a significant portion of my life dealing with these issues; and yet I felt overwhelmed. The questions were many and each seemed harder to answer than the last. Did my daughter need hospitalization, or could she be treated in an outpatient program? Once it was decided that hospitalization was necessary, which of the available hospital programs was best? How could I interview a potential facility or therapist to determine its appropriateness for my child?

What if I didn't agree with—or like—some of the professionals I met? What about those professionals who hadn't read even one book or attended one workshop on sexual abuse, yet considered themselves capable of helping my daughter? How could I be certain that a particular professional was competent? And even if I was convinced of a lack of competence, how advisable was it to change therapists (or facilities) midstream?

Should I talk to my daughter about the abuse, or leave her healing entirely in the hands of other mental health professionals? Did I have the right to inquire about her therapy sessions and the nature of her treatment, or would that be prying and intrusive? What about medication? And last but not least, how was I to pay for all these therapists, doctors, hospitalizations, and medications?

The questions were many, the answers few. I consulted many professionals and read every book on sexual abuse I could find. I also turned to friends and family to help me with some of the most powerful feelings I have ever had in my life—my rage at my child's abuser, who not only robbed her of her sexual innocence, but of much of her childhood and adolescence as well; those terrible feelings of helplessness when I realized that I could not undo the abuse and that my love and devotion alone would not heal my daughter's psychic scars; and my sadness that crimes such as child sexual abuse not only exist, but are widespread throughout our society.

The sexual abuse of children or teenagers creates a crisis not only for the victims, but also for their families and friends. It is not only the abused child who needs information and support but the relatives and friends as well. It is to you parents, relatives, and friends of the abused child that this book is dedicated. I hope that it will increase your understanding of sexual abuse, provide you with information about available therapies and treatment programs, and lend you some support as you attempt to cope with the overwhelming pain that comes with the knowledge that your child—the child you love so deeply—has been so wrongfully misused.

This book is based on my personal experience with sexual abuse, a review of the literature, some fifteen years of clinical experience working with sexual abuse survivors in psychotherapy, and on interviews with several dozen parents of sexually abused children.

Acknowledgments

I would like to gratefully acknowledge Ms. Terry Lord, whose creative input, encouragement, and extensive experience helping troubled children and their parents helped make this book possible. Her many substantive additions, careful editing, and persistent dedication greatly improved the quality of this book and increased its usefulness to parents. I would like to thank Barbara Quick for her editorial input, as well as the many dedicated doctors and therapists and their staffs who helped to save my daughter's life.

Chief among these outstanding professionals are Dr. Brenda Sigall, Dr. Carole Rayburn, Dr. Ginger Hamilton, Dr. Frederick Jacobson, Dr. Thomas Silber and the Adolescent Medicine staff of Children's Hospital in Washington, D.C.; and Dr. David Roth, Dr. Michael Edelstein, and the staff at Sheppard and Eunoch Pratt Hospital in Towson, Maryland.

I also want to thank my parents, Dr. and Mrs. Nicholas and Theodora Matsakis; my younger daughter, Magdalena; my brother and his wife, Demetrios and Cynthia Matsakis; and their two children, Nicholas and Kalliroi, for the many sacrifices they made on behalf of my hurting daughter and for their abundant love, which helped make her whole again.

A Note on the Text

To avoid the grammatical morass of nonsexist diction, I've used female pronouns in chapters 1, 3, 5, 7, and 9 when referring to the gender of your child, and male pronouns for all the rest. Naturally, you should give each chapter equal weight whether your child is a boy or a girl.

Emily's Story

Emily Smith was the girl who had everything. She lived in one of the nicest suburbs of the city. She was popular at school and always made the honor roll. She had all the clothes she wanted. She had her own room. The money for her college education was already in the bank. She had two younger sisters who adored her and her father was a prominent attorney active in both community and church affairs. It was too bad about Mrs. Smith—always so tired; not exactly an invalid, just run down. But Emily managed the household by herself.

Emily was "special" to her father from her very birth—not just because she was the first child, but because she had his blond hair and deep blue eyes. When he bathed Emily as an infant, he would stroke her vulva and, when his wife wasn't looking, would penetrate her vagina and anus with his finger. Once Mrs. Smith caught him and shouted, "Stop that!" "Don't overreact," he answered, "I was just seeing what it was like and getting her ready for when she's older." Mrs. Smith said nothing more.

As Emily grew older, her father continued to take an interest in her bathing and would fondle her genitals under the guise of washing and drying her. Sometimes he would fondle her nipples as well.

When Emily was eight years old, her mother had a major depressive episode during which she cried on Emily's shoulder and asked Emily to help her with most of the household chores. Mrs. Smith's major complaint was that she was disappointed in her marriage and that her husband was "mean" to her. At the same time, Mr. Smith began complaining to Emily that her mother was so depressed most of the time that he didn't feel he had a wife.

By the time Emily was ten years old, she was doing most of the housework and cooking. She and her sister would often eat dinner alone, or with their father, because their mother was too tired to come to the table. When Mr. Smith would help Emily clean up after dinner, he would stroke her hair, tickle her arm, and caress her back, all the while telling her how pretty she was and what a wonderful "little wife" she was, too. Soon he began rubbing her buttocks as well. Emily felt uncomfortable but didn't know what to say.

Then Mrs. Smith went into the hospital to deliver her third child and remained there for several weeks recovering from a difficult birth. One night Mr. Smith went into Emily's bedroom, sat by her bed, and began to fondle her genitals and chest. Emily woke up, but being frightened and confused, pretended she was asleep. Even when her father put his penis in her mouth and instructed her to fondle his scrotum and rectal area, Emily pretended to be asleep.

The next day Emily told herself she had had a bad dream, but that night Mr. Smith came again. This happened again and again, until Emily grew to expect his visits to her bedside to abuse her. She began to develop a disturbed sleeping pattern where she would wake up every so often and look to see if there was a pair of shoes showing under the crack in the door. She also learned to dissociate from her body and to imagine that while her father was abusing her, she was a fly on the wall, or a doll in her doll chest.

When Mrs. Smith arrived home from the hospital the visits became less frequent, but they didn't stop. Emily continued to pretend to be asleep and her father continued to assault her, all the while telling her how much he loved her, how pretty she was, and warning her never to tell anyone—especially her mother—what they did together. "It's our special secret. If you tell, you won't be able to live with me and Mommy any more and Daddy will die."

Emily was never assaulted during the day, but her father would often peek into her room while she was dressing or try to watch her in the bathroom. A few times Mrs. Smith caught him at it. "What are you doing?" she'd ask. "Don't make a big deal out of nothing," he'd snap and would choose that moment to pick an argument over something. There were times when Mrs. Smith would be tending her baby in the middle of the night and pass Emily's room. Looking in she would see her husband there. "Our little girl's gone and had another bad dream," he'd whisper, waving Emily's mother away.

By the time Emily was twelve, the assaults had reached full intercourse. Emily tried to pretend to be asleep but her father would talk to her even while abusing her. He would fill her ears with stories of woe about being married to a wife who neglected him. He wanted to leave his wife but then she would probably starve to death because she had no skills and no one else would want her. He also stayed because he loved his children and, after all, half a mother was better than none.

When Emily began to menstruate, Mr. Smith arranged to get birth control pills for her. He kept telling her that he only tolerated his marriage because of her and that as long as he "loved" her, the family could stay together and her sisters would be taken care of. Although usually loving, on occasion Mr. Smith would threaten Emily and promise to have her committed to a mental hospital if she ever told.

Emily couldn't tell because she was denying that the abuse ever happened. Denial is an amazing defense. Like many incest survivors,

Emily was able to shove the trauma into the recesses of her mind and not deal with it.

But she wasn't the only one not dealing with it. Mrs. Smith would be watching television with her husband and he would get up and disappear for an hour or so. She never asked him where he went. Once she was looking through Emily's purse and found the birth control pills. "What are these?" she asked. "Oh, I don't know," Emily answered. Mrs. Smith didn't ask any more questions.

"She knew! She must have known! She should have known!" Emily would later shout at her therapist. But Mrs. Smith acted as if nothing were happening. Instead she turned to Emily for emotional support. Mrs. Smith was preoccupied with herself and limited in her ability to function as a protective mother. She was more than glad that Emily assumed many of the household tasks and that, when Mrs. Smith was "tired," Emily would accompany her father as he did the food shopping or attended community meetings.

Emily was the perfect child until she was sixteen years old and announced that she was going to kill herself.

Up until now, she had turned down all dates, claiming she had too much homework or household work to do. She would go to group activities, but never with just one boy. Her father had told her that he would kill her if he found her with anyone else.

About the time she decided to kill herself, she stopped attending any social events and spent more and more time alone in her room. She had had nightmares since her father first started assaulting her, but now the nightmares were more frequent and more intense. She would wake up consumed with terror.

She also began cutting her legs with a razor blade. At least while she was cutting herself she could feel something. Even feeling pain was better than feeling nothing.

She announced her impending suicide very calmly. "If I don't feel better by my birthday, I'm going to kill myself. I've already gone to the library and found out what pills to take. No matter what you do, you can't stop me," she informed her parents. Her father shrugged her off, but her mother realized that her daughter was in trouble and suggested she go to a school counselor for help.

Emily went but was unable to open her mouth. She was too ashamed of the incest to talk about it. She went a few times and talked of trivial matters but could never approach her real problem. Finally she stopped seeing the counselor altogether and spent even more time alone in her room. Since Mrs. Smith had never talked with the counselor herself, or asked Emily if the counseling helped, she never knew when Emily quit.

One evening Mrs. Smith found Emily comatose in her room from an overdose of sleeping pills and tranquilizers. She called an ambulance. After Emily was out of danger, the emergency room staff recommended a psychiatric consultation. The Smiths were reluctant—but under pressure from the hospital staff, they agreed to a one-time consultation with a psychiatrist.

Because Emily was in a state of denial, she did not mention the abuse to the psychiatrist. However, because she said she still planned to kill herself, the doctor recommended psychiatric hospitalization.

It was while hospitalized that Emily was finally able to mention the incest to her therapist and begin the healing process. As required by law, the therapist informed protective authorities about the incest. Within a week, Mr. Smith was notified that, should his wife or daughter decide to prosecute, he would stand trial for child sexual abuse. Mr. Smith claimed that Emily was "crazy" and had always had problems.

Mrs. Smith also was in denial, acting as if nothing had happened and as if her life could go on as before. It couldn't. Whatever happened to the Smith family in the future, they couldn't go back.

1

What Is Child Sexual Abuse?

Toward a Working Definition

What is child sexual abuse? Is it the same as child rape? Incest? Or child molestation? Does Mr. Smith's fondling of Emily's genitals when she was an infant constitute child sexual abuse, or did sexual abuse only occur after he began having intercourse with her when she was twelve?

Although legal definitions of child sexual abuse vary from state to state, many mental health workers have adopted the definition used by the National Center for Child Abuse and Neglect (NCCAN). Here child sexual abuse is defined as contact or interaction between a child and an adult when the child is being used for the sexual stimulation of another person.[1]

The abuser may be a stranger but is more likely a relative, caretaker, friend, or neighbor. In Emily's case, it was her father. While a child is any person under the age of eighteen, the abuser can be of any age. According to the NCCAN, "Sexual abuse may be committed by a person under the age of eighteen years old, when that person is either significantly older than the victim, or when the abuser is in a position of power or control over that child."[2]

Basically, child sexual abuse refers to two forms of sexual contact: sexual interaction between a child and a much older person, and any form of sexual behavior forced upon a child regardless of the age of the perpetrator. Sexual abuse can be heterosexual or homosexual and can include kissing, fondling, penile intrusion (oral, anal, or genital), and any form of molestation, as well as sexual exploitation. Therefore, Mr. Smith's fondling of his infant daughter's vaginal area constitutes child sexual abuse. If Mrs. Smith had fondled her daughter in such a manner, it would also be considered child sexual abuse.

Also, if Emily had had an older brother and he had forced her to pose in the nude or expose her genitals for his entertainment or that of his friends, it would also be considered child sexual abuse, even if he or his friends never touched her.

Sexual abuse, even if it involves no physical pain or violence, is still an assault and/or a violent act. Some abusers use violence to get the child's compliance, but others coerce their victims through emotional appeals for the child's love or appeals to the child's need for affection, attention, and nurturing. Like many fathers involved in incest, Emily's father did not need to use violence to gain her compliance. Yet his actions were assaultive; when she tried to resist him or indicated her dislike of the activity, he punished her by withdrawing his love and threatening to abandon the family.

In her book, *Father-Daughter Incest*, Judith Herman distinguishes between incestuous and seductive fathers. Whereas incestuous fathers actually have sexual contact with their daughters, seductive fathers engage in a variety of sexually motivated behavior toward their daughters without necessarily touching them. For example, a seductive father may spy on his daughter while she is dressing, press her for details about her sexual anatomy, her sexual feelings, and her sexual involvements (if he allows her to have any); talk about his sex life and sexual interests and fantasies in great detail to his daughter; expose his genitals to his daughter; and in many other ways sexualize the relationship and intrude on the daughter's right to sexual privacy.

Without ever touching his daughter, the seductive father communicates to her that she is of sexual interest to him. While the psychological harm caused by an incestuous father is greater than the harm caused by a merely seductive one, the negative consequences for the daughter of a seductive father can be long-term and extremely damaging. The daughter may live in fear and anxiety, never knowing when her father will decide to act on his obvious attraction to her.

As Emily's story illustrates, sexual abuse generally does not occur just for sexual gratification, but also to satisfy some of the perpetrator's psychological needs. Mr. Smith projected many of his dependency needs and needs for approval and acceptance onto his eldest daughter. Despite his outward success, inside he was an insecure and needy man.

In many cases, child molesters claim to be sexually attracted to children. Generally, however, such people molest children to make up for their own feelings of inferiority, because they were themselves abused in the past, or because of a variety of other emotional problems.[3]

Similarly, it is a myth that the incestuous father turns to his daughter because his sexual relationship with his wife is unfulfilling.[4] Many an incestuous father has been found to be sexually active with his wife (or another adult woman) as well as with his daughter. When this phenomenon is probed, some men admit to taking advantage of what they see as their "rights" as men. Other men crave the assertion of their power or dominance. A man who molests may feel an emotional void that he seeks to fill in this intimate relationship with his own child.

How Prevalent Is Sexual Abuse?

Although it's extremely difficult to measure the pervasiveness of sexual abuse, several well-designed studies support the view that at least one in four females and one in nine males are sexually molested by their eighteenth birthday.[5] In fact, child sexual abuse may be far more widespread than available statistics indicate.

Like wife abuse and child beating, child sexual assault tends to be an underreported crime, especially within the family (when it is called incest). The Merriam-Webster Dictionary defines incest as "sexual intercourse between persons so closely related that marriage is illegal." However, this dictionary definition is too narrow in that it excludes other, equally devastating forms of sexual contact—for example, oral sex and fondling. It also excludes other sexually exploitative activity, such as masturbatory behaviors; having the child pose for provocative or nude pictures; or telling the child sexually explicit or provocative stories for the titilation of the storyteller.

Statistics about the prevalence of incest are questionable because incest victims are even less likely than rape victims to report the crime. Often there is family pressure as well as pressure from the abuser to keep the incest a secret. Typically the family system denies, overlooks, or otherwise discounts the reality of the incest and holds the victim responsible for her own victimization.[6] Although the incest may not be particularly frightening to the child at the time (due to a number of factors, not the least of which is a biochemically induced amnesia), it can cause agonizing problems as she grows older.

The NCCAN very conservatively estimates that 4.9 children per 1,000 are physically abused annually and that 2.2 children per 1,000 are sexually abused, mostly by family members.[7] According to Susan Forward, author of *Betrayal of Innocence*, more than ten million Americans have been victimized by incest, with women outnumbering men seven to one.[8] David Finkelhor, one of this country's foremost researchers in the area of child sexual abuse and author of

Child Sexual Abuse: New Theory and Research, estimates that 1,000,000 Americans are victims of father-daughter incest and that some 16,000 new cases occur each year.[9] Finkelhor's data, like Kinsey's data and the data from the three other major surveys on sexual abuse, are based primarily on the reports of white, middle class women. Since statistics for poor and minority women are usually underreported, the actual overall rates of incest may be significantly higher.[10]

Christine Courtois, author of *Healing the Incest Wound: Adult Survivors in Therapy* and counselor to hundreds of incest survivors, writes that "a very substantial percentage of the female population, possibly as high as twenty percent, has had an experience of incestuous abuse at some time in their lives, twelve percent before the age of fourteen, sixteen percent before the age of eighteen. Possibly five percent of all women have been abused by their fathers. Boys are also sexually victimized within the family, but in smaller numbers."[11]

Children, both male and female, may not report the abuse because they fear retaliation, the police, and hospitals, or that they will be blamed or beaten or otherwise punished for "telling." They may also be unable to report the abuse because they, like Emily, have almost totally repressed their memory of it. Such amnesia can be physiological as well as psychological. Not only does the child need to forget in order to cope with the experience, but certain biochemical changes can occur during trauma which induce this amnesia.

According to Van der Kolk and others who have studied traumatized persons and animals,[12] under conditions of extreme stress (such as combat, rape, physical or sexual assault), the body goes into a state of "emergency alert" during which a host of bodily changes can occur. These changes can include increases in adrenalin, heart rate, and blood sugar level; hyperventilation; and shifts in certain neurotransmitters and the endocrine system.

As a result of these bodily changes, it's not unusual for the trauma survivor to go into a "fight-flight-or-freeze" mode. Either she receives a supercharge of adrenalin which enables her to fight or flee from the enemy or source of danger, or she receives a nonadrenalin charge which creates a "freeze" response. In combination with a series of complex endocrine and neurological changes, the "freeze" response can include a state of amnesia, or partial amnesia, regarding the traumatic event (or series of events). The "freeze" and amnesia reactions are considered to be ways in which human beings cope with the vast overstimulation of the central nervous system that occurs during trauma.

Emotionally, the traumatic event gives rise to fear, grief, and rage. There is also heightened anxiety at confronting one's powerlessness and potential death. These emotions can be so painful and intense that the victim needs to repress them, either totally or in part. Emotionally, the child protects herself from these unbearable feelings by tuning them out, either completely or in part.

Sam, now forty-two, wasn't sure how often he was sexually abused as a child by his brother. He remembered a particularly violent incident in which his brother threatened to put a wire hanger in Sam's anus. According to Sam, this one-time occurrence did not mean that he had been an abused child. In some of his therapy sessions, Sam recalled additional incidents of abuse by his brother, but in other sessions he denied having been abused, expressed resentment about the label of "abused child," and trivialized the wire hanger incident as "boys' play." Whether or not Sam considered himself to be sexually abused, he most definitely was.

Males especially tend to remain silent or be ambivalent about disclosing their abuse, because they do not want to be seen as powerless, or suffer the shame of appearing to be passive victims.[13] In our society, victims are not perceived as "masculine." Finkelhor gives three additional reasons why boys tend not to report abuse:

- "Boys grow up with the male ethic of self-reliance," and with messages such as "don't complain" or "don't have others fight your battles." Consequently, it's harder for them to seek help when they hurt.

- "Boys have to grapple with the stigma of homosexuality surrounding so much sexual abuse."

- "Boys may have more to lose from reporting their victimization experience, e.g., loss of privileges and curtailing of freedoms."[14]

Official statistics do show that child sexual abuse, like other forms of child abuse, is on the rise. According to the most recent available official statistics, since 1980 physical abuse of children has increased by fifty-eight percent and sexual abuse of children has more than tripled.[15]

Is the Sexual Abuse of Children a New Phenomenon?

There are many theorists who feel that statistical increases do not reflect a true increase in child sexual abuse, but are merely indicators of increased public awareness of the problem and improved reporting methods. However, researchers in the field (myself among them) contend that this is not actually the case. Child sexual abuse is truly on the rise in our society. The following factors are implicated:

- Child pornography and the sexualization of children

- The sexual revolution

- The backlash against sexual equality

- Untreated child sexual abuse from previous generations

- Changes in family life—for example, the increase in single-parent households or households in which both parents work, leaving children unattended for significant periods of time[16]

The sexual revolution attempted to eradicate the Puritanical belief that sexual activity outside of marriage is sinful, and tried to legitimize a wide range of nonmarital sexual activity that had previously been socially unacceptable, if not unmentionable, in many circles. "If it feels good, do it" was the message.

However, as with any historical change, there is a tendency to go to extremes. In the wide swing from "sex is bad" to "sex is good," some people and groups disregarded appropriate limitations and boundaries. Although the sexual revolution was helpful to many people in reducing their guilt over their sexual feelings and activities, it was harmful when interpreted by certain individuals to mean that sex is "good"—in other words, harmless and satisfying—under almost all circumstances. Clearly, sexual behavior that falls into the category of rape or child sexual abuse is not "good" for the victim and, ultimately, not "good" for the perpetrator either.

Rapid social change in general can be associated with the rise of child sexual abuse. According to Justice and Justice, who wrote *The Broken Taboo: Sex in the Family,* changes in our society have led to greater stress for both adults and children. Greater geographical and vocational mobility, for instance, have made human relationships more fragmented. The family—which historically has served as the shock absorber for stress—cannot meet the demands placed on it in this new environment.

Our society is changing rapidly, and traditional roles are changing with it. Parents are now "buddies" with their children. There is less differentiation between adults and children: they dress alike in some cases and are credited with similar emotions. Children are now being taxed with greater decision-making responsibilities about their own conduct and values. Thirteen-year-old girls are expected by their peers to have boyfriends and wear makeup, and fifteen-year-old boys are "nerds" if they haven't "done it" yet.

A lack of distinctions between adults and children is nothing new: before the industrial revolution, children were traditionally depicted in painting as miniature adults; they were also saddled, in the days before child labor laws, with adult responsibilities. Our ideal of childhood as a protected and idyllic time of life is fairly modern. In some ancient societies, such as Egypt and Rome, sex with children and incest in particular situations were part of the cultural norm.

All of our definitions of childhood—as well as adult responsibility—are in the process of changing. Grown men and women strive more frantically than ever to appear youthful and vigorous, and children are being sexualized. Many of today's most seductive high-fashion models are as young as thirteen or fourteen years old. Youth is an ideal that is pursued by millions of adults with billions of dollars.

This blurring of identities has created confusion among both adults and children. Instead of nurturing their children, parents sometimes turn to them for gratification, and sometimes this gratification is pursued sexually. Unlike the sexual use of children in ancient cultures, childhood sexual abuse in modern times is cloaked in secrecy, adding guilt and fear of exposure or punishment to the child's physical and emotional victimization. In this sense, it is indeed a new problem.

How to Tell If Your Child Has Been Abused

When a Child Tells

The most direct sign of abuse is a statement from your child that she has been abused. In the majority of cases, such a statement is not a lie but a definite indicator that abuse has occurred. Children, especially children between the ages of two and seven, rarely make false allegations about abuse unless they have been influenced by an adult, are pathological liars, or have some other overwhelming motive.[17]

In a study of sexual abuse, Klajner-Diamond, Wehrspan, and Steinhauer[18] found that the majority of false allegations were adult-initiated and occurred under one or more of the following conditions:

- The adult suffered from post-traumatic stress disorder as a result of being sexually or otherwise abused or traumatized in the past

- The adult suffered from a serious psychiatric disorder and/or had a symbiotically disturbed relationship with the child

- There was an ongoing custody battle

- The professional involved was convinced that abuse had oc-curred prior to investigating the situation

Those false allegations not initiated by adults were initiated by two types of older children and adolescents:

- Those who had been previously sexually abused and were now seeking revenge or retaliation

- Those who were using the allegation of abuse to cover their own voluntary sexual behavior

If your child tells you that she has been sexually assaulted, believe her. Do not accuse her of lying or making up stories to tor-ment you or make trouble. Far better that you err in believing a lying child than make the disastrous mistake of disbelieving an abused one. Many of the sexual abuse survivors I've seen have tear-fully stated that they didn't know which was worse—the actual abuse or being accused by a parent of lying, "asking for it," or "secretly enjoying it." Many children have been beaten or otherwise severely punished by a disbelieving or blaming parent.

If your child's description of the assault is incoherent or incom-plete, this does not mean that the assault or assaults did not occur. Sexual abuse is a trauma and, like most traumas, may be only par-tially remembered. The inability to remember in a coherent or com-plete fashion is rooted in the biochemical changes that occur in individuals when they're traumatized. Adults also have trouble remembering traumatic incidents; for example, combat soldiers sometimes cannot recall the details of a particularly savage battle. Similarly, sexually abused children have usually suffered from so much fear and confusion that they may have only a fragmentary or otherwise cloudy memory of the abuse. If the abuse was frequent or severe, your child probably had to block out the memory of all or parts of the experience in order to cope. Do not expect perfect recall as a sign that your child is telling the truth.

Four-year-old Donna reported to her mother that one of her father's friends took her into her bedroom and "tickled me all over. He did it to me in the kitchen, too." When Donna's mother asked her if the man had "tickled" her in any other room of the house, Donna said "yes," but couldn't remember which rooms exactly.

The male friend said that Donna was making it all up because she couldn't remember the exact location of all the incidents. Yet Donna's mother was frequently awakened in the middle of the night by her daughter, who was having nightmares. "Hold me, Mommy. I'm scared of that man. I have bad dreams about him."

Obviously, the mother's unwillingness to believe her daughter sprang more from an impulse to deny something unpleasant and frightening than from any lack of detail in Donna's recollection.

Although legal precedent has generally considered children's memory to be "unreliable," research suggests the opposite to be true. By the age of five, children can remember events that occurred up to a year previously. As with adults, it's easier for children to distinguish out-of-the-ordinary events, in contrast to things that are part of their daily routine.[19]

However, children under two can easily misinterpret an event or mix up two or more events and turn them into one episode. In this sense, they actually tend to minimize, rather than exaggerate, the occurrence of abuse.

Children are also highly susceptible to adult suggestion, particularly if the suggestion is given by an adult whom the child wants to please.

It's not until after the age of seven or eight that children can locate past events in terms of the hour, day of the week, or day of the month. Klajner-Diamond, Wehrspann, and Skinhavven found that children of any age can place "an event in context, knowing ... whether it is night or day, or whether it occurred on or near an important event such as their birthday or Christmas."[20]

Judith Herman, in *Father-Daughter Incest,* found that many of the incest victims in her sample harbored considerable hostility toward their mothers, first for not protecting them from the incest, and second for disbelieving or blaming them when they tried to tell on their fathers. Not all incest victims in her experience tried to tell their mothers, but many of those who did reported either being ignored or chastised. Either the mother needed to deny the incest because it would mean the end of her marriage, or she needed to blame her daughter because she lived in fear of her husband or had a limited understanding of family dynamics, including incest.

Other mothers were unable to accept their daughter's revelation because they themselves had been incestuously or otherwise abused as children. When the mother had blocked her traumatic memories as a coping mechanism, she was often unable to truly listen to her daughter or accept that her daughter was being abused, too. Sometimes the mother had been blamed for the incest that victimized her when she was a child and, if she did not receive any help, simply repeated the pattern of blame with her daughter. Dr. Herman also found that while some daughters tried to tell their mothers about the abuse, they did so only indirectly, by complaining about physical problems, or by saying that they hated their fathers without specifying why.

Sons may have an even greater difficulty telling their mothers or fathers about being abused. They may feel they have failed to fulfill their parents' expectations of them to be strong and manly. Their code of honor may place an even greater taboo on "tattling." Finally, in many cases, they have to deal with the added stigma of homosexuality.

Placing Blame

No matter what you think or have been told in the past, or how seductive or attention-seeking you may find your child to be, the abuse was not your child's fault. The adult or older person involved is responsible. It is he who abused his authority or power in order to exploit your child. Blaming your child for the abuse will only reinforce your child's sense of shame, guilt, and powerlessness, and will leave her feeling abandoned.

Don't ever make such statements as, "You must have asked for it. You must have liked it. You've always been too weak to stand up for yourself. You deserve it—always wanting attention." Even if you feel like making such a comment, don't. Realize that your child is already full of self-blame and doesn't need any more guilt.

Do not chastize yourself for having such blame-the-victim thoughts; such thinking is rampant in our society. It is part of the system of denial that perpetuates child sexual abuse. It would not be unusual if you, like many others, saw your child as somehow being responsible for the abuse. However, if you verbalize your blaming attitudes, you will devastate your child and hamper any subsequent attempts you make to communicate with her or give her help. If these thoughts keep troubling you, write them down and discuss them with a friend or therapist.

Physical and Behavioral Signs of Abuse

There are definite signs to look for if you suspect that your child is being abused. These include torn, stained, or bloodied underwear; pain, itching, or bleeding in the genital area, the rectum, or the breasts; venereal disease, genital infections, or other genital problems inappropriate to your child's age; urinary tract infections; difficulty sitting; psychosomatic symptoms such as choking, gagging, and gastrointestinal problems; excessive or open masturbation (caution should be used, however, when interpreting this as a symptom); and sexually seductive or highly eroticized behavior. Some abused children place objects in their body openings. Others withdraw from all forms of physical touch. Abused children frequently display advanced knowledge about sex in their communications or in their drawings and play. They may mime sexual activity with dolls or tell stories about sexual activities or events.

Some behavioral signs of sexual assault include phobias and sleep problems—sleeping excessively, inability to sleep, nightmares, night terrors—and social problems such as having difficulty separating from parent or caretaker, difficulty making friends, or difficulty maintaining friendships (again, such behaviors are not necessarily signs of abuse). Abused children may act like adults or remain extremely childlike well into adolescence.[21] Emily, as a result of the intensive therapy she received, at age eighteen could hold psychologically sophisticated conversations about various psychiatric disorders. Yet she still needed to play with dolls and sometimes preferred to play with her younger cousins rather than mingle with adults or other teenagers.

Tony, age twelve, who was a top student in his class and was extremely responsible toward his younger brothers and sisters, sucked his thumb every night.

Incest survivors may parent their siblings, take on inappropriate household tasks, suck their thumbs, or revert to baby talk. You may notice that your child is depressed, is having nightmares, or suddenly refuses to go to school. The important point is that your child changes radically from her usual personality and behavior. Use your intuition as a parent: pay attention when you feel that something is wrong.

Teenagers may refuse to date, talk to boys, or otherwise connect with the opposite sex. They may wear multiple layers of clothing, androgynous clothing, or dress only in black to signify their mourning or hide the shape of their bodies. (Again, the sole fact of a teenager dressing oddly is not in itself a signal of abuse: many teenagers dress oddly!) A surer sign of distress is an eating disorder such as anorexia or bulimia. Drug and alcohol addictions, as well as food addictions, are often symptomatic of abuse. Sexually abused children of all ages may engage in delinquent acts and other forms of antisocial behavior. Many runaways, incarcerated adolescents, and child and teen prostitutes are found to have been sexually abused children. Sexually abused children may also engage in acts of self-mutilation or attempted suicide.[22]

In an undetermined number of cases, multiple personality disorder can develop in victims of childhood sexual abuse if the abuse occurs before the age of five and is severe and repeated, involving a highly disturbed parent or caretaker. Out of self-protection, the child develops distinctly different identities, complete with their own personality characteristics, as a way of compartmentalizing and suppressing traumatic memories.

If your child displays any of the above symptoms, this does not necessarily mean that abuse has occurred, only that you should keep it in mind as a possibility. Furthermore, if your child suffers from some of these symptoms, this does not mean that she is mentally ill. In the sexually abused child, these symptoms must be viewed in the context of the child's victimization. They should be seen as coping mechanisms or survival techniques rather than as signs of insanity. Even self-mutilation can be understood as a coping mechanism. As Emily explained, it was "better" to feel the pain of the razorblade on her legs than to feel "nothing at all—totally empty." The physical pain was easier to focus on and bear than the emotional pain and her sense of betrayal.

Sexual abuse can also be suspected if a child displaying any of the above symptoms has spent time with someone who[23]

- Abuses alcohol and/or drugs
- Is physically violent or came from a violent home
- Displays irresponsible, nonadult behavior
- Is emotionally immature, withdrawn, insecure, or inflexible and bossy

As all the latest research has indicated, sexual abusers by no means always fit the stereotype of the lonely, stuttering scout master or the alcoholic lurking behind a tree in the park. Like Emily's father, child sexual abusers can be pillars of our society: doctors, lawyers, teachers, even clerics. If your child is showing signs of abuse, *no one* is above suspicion.

Discussing the Abuse With Your Child

Suppose your child has told you that she has been abused. Or perhaps you suspect abuse because of significant behavior changes such as those just described. What next? You will eventually need to take your child to both a physician and a mental health worker who is trained in sexual abuse. But first you may decide to ask your child a few questions on your own. This is a delicate process that will require a great deal of care and sensitivity on your part. Remember that no matter how careful and sensitive you are, you cannot be your child's therapist, healer, or doctor. Your child will need professional help.

First establish what level of information and understanding your child already has about her body and adult sexuality. If she does not have a vocabulary for sexual organs or behaviors, you will need to teach her the words. You will also need to clarify what sexual abuse or "wrong touching" is, in terms your child can understand.

Use your own body or a doll (preferably an anatomical doll) or draw pictures to identify the sexual organs and demonstrate "wrong touching." For example, you could point to your own sexual organs and label them, if you feel comfortable doing that. Or you could point to the organs on a doll, a figure drawing, or a picture. For the opposite sex, you could use a doll, a picture, or a figure drawing.

Don't go through this exercise with your child unless you're completely comfortable with it: a qualified professional may have an easier time and may make your child feel more at ease. If you decide to proceed yourself, remember to emphasize that all the sexual organs are "good," that they are normal parts of the body, and that it usually "feels good" when they are touched or caressed. However, it is not "good" when they are touched without permission or by certain people in certain ways. There are numerous books available which can help you teach your child about human anatomy and "good and bad" touching. Some of them are listed in the references at the end of this chapter.

Be specific not only about oral sex and intercourse, but also about "tickling," exhibitionism, fondling, and masturbation. Many parents wonder if they should bring up oral sex and intercourse if their child hasn't introduced these subjects first, or hasn't in any way indicated that these behaviors have occurred. The answer is yes, if you feel you can do so without extreme anxiety on your part.

In general, children feel so much shame, guilt, and fear surrounding the abuse that they are highly unlikely to volunteer such information on their own. It's the rare sex-abuse survivor who can straightforwardly say, "Yes, I was penetrated here and I was made to do such and such." Even forty-year-old survivors with the benefit of several years of therapy have difficulty making such statements.

When you ask specific questions about specific sexual activities, you are giving your child permission to talk. Even if she cannot disclose the fact that she was abused the first time you inquire into the matter, the fact that you have been so open will make it possible for her to come to you at some future point in time when she is ready to disclose the abuse or when she has some other sexual concern.

You may wonder, "But what if my child did not experience oral sex or intercourse? Won't I be traumatizing her by asking such explicit questions? Especially if I have to explain to her what oral sex and intercourse are!" Once again, it's better for children to have knowledge about sexual behavior than to remain ignorant. It's their very lack of knowledge about sexual activity that can make them vulnerable to abuse.

An abuser can say, for example, that he is "doing nothing" or that he is "fixing something," or that in order for the child to grow properly she needs him to do this to her, and so on. The ways in which an abuser can take advantage of a child's ignorance are countless. If your child is armed with knowledge, she will know, "This is oral sex, or this is intercourse. This is sex, not play (or whatever)— and this isn't supposed to be happening to me."

Even if your child wasn't subjected to oral sex or intercourse, in asking her about the possibility you are educating her about sexual realities, helping to prevent any future abuse, and communicating to her that you are willing to discuss such matters with her. However, if you cannot talk about sexual matters without intense feelings of anxiety, fear, guilt, or shame, you may want to use the help of a qualified professional or wait until you can discuss the matter more calmly. If you're anxious when you discuss these matters with your child, let her know that your anxiety stems from your concern about her welfare, not from your view that she did something "wrong" or that her sexual organs or sexuality are "sinful" or shameful in themselves.

Let your child know that you are asking about sexual abuse because you have her welfare in mind, not because you want to blame or punish her. Emphasize that she does not have to tell you everything that happened, only whatever she feels comfortable sharing; and that no matter what she says, you will not hit her, yell at her, have her put in jail or a mental hospital, or call her "crazy" or "bad." Neither will you immediately go out and kill or harm the abuser.

All these points are important because abusers frequently tell children that if they "tell," their parents will blame, punish, abandon, or "put them away" in an institution. Or they may have said, "Your mother and father won't understand our 'secret.' They'll hurt me if you tell." If the abuser is someone for whom your child feels affection, such appeals can be extremely persuasive.

In speaking to your child, your tone of voice and attitude are as important as the kinds of questions you ask. Reassure her that you love her and are on her side *no matter what*. Tell her that she is not alone; that thousands of children are hurt the way she was hurt every year. Reassure her that you want to protect her from ever being hurt like that again.

Phrase your statements in terms that are appropriate for her age. For example, if she is six, you might say, "Sometimes big people touch little people in ways that are wrong. When big people do this, it is not the child's fault. Ever! If someone touched you in a way that is wrong or that you didn't like, I want you to be sure to tell me."

You want to encourage your child to open up to you as much as possible, yet you do not want to pressure her for information and upset her even more. Generally children are ashamed, afraid, or in denial or repression about their abusive experience. In some cases, they may remember it only on an unconscious level. You need to give your child permission to talk by asking open-ended (but not leading) questions and without making her feel as if she were being questioned by the FBI.

You could say, "If you were abused (hurt, touched in the wrong places, or whatever) it must have been terrible for you. Even if it felt good, you probably were afraid, or confused. You can tell me as much as you want about what happened—but if talking about it is too hard for you, we don't have to talk anymore about it right now.

"You can tell me more later, whenever you want to. I am always ready to listen to anything you want to tell me. If you want to talk to somebody else, there are people who help children who may have been touched in ways that are wrong. I can take you to meet one of these people if you like. Their job is to help you, not to tell on you, or punish you."

Watch your child's face and body as you talk with her. Is she uncomfortable? Does she have that blank look which may mean that she is feeling anxious? If so, ask, "Is talking about this too hard for you now? Shall we stop?" If your child seems hesitant to talk with you or afraid, forget your pride and ask her if she would feel better talking to someone else. If she cannot think of anyone, suggest a favorite relative, neighbor, older friend, or your minister, rabbi, or priest. It's essential that whoever is chosen be someone you can trust to be open-minded and sympathetic. You can also repeat your suggestion about seeing a counselor who specializes in child sexual abuse.

If your child has been sexually abused—no matter how unwilling she is to talk—on some level she knows she is hurting or that there is something wrong. While she may have repressed the memory or be in denial about the abuse, a part of her may want to talk about it and get help. Even if your child refuses to talk to you or anyone else, it's important that you remind her that help is available when she's ready for it.

If your child is young and has never been to a therapist or counselor, you may need to explain what a counselor is and that what she says to that counselor will be confidential. Younger children can be told that counselors are special people who try to help others by listening to whatever is bothering them. People can say whatever they want to counselors—even bad things about Mommy and Daddy—and the counselors won't tell.

Demonstration of How To Cue Recognition With (A) and Without (B and C) Excessive Leading

CHILD: He started rubbing his wiener and that stuff came out.
EXAMINER: What stuff?

A	B	C
CHILD: What do you mean?	CHILD: I don't know, I don't remember.	CHILD: That white stuff.
EXAM.: What kind of stuff? Was it white?	EXAM.: I'll help you. What color was it?	EXAM.: What kind of white stuff?
CHILD: Yeah, that's right.	CHILD: I don't remember.	CHILD: It was ... it was ... I don't remember.
EXAM.: And sticky?	EXAM.: Was it yellow, or white, or red?	EXAM.: Just one drop?
CHILD: How did you know?	CHILD: White, it was white.	CHILD: No, a whole lot.
EXAM.: And did it come shooting out all over the place?	EXAM.: How much was there?	EXAM.: How do you know?
CHILD: Yeah! That's the way it was.	CHILD: I don't remember.	CHILD: Because it went shooting all over the place. It scared me.
	EXAM.: Just one drop, or two or three drops, or a whole lot?	EXAM.: Shooting all over the place: you're kidding.
	CHILD: A whole lot.	CHILD: I am not. That's exactly what happened. I know for sure.
	EXAM.: How do you know?	EXAM.: What makes you so sure?
	CHILD: Because I remember, it came shooting all over the place.	CHILD: Cuz some of it got all over me. It was sticky. Yech!
	EXAM.: If you touched it, was it thin, like water, or sticky like glue, or solid like chocolate pudding?	EXAM.: Can you show me, using the dolls?
	CHILD: Sticky, like glue.	
	EXAM.: How do you know?	
	CHILD: Because I got some of it all over my face.	
	EXAM.: Can you show me, using the dolls?	

Adapted with permission from "Criteria and Methodology for Assertion/Credibility of Sexual Abuse Allegation," by Wehrspann, William; Steinhaver, Paul; Klajna-Diamond, Haling, *Canadian Journal of Psychiatry*, Vol. 32:7. p. 616, 1987.

Regardless of who speaks with your child, it's important that she not be asked leading or directive questions. In the diagram on the facing page,[24] column A is an example of using leading questions which contaminate the child's responses. Whoever talks to the child should stimulate and encourage her memory without providing the expected answer, or by giving her the expected answer sandwiched between other alternatives. Columns B and C are examples of correct styles of questioning.

Your goal in talking to your child is to confirm the abuse and to get information about the abuser. Once you are relatively certain that the abuse occurred, you can take positive steps to help your child cope with, and eventually overcome, some of the initial and long-term psychological consequences.

The Psychological Consequences of Sexual Abuse

Some children are severely affected by sexual abuse, while others have only a few, temporary problems. Some even appear to be relatively unaffected by the experience, although in many of these cases it is only a matter of time until one or more psychological symptoms emerge.[25] In Emily's case, observable symptoms did not appear until she was well into her teens.

A sexually abused child may appear to be functioning normally until another major loss or life stressor—such as the death of a parent, a mugging, or a serious car accident—brings the effects of the abuse to the surface. Major transitions—such as graduation from school or marriage—may also resurrect memories of the abuse. It is not uncommon for a woman to have her first conscious recollections of abuse on her wedding night. Or a woman's memories may resurface when her own daughter reaches the age she had been when she was abused. Publicity about sexual abuse, involvement in a safe and loving relationship, or an experience with massage, hypnosis, or acupuncture can all precipitate repressed memories of abuse.

A crucial element of the trauma of sexual abuse is betrayal. While a child might expect indifference to her needs from a stranger, she expects caring concern or at least the absence of malice from family members and others who assume caretaking or nuturing roles. The child who is abused by strangers suffers less than the child who is abused by an individual she trusted. Such a child learns to associate nurturance and love with eventual betrayal, making it difficult for her to completely trust anyone.

This section on psychological consequences is not meant to frighten you; nor should you assume that your child will necessarily experience any or all of the problems listed. The effects of sexual abuse depend on many factors, including the severity and frequency of the abuse, the difference in age between the abuser and the victim, the relationship between the two, the child's support system, and other life stressors. In general, the more serious reactions tend to appear in children who are victims of incest and who are violently as well as sexually abused. Those who are subjected to actual intercourse and other types of penetration are usually the most severely harmed.

There are no hard and fast rules, however. Fondling in the case of one child can be as traumatic as sodomy for another. As one survivor stated, "My uncle licked me and rubbed me and it scarred me forever. I don't think I'll ever really get over it."

Defense Mechanisms as Coping Strategies

Denial and repression as defense mechanisms are especially prevalent among children who have been abused by members of their own family. It is these children, rather than children who were violated by strangers, who tend to suffer the most severe and long-lasting negative effects. The greater the degree of trust between the child and the abuser, the greater the sense of violation and damage to the child.[26]

Dissociation and blunting are common defense mechanisms of victims. Emily experienced dissociation when she imagined herself as a fly on the wall. Blunting is a minimization or trivialization of feelings. Unlike denial and repression, in which feelings are buried entirely, in blunting, feelings are acknowledged but discounted. A child who is blunting might say, "What my cousin did to me? I guess it affected me, but not that much. Sometimes I think about it, but not a lot." Blunting can also be physiological. A child can say, and believe, "It didn't hurt much," even though she may have suffered genital lacerations and other physical injuries requiring medical attention.

Dr. Courtois writes, "This disconnection or blunting is a survival strategy which often persists into adulthood. It may be quite functional in allowing the victim to cope, but it also masks reactions to the trauma and prevents resolution. Additionally, it causes incest survivors to appear asymptomatic or less injured when in reality they are emotionally deadened as part of the trauma response."[27]

Multiple personality disorder represents perhaps the most extreme form of dissociation. The multiple personality reflects the inability of a very young child to cope with intense and repetitious abuse. Although our knowledge of multiple personality disorder is limited, it is generally felt that the abuse survivor develops an entirely different personality to cope with the abuse. Or she may develop more than one distinct personality as an expression of her various feelings and reactions to the abuse. Usually one of the personalities is dominant; depending on the degree of integration within the abuse survivor, the dominant personality may or may not be aware of the other personalities.

As many as one hundred different personalities in one individual have been recorded. About half of the recorded cases of multiple personality disorder have ten or more personalities. The individual can switch rapidly from one personality to another, usually within a few minutes. Each personality varies in its awareness of the other personalities and, over time, some personalities diminish or disappear entirely. Some personalities have no knowledge of the other personalities; some have partial knowledge, and some may be fully aware of the others. Some of the personalities communicate with each other; some do not.

Don't become alarmed. Unless your child was severely abused in a repeated fashion before the age of five, there is little chance of a multiple personality disorder developing. The sort of abuse that can lead to this disorder is usually inflicted by a highly disturbed parent who is delusional, obsessed with the occult, witchcraft, or some religious perversion that condones child sacrifice and exploitation. If your child has been abused by a babysitter, a neighbor, or even a relative after the age of five, and if the abuse was not repeated, severe, and did not involve witchcraft, religious overtones, or a psychotic or semi-psychotic abuser who was closely related to the child, it's highly unlikely that she'll develop a multiple personality disorder.

Your child may, however, invent a name for an imaginary friend who represents the abused child. For example, Mary, a thirty-year-old secretary, was sexually and physically abused by both parents and two uncles from the time she was three years old until she was twelve. Her mother was psychotic, in that she heard voices that told her to abuse her daughter. This mother was also a domineering personality who encouraged her husband to abuse their daughter.

At age twelve, Mary started hiding in the library after school and coming home after dark to escape the abuse. As soon as she could, she began working. At age eighteen, she ran away from home. She tried to commit suicide several times but has not been suicidal since receiving extensive therapy for her abuse. Yet, with tears flowing down her cheeks, she still speaks fondly, and sadly, of "Katie."

Mary explains: "Katie is the battered little girl in me. The little girl who is afraid and wants a real mommy and daddy. I talk to

Katie every day. I tell her I will take care of her, that I will protect her, that I won't make her feel unsafe. I tell her that even though nobody in her family loved her, *I* love her.

"Whenever somebody asks me to do something different or new, I ask Katie, 'Will you be scared if I do this?' If I want to do it, and she's a little scared, I promise her that I will stop the minute she starts crying.

"For a long time I didn't want to acknowledge that I was abused; that Katie lived in me. But until I faced the truth that Katie, that sad little girl with the torn vagina, was a part of me, I could never be free."

Mary's abuse was extreme. Since it began before the age of five in an extremely disturbed home, she was at risk for developing multiple personality disorder. For whatever reason, she did not. Instead she found a name for her abused self, Katie—and a way to nurture her inner child. Perhaps your child will represent the abused part of herself through an imaginary friend, or project her abused self onto a doll or animal. This a child's way of coping.

Common Symptoms

For an infant, some symptoms resulting from sexual abuse include failure to thrive, withdrawal, fretfulness, whining and crying, clinging behavior, episodes of impaired movement, feeding problems, and acute anxiety. (Of course, all of these behaviors may be symptomatic of other problems as well, and do not necessarily point to sexual abuse.)

In early childhood, sexually abused children may exhibit thumbsucking, self-injurious behavior, bedwetting, speech and sleep problems, as well as seductive or overtly sexual behavior or fear of the opposite sex. Because sexual abuse functions to overstimulate and eroticize some children, beginning from the age of two and extending into early and late adolescence, abused children may:

- Masturbate frequently
- Become exhibitionists
- Invite others to participate in sex play
- Become sexually abusive toward younger children

In middle childhood, the earlier symptoms may continue, and new ones, such as nightmares, depression, and eating disorders, may develop. Some children complain of mental confusion, and some even manifest psychotic or borderline personality states. At this point, some children begin having problems in school. Some skip school, while others try to compensate for their negative self-esteem by being excellent—if not perfect—students. Feeling shamed, humiliated, and disgraced by the abuse, some children act out their anger, creating problems at home and school with aggression and defiance. Others try to purify themselves by being especially well-behaved or virtuous.[28]

A child's efforts to be "perfect" can begin as early as age five or six and can extend into adulthood. Untreated abuse survivors as old as sixty or seventy can be plagued with the need to "purge" themselves of the abuse through self-denial and self-sacrifice. Others become over-achievers who get no pleasure or peace from their accomplishments, being unable to blot out the feelings of being damaged or unworthy.

The abused child can easily be overwhelmed by fear: fear that everyone is a potential attacker; fear of her own anger and the anger of others, especially authority figures. Such children often adopt a submissive or "people-pleasing" posture to avoid being the target of any anger or criticism. For example, they may have trouble saying no, especially to older people or people on whom they're dependent. In incestuous homes especially, the abused child is often stuck in the role of the passive and helpless victim, learning to sit quietly, to go along with everything the adults say, and to try to be invisible. Such a child may assume the role of peacemaker or caretaker within the family.

Typically, unless they are in treatment, abused children feel alone, unprotected, and vulnerable. These feelings extend into adolescence, when additional symptoms may develop, such as gastrointestinal problems, headaches, and other pains; trouble with menstruation or urinary tract infections; anxiety attacks; rage reactions and hostile, angry behavior; self-mutilation or destructiveness; social isolation; withdrawal, feelings of helplessness, hopelessness, and powerlessness; as well as food, alcohol, or drug addictions.

Many parents try to deny or trivialize the reasons behind the symptoms they observe. One mother passed off her daughter's nightmares as indigestion. Even when the nightmares persisted, the mother rationalized that they were temporary. The first time Sheila's mother saw her daughter go numb, she didn't understand what was going on. Sheila's eyes were glazed and had a faraway stare; her body was limp. She was sitting on the floor in front of a mirror, trying to comb her hair. But she moved her arm in slow motion, as if it were half-paralyzed.

"Are you all right?" her mother asked. Sheila failed to reply or even acknowledge that anyone had spoken to her. Even when the mother repeated the question, Sheila didn't respond.

"I need to lie down," Sheila finally said. An hour later, when Sheila emerged from her bedroom, her mother saw that she had cuts on her legs. Her mother reasoned that the cuts were caused by careless shaving. It was not until she found her daughter cutting herself with a razor blade and trying to make holes in her leg with a knife that this particular parent realized that something was seriously wrong.

Besides being symptomatic of numbness, self-mutilation may also be the victim's desperate attempt to draw attention to her plight and get help. Since rage against the abuser may be too risky, it often gets turned in upon the self.

Patterns of self-punishment and self-loathing may persist into adulthood. A recent study found that fifty percent of adult victims of child sexual abuse were over twenty pounds overweight and/or were completely asexual. About twenty-two percent had multiple personalities; eighty percent experienced flashbacks or had nightmares; ninety-five percent had an impaired self-image; and eighty-four percent had attempted suicide. They tended to be compulsive eaters, chronically anxious, and hypervigilant.[29]

Other symptoms include fear of doctors (especially gynecologists); fainting spells; out-of-body experiences; epileptic-like seizures; and self-destructive behavior, especially in relationships. For example, it's not uncommon for abuse survivors to sabotage, destroy, or run from positive relationships and become involved in self-destructive ones instead. The selection of inappropriate partners is especially prevalent among incest survivors. Sometimes the survivor has such low self-esteem that she doesn't feel that she deserves anyone better. She may see herself as a social outcast, unable to be part of a functioning group. As such, she is easy prey for a man who would be "unacceptable" to a more socially integrated, emotionally stable woman. As a result of her early experiences, she has never learned how to interact in an emotionally healthy relationship.[30]

The incestuously abused child may be starved for nurturing, yet often—like Emily—must take the mother role in the family. Despite her need for protection and security, she may be forced to act like a parent toward her parents and siblings. Because of her vulnerability as an adult, she is easy prey to abusive men and can slip into a relationship with a physically, sexually, or emotionally violent man. These women are more likely to be victims of rape and battering.[31] Prostitution, lesbianism, and bisexuality are also possible outcomes.

Suicidal Tendencies in Sexual Abuse Survivors

The high rate of attempted suicide among these survivors reflects suppressed rage at the abuser that is turned in upon the self. It is also an expression of the self-hatred, guilt, and shame that are the legacies of abuse. James, who had been sexually abused by his father from age four to twelve, attempted to kill himself several times. He became a drug addict at nine, but was forced to give up his drug addictions at age sixteen after he was caught forging checks to buy drugs.

Today, without the buffer of drugs, he is beginning to feel his feelings regarding the abuse in their full strength. Intellectually he knows that he isn't responsible for the abuse; but, emotionally, he still feels that he "caused" it because of his "unworthiness" or some other fancied inadequacy as a child.

Every time he makes a mistake at work or is criticized by someone he cares about, James interprets this as further proof that he is "no good" and will never make it. His suicidal thoughts then return. The last time there was tension between James and his girlfriend, he bought drugs and planned to overdose on them.

While to an outsider it might seem that James is overreacting, his extreme responses to vocational and interpersonal conflicts are entirely normal for trauma victims.

Like many abuse survivors, James is highly sensitive to the reactions of others, vulnerable to their evaluations of him, and unable to see their responses in perspective. Each time he makes a mistake at work or hears a criticism of himself, he experiences it as a catastrophe—a catastrophe similar to the abuse by his father. Psychologically, any "failure" on James' part puts him back in the trauma situation where, if he didn't please his father, he was abused.

In therapy James and I have discussed the fact that his father found fault with him as an excuse to abuse him. Even when James lived up to his father's unrealistic, contradictory, and often perfectionistic expectations and demands, his father was abusive anyway. Despite our many sessions on this topic, it will take much more time and many tears before James is finally released from his feelings of self-blame.

Like other survivors, James often becomes suicidal when he realizes that he has difficulties with intimacy. He feels that it is his fault that he can't open up to others. At this stage of his healing, he still needs the wall around his heart to protect himself from the possible betrayal and abuse which he has learned to expect from those he loves.

On the other hand, he wants to tear down the wall, because, like every other human being, he craves human companionship and intimacy. "I can't love. I'll never be able to love. When am I going to be rid of the past?" he shouts, then melts into tears. "It's bad enough what happened to me, but why do I have to keep paying the price? And how many years will it take for me to get over it and be able to have a good relationship with a woman?" Other abuse survivors feel like James: frightened that they will never be healed, afraid that they will always be lonely, as isolated and scared as they were while being abused, and angry at themselves for their symptoms. Such feelings often precipitate suicide attempts: the abuse survivor feels trapped by her feelings, just as, during childhood, she was trapped by her abuser. In such instances, suicidal thoughts and attempts may be more indicative of a desire to escape than a desire to die.

Another reason attempted suicide rates are so high among sex abuse survivors is that, in many cases, the abuser continues to follow or harass the victim, or intrude into her life.

For example, Joanne, age twenty, becomes suicidal whenever her uncle, who sexually abused her from the ages of ten to twelve, comes into town and wants to visit. Just hearing his voice on the telephone gives Joanne a migraine headache.

Even though she is now a young adult, when she has contact with her uncle, Joanne once again becomes the little girl who was powerless to stop the abuse. Joanne hates herself for not being able to say, "No, I don't want to see you. You are a horrible man." Yet unconsciously she fears the punishments he threatened her with as a child. She hates the fact that he still has power over her and that even though she doesn't want to see him, there are family pressures to do so—pressures from which she is not totally immune.

The tension between what she wants to do and what she feels she should do, and her anger at herself for still being "stuck" in a little-girl position, have on several occasions precipitated suicide attempts by Joanne.

A Little Perspective

Before you become too discouraged, remember that the long-term negative consequences of sexual abuse do not have to happen. When there is positive intervention and support for victims, they can overcome their traumatic experiences and sidestep many of the consequences described above.

Your role as a helping adult is to see that positive intervention and support are forthcoming.

To What Extent Can a Child Fight Back or Say No?

It's important to consider the situation from the perspective of a child. Adults and older children wield great power over young children by the sheer fact of their greater size, greater age, greater knowledge, and sexual sophistication. A child's instinct is to emulate adult behavior, not to question it. Extremely young children, and even some preadolescents, might well not recognize that they are being sexually abused, especially if the sexual abuse is gentle, or it is accepted behavior in the family, or somehow perceived as an expression of nurturing or affection.

Emily never perceived her father's assaults as "positive"—yet some incest survivors relate that initially they believed the actions of their sexual abuser to be expressions of love and caring. This can be the case when an abuser tells a young, dependent, and sexually naive child that he is helping her to grow up or to be a better wife to her future husband, or that he is "saving" her from being hurt by other males who do not love her the way he does.

Children who are sexually naive or sexually misinformed can be easily misled by the abuser's insistence that he is showing love or affection. Abusers may simply command obedience by virtue of the authority they have as adults. "If a big person says it's okay, then it must be okay," reasons the child. Or, "If a big person tells me to do something, then I have to do it." This is especially the case if the "big person" is the child's father, stepfather, uncle, grandfather, or respected family friend. In some cases, threats or physical force may be used to coerce the child into compliance. Or the abuser may make threats on the child's family, friends, or pets. In the majority of cases, however, the abuser insists that the abuse is a gift of love, attention, and affection, which leads to enormous guilt and confusion on the part of the child. The guilt and confusion in themselves can render a child passive and compliant.

The Child Abuse Accommodation Syndrome

When the abuse is repeated, as is frequently the case, the child might develop what is called the child abuse accommodation syndrome. Roland Summit, who developed the idea, describes the syndrome as consisting of five steps: (1) *secrecy*, (2) *helplessness*, (3) *entrapment and accommodation*, (4) *delayed and unconvincing disclosure*, and (5) *retraction*.[32]

Secrecy refers to the taboo surrounding the open discussion of child sexual abuse in most families, and the abuser's insistence that the child keep the abuse a secret. This secrecy communicates that the activity is "dangerous" and "bad." Summit writes, "The secrecy is also the promise of safety: 'Everything will be all right if you just don't tell.'"[33]

In the face of an older, more powerful person on whom they may also be economically or emotionally dependent, children are functionally *helpless*. Entrapped by the secrecy and helplessness, the child learns to *accommodate* and placate the abuser and develops psychological defense mechanisms, such as dissociation. Even if she does reveal the abuse at a later point—or if it emerges accidentally—her account may be *unconvincing* to others and she may eventually *retract* it.

Some Commonalities of Trauma

The child abuse accommodation syndrome does not usually develop unless the abuse is repeated; but this does not mean that even a one-time assault cannot be highly traumatic. Browne and Finkelhor have analyzed experiences of victimization, from being terrorized by an earthquake to being assaulted by a relative. They've identified four factors that can create trauma: *betrayal, stigmatization, powerlessness,* and *traumatic sexualization.* Child sexual abuse is one of the most traumatic experiences possible because it involves all four of these factors.[34]

Betrayal is involved when the abuser tells lies about sex, about the meaning of what is going on, or about other matters; or when the abuser manipulates the child into compliance. Children feel especially betrayed when the abuser is a family member or trusted adult. The degree of relatedness is not as important as the degree of closeness and trust the child felt for the abuser. In some cases, a child may feel more betrayed if violated by a close family friend than by an emotionally distant or rejecting parent.

Stigmatization is also involved in that children learn to feel that they're bad because of their involvement in the abusive sexual activity. This message comes from the abuser, from others, and from society in general. Stigmatization is especially strong when the child, the child's family, or the abuser holds religious attitudes which condemn sexual activity in general as evil. Sexual abuse survivors often feel "dirty," or like "spoiled goods"; they wonder if the abuse "shows." Victims of car accidents, military invasions, floods, and fires may suffer from feelings of powerlessness and, in some instances, betrayal—but they do not have to live with such belittling and stigmatizing labels. While many adult survivors of parental alcoholism have "come out of the closet," adult survivors of parental sex abuse are far less likely to discuss their pain beyond the confines of a therapist's office.

Powerlessness is another experience common to victims. As Browne and Finkelhor explain, powerlessness refers to the child's feeling that she can't control what is happening to her. Her desires with regard to her body, as well as any of her other needs and desires, are continually eclipsed by the emotional and physical power of the abuser. The child experiences powerlessness over her body when she is assaulted. With each repeated assault, the sense of powerlessness increases. The child's dependency on her abuser and the abuser's threats or manipulation all serve to reinforce her sense of powerlessness, as do any failed attempts to stop the abuse.

Traumatic sexualization occurs when the child is sexually stimulated or made to respond sexually in ways that are not appropriate for her level of emotional development. This is more severe in instances where the abuser sexually stimulates the child or forces the child to be sexually active than in instances where the abuser is content with a passive victim. Traumatic sexualization also involves the abuser's lies about sexual behavior norms. If the abuser has a fetish about a certain part of the body, the child may have an exaggerated sense of its importance.

Emily's father fussed over her breasts, often saying they were the most beautiful breasts in the world. Later, when other men did not respond to her breasts so extravagantly, Emily felt confused and deficient in some way. Her father had frequently bought her gifts as "tributes" to her breasts. While caressing them, he would ask her what she wanted, saying that any girl with such beautiful breasts deserved whatever money could buy. In subsequent relationships, Emily would sometimes regress psychologically when a lover touched her breasts. She would go back into the trauma mentality and respond as if she were the age when the trauma first occurred. Her out-of-the-blue requests for expensive gifts in the middle of lovemaking were a source of distress both to her and her partners.

When Emily was seeking a promotion at work, she wore an extremely tight sweater. When her boss seemed scarcely to notice her bosom, and her request for a raise was denied, Emily felt confused, frightened, and ashamed.

At the very least, sexual abuse tarnishes and confuses the child's view of the meaning and importance of sex and touch. Although the degree and kind of traumatic sexualization vary significantly from one situation to another, traumatic sexualization is present in all forms of sexual abuse.

Post-Traumatic Stress Disorder

Like other victims, sexually abused children are prime candidates for developing Post-Traumatic Stress Disorder, or PTSD.[35] Basically, PTSD is a normal reaction to an abnormal amount of stress. PTSD has been identified in former prisoners of war, Vietnam veterans, survivors of the Nazi holocaust and the bombing of Hiroshima, as well as among incest and sexual abuse survivors. Anyone who has undergone a trauma outside the normal range of human stress can develop PTSD (the death of a loved one or loss of property is often traumatic, but is still within the normal range of stressful human experience). Traumas severe enough to cause PTSD are of such magnitude, horror, or duration that they overwhelm your emotional and physical coping mechanisms.[36]

Children who experience a one-time rape or assault can develop PTSD; but it is those who are repeatedly abused sexually who are more likely to develop this disorder. The more traumatic the abuse experience—the greater the violation of trust, the more violence, the more humiliation involved—the more likely the victim is to develop PTSD.

According to Sarah Haley, an experienced psychotherapist who has worked with hundreds of PTSD cases, trauma consists of being made into an object. "Whether one's assaulter is a hurricane, a rapist, or an incestuous brother, at the moment of attack, one does not feel like a human being with the right to safety, happiness, and health."[37]

At that moment one becomes an object vulnerable to the will of a power or force much greater than oneself. When the assailant is a natural force, such as an earthquake, the catastrophe can somehow be explained away as an accident of fate. However, when the assailant is another person—especially a trusted family member or friend—the victim's trust in other human beings, and in society in general, can be severely shaken or shattered entirely. Trust in others is most severely shaken when the assailant is a member of one's own family, as is the case for incest survivors or children who are physically abused by their parents or relatives.

Victims with PTSD find themselves re-experiencing their trauma, experience a numbing of their emotions, and can also suffer from sleep disturbances, hypervigilance, memory and concentration difficulties, depression, anger, anxiety, alienation, and self-destructive behavior.

PTSD, however, is more than a list of symptoms. The fundamental force underlying the symptoms is the child's re-experiencing of the trauma, followed by her attempts to bury the memories and feelings associated with it. She will repeat this sequence over and over, hoping against hope that with enough repetitions, the trauma will go away. The child can become so absorbed with this sequence that she has little energy or emotion to put into everyday living—school, friends, family, and herself.

There is a high correlation between drug, alcohol, and food addictions and sexual abuse, because abuse survivors frequently turn to an external substance in order to numb their memories or feelings. Healing from PTSD involves bringing the repressed memories to the surface of the conscious mind, and experiencing the feelings associated with those memories.

The Special Case of Incest

Of all sexually abused children, those who are the victims of incest run a particularly high risk of suffering the worst negative consequences. This is especially the case if the child has a trusting, close relationship with the abusive family member. Anna Freud wrote, "Far from existing as only a fantasy, incest is also a fact. Where the chances of harming a child's normal development and growth are concerned, it ranks higher than abandonment, neglect, physical maltreatment or any other form of abuse. It would be a fatal mistake to underrate either the importance or the frequency of its actual occurrence."[38]

Yet even as late as the 1970s, the popular press—as well as some professional publications—espoused the view that incest itself was not harmful. Media programs and men's magazines have even featured fathers who ingenuously state that in sexually touching their daughters they were only giving them pleasure and a sexual education. The daughters "liked it," these fathers often say (implying that the daughters are to blame). Unfortunately, cetain sociologists, psychologists, and other therapists agree with the views of such fathers.

The core argument of this "pro-incest" lobby is that incest is a form of sexual liberation for both the child and the parent, and that great harm can be done by denying the child this expression of parental "love." Any damage that does occur, the argument continues, is because society punishes incestuous behavior and makes the participants feel guilty and ashamed.

This argument projects the sexual needs and desires of the adult onto the child. Children crave their parents' affection, acceptance, and nurturing—but it is outside the realm of a child's experience to "crave" orgasm or genital stimulation by another person.

Some credentialed therapists argue that sex between adult and child helps promote the child's sexual expression—provided, they stress, that there is no physical damage or violence done to the child, and that the child freely chooses to participate in the sexual activity. The answer to this argument is that children, in relation to adults, are powerless: they are not in a position to "freely" choose to participate.[39]

The powerlessness of children is underscored by their economic and emotional dependence on their parent or caretaker for survival. Even if an adult's sexual advances are resisted, the child can easily be overpowered by the adult's larger size. But usually force is not necessary because most children readily comply with adult demands, especially when these involve closeness or affection. As

Herman writes, "...the child does not have the power to withhold consent, (and) she does not have the power to grant it."[40]

Study after study shows that the overwhelming majority of children who experienced incest remember it as being, at the very least, an unpleasant activity. Most found it frightening and completely undesirable. This does not mean that all incest survivors are deeply and irrevocably damaged. Yet many do suffer long-lasting scars and, as a group, they are more apt to undergo additional psychic stresses in adulthood. More than the victim of sexual abuse by a stranger, the child violated by a relative has been found to suffer from intense guilt and shame, low self-esteem, depression, self-imposed social isolation, mistrust of others, and self-destructive behavior, such as substance abuse and prostitution.[41]

Incest survivors are also likely to experience greater sexual difficulties and problems establishing long-term intimate relationships.[42] Even after several years of therapy, Emily found it difficult to trust men. Generally she felt that most men were interested only in exploiting her sexually. However, even when she found men who expressed sincere, caring interest in her, she was highly suspicious of them and would "test" their caring concern for her by showing

---

Manifestations of Childhood Incest Observed in Study Group

- Sexual dysfunctioning
  - Nonorgasmic to not being able to be touched by a male
- Self-destructive behavior
  - Substance abuse
  - Suicidal behavior
  - Destructive relationships
- Emotional and physical abuse toward children
- Impulsive behavior
  - Eating
  - Spending
- Marital problems
- Difficulty sustaining intimate relationships
- Depression

- Poor self-esteem
- Promiscuity
- Somatic complaints
  - Chronic pain
  - Headaches
  - Nausea
- Feelings of detachment
- Lack of trust
- Feelings of powerlessness
- Needing always to care for others
- Difficulty with authority figures
- Inability to deal with incestuous behavior toward children
- Difficulty in parenting
- Reinvolvement in incestuous assault

Reprinted with permission from "Adult Survivors of Incest," by Mattie Lowery, in *Journal of Psychosocial Nursing*, Vol. 25, No. 1, pp. 27-31 (1987).

up late, breaking dates, verbally abusing them, or by accusing them of not really caring for her, only for her body.

"If he really loves me, he'll put up with my behavior," was her unconscious thought. Yet when she realized she was pushing away potentially loving companions, she would become overwhelmed with despair and fear that she would never be able to form an enduring bond with a man. At this point she would either totally reject the man in her life, feeling that she was unworthy of him, or she would run to him in desperation.

But because she hated her desperation and dependency needs (feelings she associated with the abuse), she would alternate between allowing herself to be close to her partner and rejecting and mistreating him. When she allowed herself to be close, she feared that she would ultimately be abandoned. Sometimes she would reject the man first, as a defense against the anticipated rejection. At other times, she would work at placating him, to fend off rejection. Even if the man did not require such submissive behavior, Emily had learned at an early age that this is what 'men" require. Maintaining this submissive position would lead to extreme dissatisfaction with the relationship on Emily's part, causing her either to hate herself for acting like a second-class citizen, to break up, or to argue incessantly with her lover.

Emily fears becoming dependent on men, because when she was dependent on her father, he misused her. On the other hand, she longs to finally find a man on whom she can rely. She has difficulty setting limits in her relationships with men because she was raised in an incestuous situation where there were no limits. Because she couldn't say 'no' to Daddy, she doesn't trust that she can say 'no' to men when they make demands on her that she doesn't want to meet.

Almost everyone struggles with the complex issues of dependency and limit-setting in intimate relationships. But these issues are even more problematic for abuse survivors because of the ways in which their dependency needs, and their ability to set limits, were discounted and violated by the abuser.

A distressing number of survivors are vulnerable to revictimization in their adult life. A high percentage of battered wives and adult rape victims have histories of incestuous abuse as children. This is true not only for female incest survivors, but for males as well. Male incest survivors who subsequently engage in prostitution or promiscuous sexual relationships are also more subject to violence and sexual assault as adults.[43]

Although the symptoms discussed in this section might seem common to almost any group of people who seek professional help, research has shown that therapy patients with histories of incest abuse are "significantly more disturbed" than patients without such a history. They have more problems developing healthy relationships—particularly sexual ones—more stressful marriages, more physical problems, and more complaints in general.[44]

Externally, incest survivors often function as caretakers—both as adults and children. Yet underneath they are needy children, desperate for parental love, approval, and nurturing. In most cases, they feel cut off, or have cut themselves off, from the nonoffending parent or—in the case of sibling incest, aunt, uncle, cousin, or grandparent incest—from both parents. Cut off like this, the child may experience genital contact with the offending relative as a form of love and acceptance. At the same time, the incest confirms the child's sense of being evil. Unlike survivors of sexual assault from a stranger, incest survivors typically have nowhere to turn and no one in whom to confide. In most cases, they bear their terrible secret alone, realizing that if they disclose the truth they may destroy the family unit. For example, it was clear to Emily that if her father followed through with his threat of leaving the family, she, her mother, and her sisters would have no means of economic support.

The early confusion of sexuality with love, pain, betrayal, and powerlessness can creates profound confusion in subsequent relationships. However, incest—or any other form of sexual assault—does not automatically lead to all the mental health problems described above. Sexual abuse is traumatic, but its effects can be either increased or decreased by other factors in the child's life, such as the child's self-esteem and level of functioning prior to the assault, the existence of an emotional support system, other family problems (poverty, physical illness in the family, alcoholism, and so on), and the way in which the incest is handled by family members, mental health professionals, and protective authorities once the incest is disclosed (if it ever is).

If you are the parent or relative of an incestuously abused child, do not assume that this child will automatically be permanently and deeply damaged. Although the results of incest are never positive, there is much that you—together with other supportive family members, neighbors, friends, and sympathetic and knowledgeable mental health professionals—can do to soften the blow for your child. Positive and immediate action on behalf of the child can help turn the situation around and save her from a life of inner torment and repeated victimization.

To accomplish this goal, you will have to shed any denial you have about the incest, and be willing to suffer painful feelings along with your child. Exceptional patience is also required as your child embarks on the path to recovery. When you become discouraged and overwhelmed, remember that healing is possible, not only for your child, but for you as well.

Jeb's Story

The Jones family was the everyday American family so familiar to us all. They were active in their church, attended all PTA functions, and were so "normal" that it was beyond anyone's comprehension—including theirs—that their family life would not continue down its well-defined, traditional path.

But that was before Jeb, the middle child, was sexually abused. Jeb is the eleven-year-old son of Nellie and Bob Jones. Bob is a successful salesman who often travels for his company and Nellie is a stay-at-home wife and mother. Jeb's brother, Bob Jr., is sixteen—a tall, athletic teenager, very popular with his schoolmates as well as with his neighbors, who feel warmed by his ready smile and serene self-confidence. Jeb's baby sister, Annie, is five; with her red hair and freckles, she seems a Norman Rockwell drawing come to life.

The Jones family lives by traditional values. Mr. and Mrs. Jones follow the same sex-role models as their parents, and both believe that showing feelings is a sign of weakness. Like many men, Bob Jones believes that men shouldn't cry. The Joneses have an image to protect and a set of values to impart to their sons, and these do not include acting like "babies."

Mr. Jones is dedicated to his family, and shows it through the expensive presents he showers on them whenever he returns from one of his frequent business trips. Mrs. Jones prefers to cook her way into her family's heart. Both Mr. and Mrs. Jones consider theirs to be a successful marriage since they are both sexually faithful. For them, sex outside of marriage is evil; they believe that touching and caressing belong only in the bedroom.

Jeb is drawn to books, music, and other creative ventures. He is considered to have the artistic talent in the family and often wins school prizes both for his drawing and his acting abilities. Mr. Jones, however, does not think these activities are as worthwhile as Bob's athletic cups and medals, and has remarked that only "sissies" or "queers" end up being musicians or artists.

When Jeb was eight, the Joneses enrolled him in the local cub scout pack to have him associate more with "regular" boys. Jeb was thrilled that his father took the time to drive him to the first meeting and even hung around for a while to chat with the cub master, Mr. R. Jeb was grinning from ear to ear, determined to be the best cub scout in the pack so that he would impress his father. He overheard

Mr. Jones whisper to Mr. R., "Try to toughen him up a little. He's a little too interested in girlish things. I know he's kind of small and weak-looking but he'll be fine with some toughening up. It's all he needs."

At the cub scout meetings, Mr. R. made a point of calling on Jeb and bringing him out. He also made a point of complimenting him on his artistic talents and frequently had him draw posters for scout activities. He often patted Jeb on the back—as he did the other boys—and was generous with his smiles and kind words.

All the boys liked Mr. R.'s warmth and friendly manner and didn't shrink from his rough hugs or pats on the back. But Mr. R. was particularly important to Jeb because he was receiving from his scoutmaster the praise, attention, and affection he craved from his father.

When the pack had parent nights, Mr. Jones tried to attend, but usually he was off traveling. He only managed to go on one of the weekend camping excursions, but Mr. R. helped Jeb feel part of the group. Mr. R.—a pedophile—had quickly spotted Jeb as a potential victim, both for his delicate build and his emotional vulnerability.

On the fourth camping trip, Mr. R. called Jeb into his tent to show him some camping skills. At that time he put his arm around Jeb, as he often did. Jeb scarcely noticed until Mr. R. started rubbing his hand all up and down Jeb's back. Jeb shrank away. No one had ever touched him like that before.

Mr. R. laughed. "Don't be afraid. I'm just trying to help you relax. Tonight you're sleeping on the hard ground, remember? I'm only trying to limber up your muscles."

Over a period of time, Mr. R. extended his rubbing to Jeb's legs and the front of his chest. Jeb liked the warm feeling and the affection and he also liked that Mr. R. seemed to like him more than he did the other boys. Without making Jeb his obvious favorite, Mr. R. found subtle ways to give Jeb recognition.

One night after all the boys were asleep, Jeb woke up to find Mr. R. rubbing his genitals. "Don't worry," Mr. R. said, "I'm only trying to keep you warm." The next night, Mr. R. invited Jeb into his tent before it was time to go to sleep. Mr. R. ordered the other boys to turn in, but let Jeb stay with him so he could "show him something special."

Mr. R. began his assault by praising Jeb for being a model scout. He caressed Jeb until Jeb achieved an erection, then unzipped Jeb's pants and fellated him. "Now do the same to me," Mr. R. said and forced his penis into Jeb's mouth.

Jeb had never seen an erect adult penis and was confused and frightened. "I'm only doing this because I love you. You love me too, don't you? Don't you want to make me happy?" asked Mr. R.

For over two years, Mr. R. fondled Jeb and forced him to fellate him on every possible occasion. Initially, Mr. R. bought Jeb's silence by saying, "This is our secret. Don't tell the other scouts because they'll be jealous. Don't tell anyone, not even your parents, because this is our special secret."

Despite Mr. R.'s assurances that the abuse was "love," Jeb was confused and frightened. Sometimes he avoided Mr. R. or tried to protest but Mr. R. would talk him around. When the loving words no longer worked, Mr. R. began to threaten Jeb. "If you don't do what I want, I'll tell the police and they'll put you and your father in jail. You don't want that to happen, do you? You don't know the terrible things I can do if you don't make me happy."

Although Mr. R. usually was vague in his threats, this vagueness increased Jeb's fears by giving his fantasies full expression. As the months went by, Jeb's vision of jail had turned into a series of nightmares of incredible violence and pain.

When Jeb tried to quit the scouts, his parents insisted that he stay. "Give me one good reason for quitting," Mr. Jones demanded. But Jeb couldn't. A part of him had repressed the memory of the abuse and another part was afraid his parents would blame him. Instead Jeb lamely said that he wanted to spend more time reading and drawing.

"But that's sissy stuff," Jeb's father retorted. "In cub scouts you learn how to do things. That's why I sent you there."

"But I don't like Mr. R."

"Why not? Mr. R. is a wonderful leader. Everybody likes him. He has dedicated himself to the troop and has shown you so many things. He always tells me what a good job you are doing, too."

Jeb gave up.

The semester after the abuse began, Jeb started having problems paying attention in school and became a loner, sitting by himself at lunch and dropping his after-school activities. Jeb's parents chastised him for doing poorly in school and punished him for his bad grades. Jeb hoped they would also make him quit scouts to devote more time to homework; but when he suggested leaving, they said, "Scouts is good for you. It'll help you grow up strong."

Jeb spent many hours alone in his room, trying to study but having periods of numbness alternating with periods of banging his head against the wall and plucking out his eyebrows. The Joneses panicked. Thinking that their son was reacting to the punishments they had dealt out to him, they said they would drop these if only Jeb would stop the headbanging and tell them what was wrong.

Jeb wanted to, but he was too confused and frightened to do so. Mr. R. had said, "If you tell, they'll think you're a sissy and a girl. And you *are* like a girl. You're small and frail just like your sister

and you like to read and draw just like a girl. Look at your brother—
he's a real boy. You must really like the things we do together because you never stop me. You must be a girlish boy because only a
girlish boy would like the things we do. Also, your penis is very
small, which is another way anyone can tell you're a sissy. When
you grow, you'll probably be a queer and do exactly what I'm doing
to you. Don't try and fight me. I'm stronger than you'll ever be.
After all, you're only a girl."

To prove to himself that he wasn't a weakling and to show his
hatred of girls, Jeb began tormenting his sister Annie.

On his tenth birthday, Mr. R. gave him the present of anal intercourse. "Now you really are a queer," he said. When Mrs. Jones
found blood on Jeb's sheets, Jeb said he didn't know where it came
from. When blood continued to appear, Jeb was taken to his
pediatrician who told the Joneses that Jeb had a ruptured anus and
that he had obviously been sexually abused.

Jeb denied it. What could he do? If he told the truth—and by
now he had so many confused feelings that he no longer even knew
the truth—his father wouldn't love him. After all, now he was a
queer and a girl.

As his parents and the doctor continued to question Jeb, he burst
into tears. "You look like a whipped dog," shrieked Mr. Jones, now
hysterical with anger, fear, and grief. "Stand up straight, stop crying,
and tell us who hurt you."

"Promise your son that you won't punish him, no matter what
he says," said the doctor.

With that assurance, Jeb revealed that it was Mr. R. who had been
doing things to him, but he blocked out the details.

At first Mr. Jones went into denial. These things simply did not
happen to boys from "good" families. Jeb must have been watching
too many movies or maybe some kid at school was warping his
mind. Or maybe Jeb had hurt himself while playing with himself
and wanted to blame the scout master rather than admit that he
masturbated.

How could an upstanding citizen like Mr. R. be a child molester?
Only savages or lunatics from certain poor ethnic groups did such
things.

The doctor gravely restated that he was certain that Jeb had been
molested. With Mrs. Jones sobbing uncontrollably, Mr. Jones went
into a white rage, swearing to get a gun and kill Mr. R. With his
parents in such emotional turmoil, Jeb felt even more guilty and
frightened.

"You don't need a gun, Mr. Jones. You need professional
psychological help for all three of you and you need it now. This is

a major crisis in your lives and you all need to talk it through with someone who can help you."

At first Mr. Jones felt that Jeb would get over it on his own. "Boys are tough. They can bounce back from a lot." Only after Mrs. Jones confessed that she had been hiding certain of Jeb's behaviors—like talking baby talk, wanting to play with much younger children, and hitting his sister—did Mr. Jones agree to counseling, but only for Jeb.

The therapist they found was a social worker with no special training in child sexual abuse. She laid a guilt trip on the Joneses for not participating more actively in Jeb's life. Mr. Jones was made to feel guilty for traveling and Mrs. Jones for not being a den mother. "If one of you had been involved, even gone on some of those camping trips, this never would have happened."

There was an element of truth to that, since it has been shown that the presence of a protector usually frustrates the plans of a child molester. However, this did not mean that the Joneses were negligent, nor that their behavior caused the assaults. It's impossible for a parent to be with a child twenty-four hours a day.

The therapist wanted to focus on the family interactions and was only occasionally concerned with Jeb as an individual. She would sometimes demand that Jeb tell her all about the abuse; and when Jeb couldn't, she got angry. Jeb withdrew even further and repressed his memories even more.

The social worker put the whole family through a series of expensive psychological tests and then interpreted the results to them, even though she wasn't qualified to do so. Her interpretation of Jeb's results was as negative as possible. She stressed that Jeb was developmentally somewhat delayed and had some regressive qualities.

These characteristics often result from sexual abuse. They are temporary symptoms of stress and the child's wish to return to an earlier stage of life when he felt protected and taken care of. The therapist, however, claimed these results to show that Jeb was a seriously disturbed child.

When Mr. Jones asked the therapist if Jeb would turn into a homosexual because of the abuse, she shrugged her shoulders and said, "I don't know. Only time will tell." Uneducated in sexual abuse, the therapist had not realized the kind of physical and emotional power that an abuser has over a child. She interpreted the fact that Jeb didn't tell on Mr. R. as a sign that on some level Jeb enjoyed it and therefore had homosexual leanings.

If the therapist had bothered to study the subject before taking Jeb on as a patient, she would have known that it's almost impossible for children to "tell" on their abusers. She would also have been able to reassure the Joneses that child sexual abuse does not necessarily cause homosexuality.

Jeb's parents were intimidated by the therapist; but when they saw no improvement in Jeb's schoolwork or disposition, and when he increased his bullying of his sister, they decided to look for help from another professional.

Their first therapist accused them of wanting to escape from the knowledge that they and Jeb were all seriously disturbed people.

The next helping professional consulted by the Joneses asked them, "Has your son bonded with this therapist? Does he trust her? Does he talk freely? If he has, you might want to overlook some of the therapist's limitations. But if he hasn't, you might want to consider changing."

Jeb wanted another therapist. He was very clear about it and his parents agreed. They got recommendations from a local rape crisis center and interviewed different therapists for personality, approach, and familiarity with child sexual abuse.

The therapist selected went right to work on establishing a relationship of trust with Jeb. They played games, drew together, and talked very generally about feelings. She tried to alleviate the guilt Mr. and Mrs. Jones were feeling and assured them over and over that it was possible for Jeb to heal.

It took Jeb a good three months before he could talk about Mr. R. with his new therapist. The new therapist did not see Jeb as resistant to therapy or difficult; she understood that as a sexual abuse victim, Jeb had lost much of his trust of others and would have great difficulty trusting her—or anyone else.

At first Jeb was afraid that his therapist would punish him for the abuse; but she gave Jeb permission to feel his feelings without any possibility of being punished for them. She frequently gave Jeb, and his parents, little talks on some aspect of child abuse and how people can recover. For Jeb, she pointed out that it was not "queer" or "girl-like" to have emotions such as fear, and that one's penis size had nothing to do with one's worth or sexual leanings. She also challenged Jeb's belief that the abuse was his fault, that he was not a good son, and that the assaults were his punishment for being inadequate.

The therapist tried to build Jeb's sense of power and self-esteem by helping him improve his communication and social skills. She also helped Jeb differentiate between power and abuse, which he had confused because of his experiences with Mr. R.

Seeing how effective counseling was for Jeb, Mr. Jones became more willing to use it for his other children, who were also suffering. Bob Jr. and Annie were not blind. They lived in the house and had seen their quiet brother turn into someone who banged his head until it was bruised, pulled out his eyebrows, and beat up his sister. When the children asked their parents what was wrong, the Joneses would shrug their shoulders and mumble something about "going through a phase." Although they had meant to reassure their children, what had happened was that Bob Jr. and Annie became afraid that they too would "go through a phase," or that they had caused this to happen to Jeb.

Mr. and Mrs. Jones decided to lift the veil of secrecy and tell their children the truth. Bob Jr. and Annie were spared the gory details, but with age-appropriate language they were informed that for over two years their brother had been sexually abused by Mr. R.

Both children felt confused, guilty, and fearful. Bob Jr. felt that he should have spent more time with his puny little brother, building him up, teaching him how to take care of himself. Annie felt that Jeb had been hurt because she had wished him dead. He had hit her and hurt her, and in her childish fantasies she had wished vengeance on him. Somehow, her wishes were powerful enough to cause this punishment to befall Jeb. It was her fault.

Both children needed short-term therapy to deal with their feelings and to be educated on sexual matters. They were reassured by a professional that their brother could recover. The therapist also helped them handle their jealousy over all the attention Jeb was getting. They were encouraged to see all their feelings as normal and to recognize that they could react in a responsible manner to those feelings.

The therapist guided Mr. and Mrs. Jones through new parenting techniques to help all their children—not just Jeb. As a family unit, the Joneses had been through a terrible ordeal. Part of their healing would have to come from learning new ways of interacting and a new appreciation of each other and each other's feelings.

2

The Grieving Process

Parents whose child has died grieve. Although your child is not dead, he has lost his innocence and naivete, and you will grieve for those losses. His childhood or adolescence has been severely disrupted, if not stolen entirely. Depending on the nature and extent of the abuse, your child may be suffering from one or more emotional, intellectual, and vocational impairments. These are all significant losses, worthy of grieving. And they will need to be mourned, not only by your child during his healing process, but by you as well.

In her landmark book, *On Death and Dying*, Elizabeth Kubler Ross explains that the grieving process consists of five stages: denial, anger, bargaining, depression, and acceptance. Not only the dying, but those who are close to the dying or to a loved one who is suffering usually experience the five stages of grief. These stages do not always occur in order and a person can be in more than one stage at a time. The length of time spent in each stage varies from person to person, as does the depth of feeling.

Denial

In the first stage—denial or shock—the loss engendered by the problem is not acknowledged. For example, at first Jeb's father could not believe that the abuse had really occurred. He thought, or more accurately wished, that Jeb was only fantasizing. It's not unusual for parents, even parents who are emotionally sensitive and nonjudgmental, initially to go into a state of denial about abuse. It's only human to want to avoid painful realities: acknowledging that one's child has been so terribly victimized hurts. Like Achilles' mother, who sought to make her son immortal, parents hope that by lavishing their child with love and care and their best wishes they can protect him from harm. When, for you, that hope is shattered by evidence that your child has been violated—when the bough breaks—your world can come crashing down on you. Because of the overwhelming pain involved in facing this reality, you can easily remain in denial, especially if you feel hopeless because you are unaware that help is available.

How did you feel when you first learned that your child had been sexually abused? Perhaps you felt nothing at all, except a certain numbness or disbelief.

Such numbness or shock is not a sign of your insensitivity or lack of love for your child; it is a totally normal, natural reaction to the devastation of learning that someone you love so much has been injured. Have you ever cut your finger and not felt the pain immediately? Or suffered whiplash in a car accident, but not felt the soreness or fatigue until several days later? The body often emits a natural anesthetic which gives us some time to take care of our wounds and to do whatever is necessary to protect ourselves from further injury. When the pain is overwhelming, we may even lose consciousness entirely. Our bodies simply cannot tolerate the pain and nature, mercifully, spares us.

Just as, in self-protection, the body may temporarily anesthetize itself against physical pain, the psyche, in self-protection, can numb itself against onslaughts of unbearable emotional pain. For you as a parent, there is no greater pain than knowing that your child has been hurt. All of your natural protective instincts as a parent have been trampled on and you feel worse than if you yourself had been violated. If, in fact, you actually were abused physically, sexually, or emotionally in the past, your pain may be especially intense because you know, firsthand, how deep the wounds can go. The knowledge that your child has been abused as you once were may reopen old and forgotten wounds.

In self-protection against such pain, you may not believe the news that your child has been sexually abused. You may even accuse the informant—your child, a relative, a schoolteacher, or a police officer—of lying. Or you may feel positive that there has been some mistake: certainly it is some other child who has been abused, not yours. Even when presented with bloodied clothing, medical reports, or other undeniable evidence, you may persist in your denial.

You are not alone. Until recently, most of our society was in denial about childhood sexual abuse. The crime was shrouded in secrecy. Those few children who had the courage to "tell" were often accused of lying or making up tales.

For most people, the thought of harming a defenseless child is unthinkable. Considering children as sexual objects is even more unthinkable. Until about ten to fifteen years ago, even some physicians ignored obvious evidence of sexual or physical abuse in children. Because child abuse was so abominable to them and they could not conceive of ever misusing a child themselves, they went into denial. In failing to label the child as abused, to make inquiries about the abuse, or to report the abuse to authorities, they inadvertently perpetuated the child's agony.

These physicians were not ignorant, nor were they condoning the abuse. The crime of child sexual abuse was simply so reprehensible to them that they could not accept the medical evidence before their eyes. If a physician who is trained to be objective and observant can deny the abuse, how much easier can it be for you, a parent who is deeply and emotionally committed to this child, to deny it as well?

If you feel that the sexual abuse is a sign of your negligence or the consequence of some "sin" on your part (for which you are being punished through your child's suffering), your denial may be severe. It is much easier to deny the abuse than to feel that it was somehow your fault. This was the case with Jeb's parents, both of whom felt guilty about not having participated more actively in Jeb's activities.

Your denial may also be strong if you, like Jeb's parents, believe that sexual abuse is rare and only happens to "bad" children or children from "bad" families. The fact that your child has been assaulted does not reflect on your personality or integrity as a person or parent, nor on your child's. Unless you actually were negligent or knowingly allowed the abuse to occur without trying to stop it, the perpetrator, *not you*, is solely responsible for the abuse.

The Joneses were shocked that child sexual abuse could happen to a decent family like theirs. Yet the sexual abuse of children, like other forms of violence, is blind to differences of race, class, or social standing. The crime is widespread and affects all socioeconomic levels. It can happen to a child of any race, background, religion, or geographical area. A child of a prosperous family or a child of the suburbs can be victimized just as easily as a child from a broken home who lives in a slum with an alcoholic parent.

It's normal for you to be in denial at first, at least until you gather the inner resources to absorb your shock. However, you can do your child harm if you continue to deny the problem. You may be unable to assess the extent of the damage to him. When your child displays symptoms of abuse, you may pretend they aren't there or dismiss them as "unimportant." You may even resist your own healthy impulses as well as the attempts of others to get help for your child.

In one instance, a preschool boy had been sexually abused by a teenager for more than two years. This teenager had also abused several other children in the neighborhood. When the abuser was caught, parents of the victimized children met to compare notes. Initially, the preschooler's mother felt that she did not need to attend because she could not accept the fact that her son was one of the victims. However, when her son asked her to suck his penis, she became alarmed and wanted to put him in therapy. But her husband was still in denial. He saw therapy as unnecessary, even though his son had approached him, too, for sexual stimulation. The mother eventually took her son to a therapist without her husband's approval.

In some but definitely not all cases, a parent's denial may stem from the fact that he or she was sexually abused as a child but has repressed the memory. For example, Lisa's six-year-old daughter would stick her fingers in her vagina at school and ask her teachers and schoolmates to smell her fingers and taste how good they were. Lisa was mortified and punished her daughter severely. However, she passed off her daughter's behavior as "normal" childhood experimentation. Even when other signs of abuse became obvious, Lisa found other explanations or blocked them out of her memory. In time, however, Lisa began to recall being molested herself as a child. Her memories were vague, but she remembered a "big man" holding her tightly in bed, telling her he loved her, and to "be quiet." Only after Lisa acknowledged the possibility that she had been abused was she able to deal with her daughter's abuse.

Sometimes denial is sustained because of fear of what others, especially one's parents, might think. Judith and Tom often let their preschool daughter run nude around the house or at the beach. It was part of their California lifestyle. Tom's mother highly disapproved and was particularly vocal when her granddaughter would race madly through crowds of sunbathers to hurl herself naked into the ocean which lay only a few hundred yards from her home.

"What's going on here? It's not safe to have her exposed like that. She could fall and hurt herself. Or someone will grab her and run off with her," Grandma would warn over and over. "She'll grow up to be flighty."

Judith and Tom shrugged off the warnings as "old-fashioned" and "conservative." However, when their child was sexually abused by a teacher at her nursery school, they denied the reality of the abuse for quite some time because they couldn't handle hearing Tom's mother's gloomy "I told you so. No one ever listens to me." On an irrational level they felt that Grandma was right: that the way they had dressed their daughter had somehow been the reason she was molested.

The reality was that the abuse occurred in a nursery school, where their daughter was appropriately dressed. Furthermore, other children with varied lifestyles were also molested. Had Judith and Tom caused their abuse, too? Of course not—but the trauma of sexual abuse is such that our minds play tricks with reality while attempting to deny what has happened. The reality hurts; the pain is overwhelming and the mind tries to protect us from having to feel that pain. When irrational guilt gets mixed in—as it did for Judith and Tom—denial can be a very powerful tool.

Parents may acknowledge the abuse but maintain denial about the severity of their child's symptoms. Some children develop more severe symptoms than others—however it's not uncommon for parents to wishfully assume that "time heals all wounds," or that their children will outgrow their symptoms on their own without professional help.

The Joneses had a particularly hard time accepting that Jeb needed help, because no one in their family had ever before consulted a mental health professional. In their view, only feeble-brained or crazy people sought mental health care. If Jeb had merely been depressed, they might have passed off his symptoms as grouchiness or teenage stuff and not have sent him to a therapist. However, his self-mutilation and their own paranoid fear that he would become a homosexual prompted the Joneses to overcome their biases and seek help for him. In cases like theirs, a severe symptom can be a blessing in disguise because it forces families who mistrust or who are unfamiliar with mental health services to get the professional help their children need. Symptoms of "craziness" may not be all that crazy as they seem, but may simply be your child's only avenue towards recognition and help.

If your child has severe nightmares or sleeping problems, or if he is having attention or behavior problems at school, or if he has developed an eating disorder or an addiction to alcohol or drugs as a result of the abuse, intensive or long-term help may be required. The abuse also may retard your child's intellectual and emotional growth. Although it's painful to acknowledge that your son or daughter is "behind" in school or in emotional maturity, these realities must be faced if they are to be dealt with effectively. Sexual abuse can scar, but healing and help for your child are available.

Anger

Once your denial is cracked, expect to be flooded with anger. Like Jeb's father you may want to rush out, buy a gun, and kill the abuser. "Why me? Why my child? What did I do to deserve this?" you will ask. In this stage, you may be angry not only at life or at God, but at society in general. "If there wasn't so much child pornography, maybe my child wouldn't have been harmed," you might feel. Or perhaps you blame the media's obsession with sex or some other aspect of our society for your child's abuse. It is at the anger stage that parents of sexually abused girls often become politicized regarding the reality of sexism, especially if they encounter sexist attitudes or negative stereotypes about sexually abused girls in their search for medical and psychological help for their daughter.

You will experience anger, if not outright murderous rage, at your child's abuser. If that abuser is a family member, neighbor, or friend, you will also experience the rage associated with the betrayal of your trust. If the abuser is someone you love—your spouse, your lover, your brother, or even your son—you will feel torn apart by conflicting emotions. In addition to helping your child, you should get help for yourself at this point. No human being can handle this sort of stress alone. If getting therapy for yourself seems self-indulgent, think of it as a way of strengthening yourself so that you can better help your child.

If your child enters a program of therapy, you may be angry on some level about the time and expense involved in the healing process. Your life, and your pocketbook, will be disrupted for therapy sessions and visits to doctors. While you may be glad to give all you can to help your child, you may also greatly resent that one person's crime is costing you so much, both emotionally and financially.

At this point, you may even feel angry at your victimized child for the burden he is causing you. Do not be ashamed of this feeling. You are a parent, but you are a human being, too. Rationally, you know your child did not choose to be abused, but emotionally you may resent the financial and emotional load your child's abuse has imposed upon your life.

You may also be angry at your powerlessness and helplessness. How you wish you could wave a magic wand and make the abuse, and its effects, go away! You're angry that you're no longer in control of your life or that of your child. An abuser has intruded not only on your peace of mind, but on your child's emotional and physical health, and has thrown the entire family off balance—perhaps even broken the family apart. You're angry because when your child was victimized, you were victimized, too.

You may also be angry at the fact that innocent people are made to suffer through no fault of their own. Because of your child's pain, you've probably begun to develop a heartfelt empathy for and identification with other victims and their families, all of which can be extremely painful. You may even have begun to ask age-old questions for which there are few adequate answers—questions such as, "Why do the good suffer and the evil prosper?" Perhaps you now challenge your religious faith and spiritual assumptions about the goodness of the universe.

Professional Misunderstanding

You might be angry at certain mental health professionals. Unfortunately, many incest survivors, rape victims, and other sexually abused people have not been spared the humiliation of psychiatric misdiagnosis. Prior to the American Psychiatric Association's acknowledgment of Post-Traumatic Stress Disorder as a psychiatric problem in 1980, some troubled sex abuse survivors, both male and female, were given negative-sounding labels such as "character disordered," "sociopathic personality," "schizoid personality," or "borderline personality," especially if they were from a minority group. Such mislabeling has sometimes occurred due to Freudian assumptions about an individual's problems being rooted in the inability to resolve childhood conflicts.

Although it is certainly true that childhood conflicts can influence behavior in later years, critical events that occur after age seven, adolescence, or even later can also have a significant impact on the personality. Therapists and mental health practitioners who adhere to the Freudian notion that the personality is "set" by age seven due to childhood patterns often have trouble recognizing the profound changes that trauma, such as sexual abuse, can wreak on the individual at any age.

Study after study has found that age, prior mental history, and educational background do not predict who will develop post-trauma symptoms.[1] Yet some therapists are unaware of these studies; or, even if they're aware of this recent work, they still adhere to the Freudian-based notion that childhood conflicts are the central controlling factors in shaping the personality.

Mislabeling can still occur because of such mistaken notions, or simply as a result of the therapist's lack of experience in helping victims of childhood sexual abuse.

Today, however, more and more mental health professionals are realizing that a significant stressor such as incest can create psychiatric symptoms in an individual regardless of pretrauma mental health. But you should be aware that there are still therapists who blame the victim or, as in the case of Jeb's first therapist, blame the parents.

Some sexual abuse survivors are now in the process of being psychiatrically reevaluated in hopes of having the negative labels removed from their records. In some cases the damage of misdiagnosis has already been done. Carey was inaccurately labeled "borderline" and "character disordered," which all but destroyed her self-confidence. Her current psychiatrist attributes her symptoms to her having been sexually abused as a child rather than to any "psychopathological" component of her personality. But Carey is still convinced that she is mentally ill. Her mother, timid by nature, feels almost homicidal toward those who mislabeled her daughter for so many years. "We thought we were getting the best care possible for Carey, but now she is damaged anyway," she says. "Where do I go to complain? How do I wash away her hurt and give her back her dignity?"

Like other parents who see the results of their child's low self-esteem, Carey's parents live in a state of nearly constant grieving and anger.

Bargaining

The bargaining stage of grieving is characterized by fantasies of "what if" and "if only." Carey's parents, like others, are not only angry at their daughter's abuser and at the therapists who misdiagnosed her, but they are also angry at themselves. Perhaps you, too, like Jeb's parents, somehow blame yourself for your child's abuse.

Do you ever think, "If only I hadn't let him visit that uncle, go to that camp, go away for that summer," or "What if I had spent more time with him—he might have told me about the abuse sooner," or "If only I had forced him to go to a counselor the first time he showed signs of a problem!"

Remember that you did not commit the abuse and, in most circumstances, there was probably no way you could have prevented it. Nevertheless, if you are in the bargaining stage, you might find yourself going to church or synagogue more often and making larger and larger contributions to charity. Or perhaps you make a secret promise never to lie, steal, or cheat again in hopes of purchasing your child's recovery with your purity. Some parents even punish themselves physically or materially in hopes that their sacrifice will ensure their child's mental health and happiness. If you really want to help your child, educate yourself about sexual abuse and support him as he goes through the recovery process.

Depression

There are many kinds of depression: the normal fluctuations in mood experienced by almost everyone; clinical depressions, which can be either neurotic or psychotic; and the depression associated with the grieving process. You may be experiencing this last type. If so, remember that this is a normal response to an extremely stressful situation.

As the parent of a sexually abused child, you are under severe stress. Not only are you coping with your child's feelings and needs, your own feelings, and the reactions of others, but you are also making complex arrangements in providing for your child's care. Perhaps you are also prosecuting the offender through legal or police actions. At the same time, you are suffering from many losses:

- The loss of your child as he once was

- The disruption to your marriage, family life, and career caused by the needs of your abused child and/or any court or police action

- The loss of your belief that the world is safe and just and your illusion that you could protect your child

You may also be experiencing a loss in status if some of your relatives, neighbors, or friends have placed a negative judgment on your child's victimization and consider you and your family "tainted" because of the abuse (this is not at all uncommon!). If you are paying medical or psychiatric bills or are pursuing litigation, you are also losing time, money, and peace of mind. The time and money you are spending on your abused child lessens the time and money you could be investing in your marriage, your other children, your career, or other aspects of your life. Although Mrs. Jones was reluctant to admit it, she resented the fact that the money she and her husband had been saving toward that once-in-a-lifetime vacation was now going to pay for Jeb's therapy bills instead. She was also sad that as a result of the abuse she had even less time for herself and even less of her husband's already limited time.

You also experience the sense of losing control over your life and your child's welfare as you realize that all your anger and your attempts at bargaining are futile: they will not make the abuse, or its effects on your child, go away.

A natural response to all these stresses and losses is depression. Even though the depression associated with the grieving process is temporary, it can still be intense and painful. You may also suffer some of the symptoms associated with clinical depression: difficulty concentrating, low self-esteem, changes in your eating and sleeping patterns, feelings of futility and hopelessness, or various physical problems such as backaches, headaches, vomiting, or constipation.

Extreme fatigue or its opposite, physical agitation, are common to depression. You find every task an overwhelming burden; you see little hope for your child or your family situation; you are tired all the time; and you receive little or no pleasure even from people or events that normally would please you.

You may have lost interest in sex. Although you may be able to engage in sexual activity, it seems to have lost its appeal. Loss of sexual interest is part of depression and, in your case, it may be partly due to the association of sex with your child's pain. You may not be able to stop thinking of your child being sexually abused when you begin to have sexual thoughts or engage in sexual activity. These thoughts can definitely interfere with your zest for sex. Since sexual activity and orgasm require energy, they are often seen as draining by the depressed person and are consequently avoided.

The possibility exists that you may be suffering from both a clinical depression and the depression associated with grieving, especially if you are an abuse survivor or have been otherwise traumatized in life. If you are unable to get out of bed, unable to feed yourself, or otherwise unable to take care of yourself; if you are having delusions or hallucinations; or if you are having disturbing, recurring thoughts of death or suicide, seek help immediately.

If you are experiencing five or more of the following symptoms, which psychiatrists recognize as being part of a major depressive episode, and these symptoms persist for more than two weeks, you owe it to yourself to have a consultation with a mental health professional trained in depression. This list of symptoms is reprinted with permission of the American Psychiatric Association.[2]

1. "Depressed mood ... most of the day, nearly every day, as indicated by self observation or by others"

2. "Markedly diminished interest or pleasure in all, or almost all, activities most of the day, nearly every day ..."

3. "Significant weight loss or weight gain when not dieting (e.g., more than five percent of body weight in a month), or decrease or increase in appetite nearly every day ..."

4. "Insomnia or hypersomnia [oversleeping] nearly every day"

5. "Moving in an agitated hyperactive manner or moving in slow motion nearly every day ..."

6. "Fatigue or loss of energy nearly every day"

7. "Feelings of worthlessness or excessive or inappropriate guilt (which may be delusional) nearly every day (not merely self-reproach or guilt about being sick)"

8. "Diminished ability to think or concentrate, or indecisiveness, nearly every day ..."

9. "Recurrent thoughts of death (not just fear of dying), recurrent suicidal ... [thoughts] without a specific plan, or a suicide attempt or a specific plan for committing suicide."

The above list is only a rough guide. If you have any symptom or problem that concerns you, discuss your concern with a trained professional. You need to take good care of yourself as well if you are going to be of help to your child. Left untreated, depression worsens over time. The symptoms can create a vicious cycle whereby depression is not only perpetuated, but deepened. Mild depressions can become moderate ones and moderate ones severe. If you become severely depressed, you will be emotionally unavailable to your child and will be unable to take the necessary actions to assure his recovery.

If you are diagnosed as having a clinical depression, do not conclude that you are a "hopeless mental case." Being clinically depressed does not mean that you're insane. It does mean that you may have a biochemical imbalance which creates negative thinking and negative feelings; that you may have a lifestyle that is not sufficiently rewarding to you; that you have suffered many losses or lived under considerable stress in your life; or that you yourself may have been traumatized.

Recent years have seen important advances in our understanding of depression: today depression is a highly treatable condition. There is no reason for you to spend the rest of your life chronically depressed and unhappy. Get help, and you will be better able to help your child.

Acceptance

Acceptance is the final stage of grief. After you have gone through the other stages, you will no longer feel so depressed or enraged about the abuse. You will simply accept it and the emotional toll it has taken on all the members of your family. Acceptance does not mean that you are happy, but rather that you have stopped fighting your own limitations and the reality of what happened to your child.

Now you realize what every parent of a troubled child must eventually admit: that while you can be supportive and loving, you do not have the power to cure what ails your child. You cannot heal him with your love, your gifts, or your desire to take away the pain. You can only seek qualified help and support him through the recovery process. In this sense, acceptance is not the same as hopelessness or passive resignation, because you are continuing to search for recovery. You have not given up. You have accepted what has happened. Now you will concentrate on the healing process.

For the Mother of the Incestuously Abused Child

If your child has been sexually abused by a family member, know that you are not alone. Countless other mothers have had their world shattered by incest, too. Of all the forms of sexual abuse, incest is the most heartbreaking and the most common; yet it is also the most shrouded in taboo and ignorance.

Reflecting on the day she was informed that her husband was having an incestuous relationship with their daughter, one mother wrote:

"I wanted to throw up. I kept feeling the vomit in my throat but it just stayed there burning. I concentrated on that physical upset to avoid facing the truth. My husband, the man I trusted and planned to live with for all my life, had done this horrible thing. It was too much. Incest was something you read about that happened in unfortunate families with no money, no morals, and no brains. Not us! Not affluent, educated people. I finally threw up and then I couldn't stop. I threw up over and over and the tears streamed down my face and I kept trying to shut out that horrible word. Incest."

Until this mother sought help and educated herself about incest, she thought that it only occurred among the "lower classes" and that she was the only middle-class woman alive who had to bear such sorrow. Far from being restricted to certain social groups, incest is endemic in our society. "Incest," writes Marjorie Leidig, a psychotherapist who specializes in treating incest survivors, is the "most underreported crime against women and girls in the U.S.—even more than battering and rape."[3]

In over 95 percent of the cases, abusers are male and victims are female. Although boys are victimized, too, approximately 90 percent of victims are girls. Mothers, aunts, sisters, and even grandmothers have been found to sexually abuse child relatives of both sexes—however they are clearly in the minority. By far, the most common forms of incest are

- Father or stepfather/boyfriend–daughter incest

- Brother–sister incest

- Uncle–niece or grandfather–granddaughter incest

It is to mothers involved in these situations that the following three sections are addressed.

For the Mother Whose Daughter Has Been Abused by Her Husband, Boyfriend, Lover, or Partner

Can there be any greater sorrow or rage than yours? In the ancient Greek play, *Oedipus Rex*, King Oedipus stabs himself in the eyes when he discovers that, unbeknownst to him, he has committed incest. Blinding himself is a means of self-punishment, but it is also a way of saying, "Incest is so terrible, so degrading, I don't want to see, or remember, what happened." This is a poeticized rendition of denial.

You can probably identify with Oedipus's wish to forget what happened. Yet just as blinding himself does not make the incest go away for Oedipus, you can no longer deny what has occurred in your family. Many mothers, however, become so frightened and disoriented by the fact of incest and its far-reaching consequences that they persist in denial, acting as if the incest is not occurring or doesn't matter, the way Emily's mother did. In some cases, they may acknowledge that the incest is occurring, but minimize its impact. They may tell themselves that it was "only a couple of weeks of fondling" when it actually involved oral sex and intercourse for over two years. Or they may believe that the incest "isn't that important" when, in fact, they and their family can never again be the same.

Underneath the denial are intense fears about how the incest will affect the family's economic security and emotional stability. In many cases, as with the Smith family, disclosure of the incest can destroy the parent's marriage, livelihood, and social standing. The prospect of getting a divorce, becoming socially ostracized and involved in court litigation against her husband may also be overwhelming for any woman. If the mother has other children to consider, is physically or emotionally handicapped, or otherwise lacks the skills or strength to stand on her own, she may see no alternative apart from accepting the incest or acting as if her daughter is telling lies.

Some but definitely not all mothers who were themselves incestuously abused as children, and who have never dealt with their past, may develop "blind spots" when it comes to incest in their homes as adults. At the first sign of incest, they may tune out or otherwise ignore the obvious, because they need to continue to suppress their painful memories of the past. If you've done this, try to forgive yourself and get on with the business of helping your child. If the abuse is still going on, and you feel unable to stop it on your own, get help from other people: make a phone call to protective authorities if this is all you feel capable of doing for now. If the incest happened in the past, give your child all the love and support and protection that you're capable of giving *now*. Everyone makes the best decision she can within her emotional means at any given moment. Your conscious or unconscious decision to look the other way may seem despicable to you now: if so, your guilt is appropriate. Let it motivate you to positive action. Reading this book is a step in the right direction.

If you've chosen to believe your child, commend yourself on having had the courage and strength to do so. Although there may be times when you slip back into denial (for a little relief), basically you have been willing to face the truth. This shedding of denial may well mark the beginning of the most painful period of your life. However, it is also a necessary first step toward healing for you and your child.

While your husband, boyfriend, or lover has done much to destroy your daughter, all is not lost. You *can* help save her. Your responses to her, your support, and the kind of help you can provide for her can make all the difference in the world. Therapists who work with families blighted by incest concur that one of the most crucial variables, if not *the* most crucial variable, involved in healing the survivor's incest wound is the strength of the mother-daughter relationship.

Yet you cannot possibly be supportive of your daughter and strengthen your relationship with her until you first take care of yourself. This involves fully realizing and appreciating the extreme stress and pain of your position.

When incest is disclosed, all the attention tends to focus on the victim and the offender. You, the mother—and any other children—tend to be ignored. Yet you need a tremendous amount of support and help, too. Not only are you trying to overcome your shock and disbelief, and cope with your own emotional reactions, but you need to make many important decisions that will affect the future of your family. At the same time, you're trying to handle the increased emotional needs and distress of your other children, while maintaining the household all alone—without any help that your partner used to provide. If your partner is in jail or has lost his job because of the incest, you may be under considerable economic strain as well. Court or police action add additional mental, emotional, and financial strain.

Others seem to expect you to act like a superwoman. You might even expect this of yourself—it seems the least you can do after what your daughter has gone through. Inside, however, you're falling apart—torn between two people you love (or once loved) and feeling betrayed, perhaps even by both of them. You have probably given much to your partner and your daughter. Perhaps you've even dedicated your life to them, and have made many sacrifices for their well-being. In return, you've been humiliated and abandoned.

Rationally you know that your daughter cannot be blamed for the incest. Yet, in your pain and confusion, you may be faulting her for it anyway. You may even feel somewhat jealous of her, especially if she is an adolescent. Any feelings of jealousy you might have are entirely normal. Had your husband or lover been having an affair with another woman, you would have been jealous of her, too. Since the other woman is your child, any jealousy you feel is mingled with strong feelings of maternal protectiveness and compassion.

Many mothers have a difficult time admitting their negative feelings toward their daughters who've been victimized. Yet in the situation of incest, negative feelings directed against the daughter—such as jealousy and anger—are to be expected. Women in our society are trained to be competitive with other women and not to show anger toward men. It's quite natural to project your anger at your husband or lover onto your daughter instead (no matter how unjust this may be).

Similarly, your daughter, who is also the product of a patriarchal culture, may be projecting her anger at her abuser onto you, or onto another woman in the family, such as an older sister. This is not at all uncommon. After all, it's safer to be angry at another woman, whom she can at least trust not to hurt her physically, than to confront her anger toward someone who has already done her so much physical harm—and whom she still fears. It may feel safer to vent anger at you for failing to protect her (even though it may not have been in your power to do so) than to feel and express anger about the incestuous abuse itself. This transferred anger is another form of denial for the victim—a way of not confronting or admitting the existence of the abuse directly.

Therapists who work with incest survivors often observe that anger at the mother comes first, before the "real rage"—anger at the abusive father, stepfather, or boyfriend—can be expressed. Dr. Leidig, for example, has found that when incest survivors first come for help, they often deny their anger toward their father, only being able to express it intellectually. As a feminist, Dr. Leidig finds it difficult to accept that her client is directing her rage at the wrong person—the mother—but realizes that "this rage must come first."[4] When the survivor finally does get in touch with her anger at her abuser, however, her anger can be "beyond furious."

Your anger at your partner may also be "beyond furious." In order for you to heal, you will eventually need to express that rage in a safe manner. You have a right to your rage. Not only has the abuser violated your child, but he has broken your marriage vows (or other commitment) and has insulted your femininity and the integrity of your family to the core. Your sense of betrayal is rightfully enormous.

At only one level of outrage, the man you've shared your bed with and who promised to be your "one and only" has gone after "another woman." Your anger is even greater if he was having sexual relations with you at the same time he was sexually abusing your child (which is not an unusual occurrence). The very fact that he needed someone besides you can bring to the fore any personal insecurities you might have about your attractiveness and desirability or about your adequacy as a wife or partner.

Your situation will be doubly stressful if you yourself were incestuously abused as a child or victimized in some other way. Under such circumstances, your fears and anxieties will go back to your own unresolved issues about having been abused. You will need help in separating the present from the past, and deserve as much support as you can find, because you will not only be feeling the pain of the present, but of the past as well. The only positive side to having been abused yourself is that you are in a unique position to understand, empathize with, and be helpful to your daughter.

You may encounter a friend, family member, mental health professional, or court or police official who erroneously blames you for "allowing," "setting up," or even "enjoying" the incest. ("Did you ever watch?" many mothers have been asked.) People with this mind-set do exist, and it is important that you be aware of them, avoid them, and never let them convince you that you are to blame for things that were beyond your protection or control.

The Blame-the-Mother Tradition

Just as society tends to blame the victim of sexual abuse, in the case of father or stepfather incest, society tends to blame the mother as well. Psychological and psychiatric accounts abound with descriptions of the "incestuous triad" and the "collusive passive mother" who either consciously and/or unconsciously "sets up" her daughter for the abuse.

In these accounts, the mother is described as overly dependent, infantile, "femininely underdeveloped," or otherwise imperfect or deranged. As a result, she foists a role-reversal on her daughter wherein she expects her daughter to function as family caretaker as well as the father's sexual servant. Almost always the mother is portrayed as sexually disinterested, cold, or frigid. Other "villains" are mothers who have to work or go to school at night, or who are sexually or emotionally unavailable to their husbands due to child-birth or physical or mental illness. The grand conclusion is that incest is the mother's fault.

While it is true that incest is related to maternal absence, it is the father, stepfather, or lover who takes advantage of the situation to molest a child. There is no evidence that these men are forced to turn to a girl child for sexual gratification because of lack of sexual access to the mother. Sex offenders have been found to be having sexual relations with their children and their wives simultaneously. In most cases, those who were having sexual relations only with children did so because they rejected their wife or partner, not because she was sexually unavailable to them.

Even if the mother is cold, frigid, alcoholic, drug addicted, depressed, personality disordered, or otherwise dysfunctional, the mother's deficiencies are no excuse for incest. Consider the reverse situation. If a father is impotent, unemployed, chemically addicted, cold toward his wife, or otherwise an inadequate husband, would that justify the wife turning to her son for sexual gratification?

Popular opinion, as well as some professional opinion, holds that the mother "always knows" about the incest. Researchers, however, are finding that many mothers are not aware that incest is occurring. Even if there are signs of abuse, the mother may not pay attention to them because (a) incest is such a remote possibility that she cannot conceive of it occurring in her family, or (b) the daughter tried to indicate the problem to her mother, but communicated in such a vague or indirect manner that the mother could not interpret her meaning. Many of the incest survivors studied by Dr. Herman did not tell their mothers about the incest directly. Instead they complained about abdominal pains, genital problems, nightmares, anxieties, fears, and other symptoms—not the incest itself.

Confronting Realities

There are homes in which the mother does suspect or even know that incest is occurring. Often these are homes where

- The mother is a substance abuser

- The father or stepfather has a Dr. Jekyll-Mr. Hyde personality

- The mother is being physically battered and feels helpless in the face of her husband's abusiveness toward herself and her children

- The mother, for reasons having to do with her past and personality, is stuck in the psychological state of denial

There are also homes where the mother is not confronted with any direct evidence of incest, but where she chooses to turn away when faced with subtle indicators of an incestuous relationship. Emily's mother noticed that her husband would disappear while they were watching television together, and that he liked to watch Emily dressing. But she never asked him to stop his voyeurism or inquired about where he went or what he did while she was left alone to watch TV.

If you are in a relationship in which you are being battered, or are aware that your daughter is being sexually misused, you have a moral *and* a legal obligation to seek help. The battering and abuse will not stop on their own accord: they will only escalate over time. As difficult as it may be, pick up the phone and call your nearest crisis hotline for information on available help.

Like many mothers in this situation, you are probably asking yourself, "What did I do wrong? Was it my fault? Why didn't I pick up the signs that my child was being abused?" Your mind is probably racing with negative thoughts. Your guilt may be so severe that it hampers your ability to act on behalf of your daughter.

Dealing with incest is neither easy nor a short-term matter. The disclosure of incest in your home may trigger a deep self-examination and a close look at your patterns of relating to others, especially to men and to your children. Without blaming yourself for the incest, you may come to see how certain problems within yourself or in your marriage or relationship may have contributed to the situation. This self-examination may be painful, but it can ultimately help you to grow.

Always remember that no personal problem and no amount of marital discord or estrangement constitutes an excuse for incest. Your husband, boyfriend, or lover is the one who committed the crime, not you. Deciding whether or not to prosecute him, and whether or not to leave him, are highly complex, individual matters that need to be talked out with caring friends and understanding mental health professionals. Your first duty, though, is to put your daughter out of danger of being abused again. If the only way to do this is to leave your husband, boyfriend, or lover (or to obtain a court order to make *him* leave), then your choice is clear.

Incest creates upheaval in every dimension of life, including your relationships with friends and relatives. Do not be surprised if some of them suddenly exclude or avoid you, or if you feel sharp pangs of grief and bitterness as you hear others talking happily about their family lives. Surround yourself with as many supportive, caring people as possible and consider joining a support group such as Parents United. This resource and others are listed in the Appendix.

Sibling Incest

Sibling incest is often trivialized as "harmless childhood experimentation." This may be the case where two siblings have engaged in playing "doctor." However, such sex play usually ceases after two or three episodes. If the sexual contact persists, especially if it occurs between a brother and a sister, one can no longer speak of it as sex play.

When it comes to sexual contact involving children, there is no such thing as "willing participation" even if both participants say they are "willing." The sister may be older, taller, and smarter, but she may also have been socialized—as the vast majority of girls are socialized—to please and be subservient to the male; she is no longer a "willing participant." Her brother is acting on "male prerogative" and on the power that males wield over females due to society's teachings about male superiority. Even if the sister claims to have "enjoyed" the sexual contact, and had sexual and even emotional needs met through the sexual contact, she is still the brother's victim. This is true even if she is not injured or coerced with violence.

If the siblings involved are two brothers who began playing "doctor," typically one brother wishes to cease the sexual contact after one or two episodes, whereas the other insists on continuing it. "Come on, you liked it last time. Why are you changing on me?" or "If you don't do it anymore, I'll tell and you'll be in big trouble," or "It doesn't hurt you, so why are you complaining?" the aggressor might say.

Sibling Incest as an Expression of Insecurity Within the Family

Another situation that may appear harmless, but which, in fact, can have far-reaching consequences, is where siblings turn to each other for emotional comfort and security because neither parent is emotionally attentive and/or where one or both parents are physically or emotionally absent much of the time. For example, homes in which both parents are actively alcoholic and children have to fend for themselves are likely sites for sibling incest. Under such circumstances, a brother and a sister may look to each other for the affection and guidance that should have been provided by the parents. This can lead to sexual contact (although, of course, this is not always a consequence).

Once again, one of the siblings usually desires to cease the sexual behavior once it has commenced, but feels powerless to do so. He, or she, may be so pressured by the dependency bond that it's im-

possible to stand up to the sibling's insistence that the incest continue.

The incest is more obviously abusive when the instigating partner
is older, stronger, or more knowledgeable than the other sibling, who
then functions like the victim in adult-child incestuous relationships.
In the case where the nineteen-year-old brother enlists the participation of his five-year-old sister as he masturbates, there is no "harmless childhood experimentation" involved.

If Your Son Has Violated Your Daughter

Sisters violated by brothers are often subject to physical and/or
psychological coercion; as adults they display many of the symptoms of survivors of father-daughter incest. In some instances where
the brother has used their father as a role model, the same girl is
victimized by both her father and her brother.

If you have discovered that your son has been sexually abusing
your daughter, much that has been written in the previous section
also applies to you. While your adequacy as a wife or lover is not
being called into question, your parenting skills may well be
scrutinized and analyzed, not only by others, but by yourself as well.
"Where did I go wrong? How did I fail as a parent for this to happen? How could I have raised such a son?" you might be asking
yourself.

Do not forget that there are other influences in your son's life
besides you. First and foremost, your son is living in a society that
not only gives men permission to abuse women and persons smaller
and less powerful than themselves, but confers signs of masculinity
and status to such men. Violence against women is portrayed daily
in the media and in pornography; your son, like other males, is not
immune to it.

If your husband or boyfriend has been abusive to you or your
daughter, you may be chastising yourself for having chosen a violent
or critical partner with whom to live. Lisa, for example, blamed herself when her twelve-year-old son was found sexually abusing her
seven-year-old daughter. "It's all my fault," she sobbed. "If I hadn't
allowed my boyfriend to hit me, my son wouldn't have learned that
it's okay for men to push women around."

Lisa left an abusive husband when her children were three and
eight. For several years she avoided dating and spent most of her
time working and taking care of her children. When she met her
boyfriend, Paul, there were no signs that he was violent. But soon
after he moved in with her, he began to use physical force to get his
way.

Lisa cowered for a while—but after a year of abuse, she made Paul leave. Yet she can't help feeling that the scars of having been exposed to violence are responsible for the incest between her son and daughter. When Lisa sought help, the psychologist told her that sibling incest tended to occur in two types of homes:

- Where the parents were alienated from each other and also neglected the children, forcing the children to turn to each other for attention and nurturing

- Where physical and/or sexual abuse were modeled by an adult male

Lisa felt full of guilt. When she had to work more than one job to make ends meet, she sometimes had to leave the children alone and was often too tired to give them much attention. Also, she was certain that her son had learned to be abusive from her husband and boyfriend.

"But you left your husband and threw out the boyfriend," the psychologist reminded her. "And you aren't responsible for your son's behavior, even if everyone is telling you that you are. What you are responsible for, however, is getting your son—and your daughter—some help."

Subsequent analysis of the son revealed that he harbored considerable hostility toward his father for abandoning the family and for abusing his mother. He also resented his mother's boyfriend for hurting his mother and for hitting him, too. The son felt emasculated when he could not protect his mother, or himself, from these men; but he also wanted to be powerful like them. Abusing his sister was a means of venting his anger and asserting his masculinity.

Every family situation is unique and complex. There are no pat answers as to why sibling incest occurs and how to maintain the family after it is found out. The only rule to remember is that your daughter needs to be protected from further abuse. If your son is unable to control himself, he may have to live somewhere else or never be left unsupervised with his sister.

In every case of such abuse, professional help, both individual and family, will be needed, and the healing process may well take a considerable amount of time.

Lisa's daughter, for example, required two hospitalizations before she was able to put the abuse in perspective—in other words, not to make the abuse the central controlling event of her life. She felt abandoned and betrayed not only by her brother, but by her mother as well. Rationally, the daughter knew that her mother was absent from the home because she was working to put bread on the table, but emotionally the daughter felt that her mother should have been there to protect her.

It was easier for this young girl to resolve her feelings towards her mother than towards her brother, whom she still fears. She is now married to a man with whom she has a loving and relatively egalitarian relationship devoid of any abuse—verbal, physical, or sexual. She is capable of loving deeply, responding sexually, and going for long periods of time without even thinking of the incest. However, whenever her brother contacts her, she spirals into anxiety and fear. She has had two major depressive episodes: when her daughter turned the age she was when she was abused, and when her son turned the age of her brother when he abused her. She also watches her son intensely for any signs that he may be sexually or in any other way abusive toward her daughter.

If Your Daughter Is Abused by Your Uncle, Cousin, Father, or Other Male Relative

The fact that a member of your family had so little respect for both you and your daughter is ample cause for volcanic rage and profound hurt. What the rest of the family thinks or feels about the situation is irrelevant. Even if they don't believe you or your daughter, it's imperative that you protect your daughter from future assaults. If necessary, you may need to avoid family gatherings or never invite the abuser or his supporters to your home again. If this causes some family members to criticize you or never speak to you again, so be it.

Although you will want to seek help for yourself and your child, it is not necessary for you to engage in joint counseling with the abuser. You may or may not want to establish a relationship with him again. The choice is yours.

If the man who violated your child also violated you as a child or young adult, you may be reexperiencing your own incest as well as blaming yourself for allowing your child to be in his presence. It bears repeating that you did not commit the crime. Your responsibility now is to protect your child (and any other children) from the abuser and to provide qualified help for your child should she need it.

In order for your child to be healed of her experiences with sexual abuse, she will need to undergo the grieving process. She will need to face her pain, sorrow, and anger. In a parallel manner, you will need to overcome any tendency to deny or minimize the fact that your child was sexually victimized, and experience your own grieving process—not only for the losses to your child but for your own losses as well.

While you are grieving, you may feel disoriented and "out of control." Given the stress of acknowledging that the abuse occurred, and the emotional, financial, and other burdens associated with providing for your child's care (and possibly prosecuting the offender), you are only responding appropriately. You will be especially stressed, since the abuser is a member of your extended family. You may have conflicting feelings toward the abuser (especially if he is your father or brother), and an enormous sense of betrayal and rage. You will also have to deal with the reactions of other members of your family (who may not be able to accept the reality of the abuse), and may have to go to great lengths to protect your child from further abusive violation. As she learns how dangerous it is to trust certain adults in your family, your daughter will need more than ever to know that she can trust *you*. Be there for her; support her through this difficult time.

3

Disclosure and Coping With the Reactions of Others

Change creates stress. Even a positive change, such as a promotion, can cause you difficulties. Your stress level can reach the crisis point when you have to deal with not just one life change, but many. Major events—such as marriage, divorce, the birth of a child, relocation, a job change, or the illness or death of a family member—can be considered crises precisely because they involve handling at least two or three, if not four or five, important life issues at a time.

Coping simultaneously with several challenges can strain anyone, even the most well-adjusted and efficient among us. A familiar story is that of the successful executive who has felt secure within herself for years but suddenly finds herself "falling apart" when faced with the death of her husband. Accustomed to feeling in control of herself and capable of managing not only her own life, but an entire business, she now berates herself for feeling so fragile, scattered, and overwhelmed. She forgets or minimizes the fact that not only has she lost a significant love relationship, but is adjusting to other losses as well: economic losses, a loss in social status, and the loss of certain friends and relationships.

Because she represents an unpleasant event, some of her former friends and associates avoid her, depriving her of social support and human comfort just when she needs them the most. The negative responses of others not only make her feel lonely, but guilty, as if she were somehow at fault for suffering losses that were out of her control.

The sexual abuse of your child is a major life crisis. Not only are you trying to help your child, deal with mental health professionals (and/or police and legal officials), and cope with your own grieving, but you must also contend with the reactions of others: those of your spouse or partner, your children, and your friends, neighbors, relatives, and casual acquaintances.

Like the widow, you may be ignored or stigmatized because you represent a painful reality that others would rather deny. Don't be surprised if some people stare into space or quickly change the subject when you tell them about your child's experience. Or perhaps you will find people to be rejecting or judgmental—people you thought would be as crushed as you were when you learned of the abuse.

Don't take these negative reactions to heart. They are not a reflection on you or your child. They indicate either your listener's ignorance about sexual abuse or the person's fears and anxieties about the emotionally charged issues of sexuality and victimization.

"I would never allow that to happen to one of *my* children," the mother of a four-year-old rape victim was told, as if this grief-stricken mother had "allowed" the rape to occur. Mothers of incest victims especially may be blamed for failing to protect their daughters from the abusive relative or for not having detected the incest sooner.

There are some mothers who are not only aware of the incest in their home but actively encourage it. However, such women are clearly in the minority. More typically the mother suspects or knows about the incest, but turns away, overcome by denial or anxiety about her economic and emotional security; or she may simply be too preoccupied with herself to focus her attention on her child's plight. In other cases, the mother has no knowledge, not even a clue, that the incest is occurring. It is these mothers who almost always seek help for their child once the incest is disclosed, and who often end up separating from or divorcing their husband.

Once others learn that your child has been abused, you may hear such comments as: "That's what happens when you don't go to church on Sunday (or synagogue on the Sabbath) ... when children are in parochial school ... when mothers work outside the home ... when there's divorce in the family ... when you have too many children ... when you have an only child ... when you give your child too much freedom ... when you restrict and overprotect your child ... when you talk about sex at home and overstimulate the child ... when you don't talk about sex at home and the child is sexually uninformed."

Perhaps one of the most devastating remarks you'll hear is that what happened to your child is "God's punishment" for one of your sins or one of your child's moral slips. Or maybe you will be told that your child invited the abuse because she was too shy and wanted attention, or was too sassy and "provoked" the abuser. Or perhaps she was too attractive and the abuser couldn't help himself, or too plain and consequently was an easy target, or permitted the abuse because she needed affirmation of her desirability.

You have a right to feel angry when you hear such comments. They are enormously insensitive and hurtful. They are also inaccurate. They reflect not only a profound ignorance about the prevalence and nature of child sexual abuse in our society, but our society's lamentable but well-documented tendency to blame the victim—and the victim's parents, too. Underlying this blame-the-victim attitude is the "just world" philosophy which holds that people get what they deserve and deserve what they get. The "good" are rewarded and the "bad" are punished. Although many people would not openly admit to subscribing to such beliefs, they are nonetheless widely held and can influence attitudes toward victims. If someone suffers, it must be because he or his parents were "bad": weak, ineffective, emotionally disturbed, morally debased, irresponsible, stupid, reckless, or whatever. Jeb's parents were subject to this sort of thinking.

Despite the obvious wrongness of the blame-the-victim attitude, it exists not only among the general public, but among some caregivers (such as Jeb's first therapist) and community professionals as well. In a recent survey of police, hospital, and mental health professionals, the American Psychological Association found that not only victims of sexual abuse and physical battering, but victims of robberies, muggings, car thefts, and even murder were often blamed for their fate. If only the victim had been more competent, more careful, or otherwise behaved "as they should," the incident would not have occurred.[1]

Such thinking was especially applied to rape victims, who were blamed for dressing too sexily, smiling too warmly, or otherwise "asking for it." If they were attacked outdoors, they were blamed for not being at home where they belonged. If they were attacked in their homes, fault was found with their behavior, attitude, or personality. Even mugging victims have been blamed for "being in the wrong neighborhood," or "carrying too much money" or "too little money," and murder victims for "associating with bad company" (even when the victim had no prior relationship with the attacker).

Behind such judgmental attitudes is a refusal to acknowledge the fact that the world is not always fair, that sometimes the "good" suffer unjustly and the "bad" go unpunished. There is such a thing as random victimization in the world—people sometimes, through no fault of their own, incur grave emotional and physical losses. Although this fact may be acknowledged intellectually, on an emotional level many people refuse to empathize with victims. The randomness of victimization is simply too painful to acknowledge.

People attribute reasons to assaults or tragic accidents, and cling to this view, because they want to believe that horrible events are preventable. Like most of us, they want to feel that they can exert some control over their lives and protect themselves and their loved ones. Their all-too-human wish is that if they behave as they should, they can avoid injury. However, the conclusion which follows—that "bad things" only happen to "bad people"—denies compassion to those people who have been unjustly violated.

"But there must have been *something* the child could have done to prevent or stop it," some may say, failing to realize both the relative physical and psychological powerlessness of your child in relation to the abuser, and the random nature of victimization. Jeb's first therapist failed to appreciate Jeb's powerlessness in relation to Mr. R. She erroneously assumed that because Jeb failed to report his scoutmaster, on some level the boy must have "enjoyed" the abuse and therefore encouraged it. But in the vast majority of cases, the impetus for the crime comes solely from within the molester or pedophile. Although it has been found that children who are emotionally or physically vulnerable, or who do not have the protection of a parent or caregiver, may be targeted by child abusers, there is often no special reason why one child is molested rather than another, except that the child happened to be in the wrong place at the wrong time. In a parallel manner, some people are maimed, or even killed, in car accidents—not because of their personalities, moral character, or their clothing, but because they just happened to get in the way of a drunk driver.

We all want to believe that life is meaningful rather than random and that we can take actions to ensure our safety and happiness. Yet for victims of sexual assault and their families, these beliefs in personal invulnerability and a just world are shattered. You and your child can no longer believe "It can't happen to me," because it did happen to you.

Since you can no longer feel completely safe and secure in the world, you may feel very anxious. You've been rendered helpless in a situation of great danger, whether physical or psychological. There is also tremendous fear for you and your child that the trauma will recur in one form or another, and that once again you will be powerless in the face of some person or force which has endangered you.

Such feelings of anxiety and helplessness are extremely painful and frightening. It is precisely these feelings that your friends or relatives are fighting when they avoid you or discount the abuse of your child.

It's fear of their own mortality, fear of emotional pain, and fear of becoming victimized themselves someday that causes people to say such insensitive things as: "I can't believe it. Are you sure she isn't making it up to get attention?" "Are you sure she hasn't been watching too many movies?" "What's the big deal? How could a little fondling hurt? She was probably too young to know what was going on anyway." "Stop feeling sorry for yourself. At least she doesn't have cancer." "That's nothing. My niece has leukemia." "She'll get over it. All she needs is a little time." "I always thought there was something overly precocious about your child."

If your child is an adolescent girl, you can expect many such blame-the-victim remarks because of the many myths in our culture about rape. As Kathryne Quinna-Holland of the University of Rhode Island points out, "From Homer's sirens to the early American witches burned for driving men crazy, to miniskirted 'nymphets' like Nabokov's preadolescent *Lolita*, history has held females from age 5 to 95 responsible for man's animal instincts." Other myths are that women "want/need/love to be raped" and that truly virtuous women or properly reared young girls "would not have allowed it to happen."[2]

Whom Should I Tell? Whom Should My Child Tell?

If your child's case has received wide publicity, you may not have a choice about whom to tell. Many people already know and you must deal with their questions whether you want to or not.

If your child's case has not received media attention or publicity, the decisions about whom to tell and how much to tell are largely up to you, your child, and the rest of your family. If your child is old enough, discuss with her the issue of disclosure. Try not to forget this step, since it's important that she, as an abuse survivor, reclaim a sense of power over her life. For someone like her, whose body was violated and whose wishes were disregarded during the abuse, it's vital for her at least to be allowed some control over who knows what about her experience.

Jeb begged his parents not to expose the abuse to his friends by prosecuting Mr. R. So his parents temporarily put aside their wish to avenge their son's violation in order to spare him further shame and social ostracism. As a result of the therapy, however, Jeb came to accept rather than deny the abuse; eventually he was able to assign the shame and guilt to Mr. R., rather than himself. When he'd reached this point, Jeb was willing to cooperate with his parents to expose Mr. R. and prevent him from molesting other young boys.

You may also want to spend some time teaching your child how to cope with the reactions of others. Stress to her that she has choices. She can be selective about whom she tells, or she doesn't have to tell anyone at all. She especially doesn't have to answer any questions that make her uncomfortable. (This may not pertain to court or police proceedings. However, even in these situations, your child may have options. She needs to know what those options are.)

Help your child anticipate how certain people might react, and prepare her for possible negative responses. You may want to warn her about the blame-the-victim attitudes she may encounter, and about people who might have a voyeuristic interest in her story. Ask her to come to you if anyone ignores her in reaction to her disclosure, gives her a hurtful response, or presses her for sexual details. Don't force her to tell anyone. Ask her if she would like *you* to tell anyone for her and how much she would like you to tell.

You need to strike a careful balance here. You don't want to give your child the message that what happened to her is so "dirty" that she must keep it a total secret. Like you, she may eventually need to talk about the abuse over and over again, as many times as needed, until some catharsis is achieved. But it will be in her interest to be open only with people who will receive the disclosure with sensitivity and discretion, who are capable of keeping it confidential, and who truly love your child and have her best interests at heart.

If the abuse involved incest, you and your child should both be aware that other members of your family—especially siblings—will have their own strong reactions to the disclosure: and confidentiality may abrogate their need to explore and express their feelings. Discuss this at the time the disclosure is made. For instance, you might want to say to the abused child's sibling, "I know that this probably will bring up a lot of feelings in you, and I don't want to minimize them. You can talk to me, and we can arrange to let you talk with a therapist who will be your special friend. But for right now, to help [the abused child] get through this difficult time, I want to ask you not to discuss the abuse with anyone else."

While your child's wishes and needs, and those of your spouse (if appropriate), need to be taken into consideration, you will also need to decide for yourself who else should know. Some of these decisions are difficult to make and you may find it helpful to discuss them with your therapist, your child's therapist, or someone else whom you trust.

A neutral third party can also provide some objectivity if family members cannot agree on whom to tell. For example, your spouse may want to tell no one, but you may want to tell certain relatives and friends who care about your child and with whom you feel you could share your pain. You may also feel the need to tell certain teachers or doctors about the abuse so that they will understand your child's special needs and make sense of her behavior.

In one instance, a mother had to tell her daughter's elementary school teacher that her child sometimes plays with her genitals because she was abused. Another had to tell the junior high school teacher that her daughter should not be forced to participate in certain co-ed activities, since she was abused and has a problem about physical contact with boys.

If you need to make a disclosure to protect your child, consider whether it is possible to communicate that she has a problem with a certain activity or event, without necessarily explaining sexual abuse as the underlying cause. This might not always be possible, however, and you may need to state frankly, "My child behaves or may behave in such and such a manner because he was sexually abused."

For example, if your child has acquired an attention deficit disorder as a result of prolonged abuse, or if she has become truant, aggressive, or otherwise a "problem child" at school, you may want to consider telling her teacher the facts. Disclosing the abuse may prevent the school system from labeling your child as "retarded" or a "troublemaker." You may want to consult with a trusted friend or therapist on this matter, or with someone who is familiar with your particular school system, before you make a decision.

If you need to disclose the abuse to someone, remember that you do not have to reveal details. People may ask you more questions than you want to answer about the sexual aspects of the abuse. Only disclose what you're comfortable disclosing: you are under no obligation to entertain other people with your child's pain. You need only give the information needed to better serve your child. If you're pressed to "tell it all," simply decline. You could say, "I don't want to discuss what happened in detail; I don't believe it's necessary. I'm telling you that my child was abused because the abuse hurt her tremendously and devastated me, too. Because of the abuse she may behave in certain ways that may seem strange to you, but which are perfectly normal to abuse survivors."

Some parents are afraid to tell teachers, babysitters, or others about their child's history, because they don't want their child to be singled out as "troubled" or "different." Try to think of yourself as educating others. Give the person a pamphlet on sexual abuse (available from your local library or child protective services agency). Tell him or her that sexual abuse has real consequences, but in most cases, with good help, many of the negative effects can be overcome.

Appeal to the teacher's or babysitter's desire to help. Make it clear that they can help by supporting your child and by keeping you posted on your child's behavior and emotional state. If there are other things they can do, be specific. Don't be afraid to reach out: it may help your child—and you—immeasurably.

Remember: You do not have to do all the telling all at once. This can be emotionally exhausting and overwhelming. You are also entitled to change your mind. You may decide to share with someone—then your gut feeling tells you to stay silent. Trust your intuition. You can always share later if you change your mind again.

Give yourself permission to make mistakes. Sometimes you may misjudge a person or situation. Perhaps you decided not to tell a certain teacher about the abuse, and then an incident arose at school which might have been avoided if you had forewarned the teacher. Or perhaps someone you trusted with this knowledge gossiped about your child, or turned white with shock and has avoided you ever since. Forgive yourself. You are not perfect and you are not supposed to be an expert on handling these extremely delicate, complicated interactions. You're not responsible for other people's reactions. Our society is only now beginning to acknowledge the reality of child sexual abuse. You cannot expect everybody—not even yourself—to handle every situation perfectly and in your child's best interest.

Communicating With Your Spouse or Partner and Your Family

At this time of family crisis, it is extremely important that you and your spouse or partner maintain open communication (unless your spouse or partner is the abuser—a case that is discussed in detail in other parts of this book). You and your spouse can provide tremendous support for each other, and your relationship can actually grow as a result of this trauma. However, if both of you—devastated by the occurrence—keep your true feelings to yourselves, your relationship can be weakened. It's essential for you each to share your fears and confusion, as well as your anger and pain. Through sharing, you'll be able to find the strength to endure the crisis together.

Problems can arise if you want to talk about the abuse, but your spouse or partner doesn't. Jeb's parents had a great deal of difficulty sharing their emotions with one another. Since they generally preferred to keep their feelings to themselves, even under normal conditions, it was difficult for them to be open during the crisis unleashed by Jeb's abuse. They each found reasons to blame themselves for the abuse; they avoided talking openly about the subject, each fearing the other's blame.

After a few therapy sessions, Mr. Jones was done talking about the abuse: talking about it was just too painful for him. Mrs. Jones, on the other hand, needed to talk about it more: it was just too painful for her to keep her thoughts and feelings bottled up. If you are in a similar situation, you'll need to find someone other than your spouse or partner with whom to share. Make the effort and find someone—your own sense of guilt and helplessness has isolated you enough already. Within the boundaries of discretion, talking is a healthy and necessary therapy that can help you handle this crisis. Perhaps there are members of your extended family who can help you cope. Don't hesitate to turn to them. One of the most valuable functions of the family unit is its capacity to serve as a coping resource during times of crisis.

It may be that your spouse or partner is an abuse survivor, and that your child's trauma has triggered buried or unacknowledged feelings about the past. If this is the case, your partner may emotionally shut down almost completely, regress, or develop symptoms of his or her own; or may react with a burst of vengeful fury. It may take a lot of talking and convincing to stop him or her from searching for or violently attacking the abuser.

Speak to your partner in terms of what is best for your child. You might say, "If you really want to help, you need to be there for her, not running all around town looking for the abuser—or in jail for assault." Or "I want revenge, too—but we have to focus on prosecuting the abuser legally, so we can be there for our child when she needs us."

Telling Your Other Children About Their Sibling's Abuse

We're a society that tends to protect children from painful realities. Yet even infants or very young children will feel the tension in your home and the grief in your heart. If they are at least three or four, they will probably be very aware of the changes in your hurt child. She may be gone a lot (to court or for counseling), or acting strangely. Depending on the age and mental development of your other children, you will need to tell them, in terms they can understand, about what happened to their sibling.

"But won't telling them frighten them? How much should I tell? Will they even understand?" You may be asking yourself these questions or others like them. You may be wondering how you can deal with your other children's feelings when you are having trouble dealing with your own.

As difficult as it might be, you may need to share both what happened to your abused child and your own feelings with the rest of your family. You don't have to be graphic or complete in your description of the abuse, but you must communicate to your other children that their sibling was harmed and that the abuse was not her fault or theirs. Emphasize that child sexual abuse is not only immoral, but illegal; that it doesn't mean their sister is "bad" or "nasty"; and that she can heal.

You may simply want to say, "Your sister was touched on her private parts in ways that are wrong by a person older and stronger than she. She is afraid and sad because she didn't understand what was happening (or because the abuser tricked her); she wanted to stop this bad person but couldn't. We are going to help [your child's name] now so this will never happen to her again."

If you decide to describe the specific sexual acts involved in the abuse, use the correct terms and distinguish between the sexual abuse and any physical abuse that also occurred. If your abused child has developed specific symptoms in response to the abuse—such as nightmares, separation anxiety, bed wetting, fear of crowds, or an eating disorder—you might want to mention these, too, emphasizing that they can and will diminish.

Speak in terms that your other children understand and do not be afraid to answer all their questions. Give simple, direct answers. You can always elaborate on them later. If you need time to think about an appropriate answer, tell your children that you can give them a better answer later, after you have had a chance to think about the question.

If you are concerned about your other children's reactions, give them a little information about the abuse and be alert for their reactions. Do they seem frightened, sad, anxious, or inattentive? Are they inattentive because they do not understand, because they are upset about their own issues, or because they are so frightened that they feel the need to "tune out" what you're saying? Don't be afraid to draw them out by asking them how they feel. You could say, "Does hearing about your sister's abuse make you scared or mad?"

This is a good time to speak about your feelings. By letting your children know how you feel—angry at the abuser, sad about the abuse, confused about why it happened, and so on—you can help them identify their own feelings. Tell them that they may have some of the same feelings you do and that these feelings are normal. Encourage them to talk about their feelings and tell them that any feelings they have are all right.

These suggestions will be difficult to follow if you and your partner, like Jeb's parents, are unaccustomed to speaking openly about sexual matters, or about feelings. Don't force yourself to share with your other children until you feel ready; or ask a trusted friend, clergyman, relative, or therapist to help.

You don't need to speak to your other children immediately; nor should you expect yourself to have the perfect words. You don't need to say everything at once either. However, it is extremely important that you get started. For too many years the issue of child sexual abuse has been hushed up and swept under the rug. Only by bringing the problem out into the open can we hope to begin to eradicate it. The best place to discuss, and prevent, child sexual abuse is within the context of a loving family.

You are not harming your other children by sharing openly with them: you are doing them a service. They need to know the facts about sexual abuse and to be aware of the psychological repercussions of trauma. In this sense, you are not only helping them to understand their abused sibling, but you are preparing them for a world that is full of abused people and trauma survivors.

You will also be helping your other children to allay any guilt feelings they may have about their sibling. Whether they talk about it or not, on some level they probably feel guilty about the abuse because of their own quite natural feelings of hostility or hostile rivalry toward their brother or sister. For example, Jeb's sister felt she had caused Jeb's abuse because she hated him so much for hitting her. Younger children especially are egocentric in that they feel they are the center of the universe and the cause of all events. Like Jeb's sister, your younger children may need to be told repeatedly— not just once—that they did not cause the bad thing that happened to their sibling.

Like Jeb's older brother, your children may have survivor guilt. "Why was my brother hurt and not me?" Your other children will also be wondering what is going to happen now to their sibling. Like Emily's younger sister, your other children may wonder, "Will my sister ever get well? Can it happen to me, too?" These fears will be especially strong if the abuser is a family member. For example, Sue couldn't wait for Emily to come back home from the hospital, not only because she depended on Emily as a mother figure, but also because she feared that if Emily didn't come back, her father might molest her. Sue could not articulate these fears, yet they brought on crying spells and an inability to concentrate at school, leading to poor grades and low self-esteem.

Talk about any specific measures you are taking to protect your abused child and your other children from future abuse. If you haven't already done so, provide them with some preventive education regarding sexual abuse. Teach them about "good" touching and "bad" touching. There are any number of books and pamphlets that can help you. Consult your local bookstore. Some books and pamphlets are also listed at the end of this chapter.

Your other children may feel jealous that their sibling is now the object of so much of your time and attention, and at the same time they may feel guilty about these jealous feelings. Assure them that if they had been harmed, you would be doing all you could for them, too—but that their sibling's position is not enviable. "What would you think if I didn't do everything I could to help your sister? I wouldn't be a very good parent, would I? Well, if something happened to you, I would do the same for you as I'm doing for your sister. But even with all my help, she's still hurting a lot—and I'm sure that she'd rather never have been harmed and get less of my attention than to be hurting as much as she is now."

Reassure your other children over and over, as often as necessary, that their feelings did not cause the abuse. If there are any ways in which they can help their sister, let them know. They want to help, too. All of you can be drawn closer together as you unite to support each other and your hurt loved one. Just be sure that you are in control. You are the adult and should be giving comfort to the children, not the other way around. They are not there to comfort you. That job should be done by your spouse or partner and by other adults.

Jeb's mother was quite naturally shattered when she learned of Jeb's abuse. She wanted to lean on her husband, but he preferred not to deal with the issue. When he did think about it, he would often go into a murderous rage toward Mr. R. and Jeb's mother would end up having to comfort and calm her husband, rather than getting any support herself.

She was greatly tempted to lean on her eldest son, Bob. Jr., for emotional support and physical protection. Ever since learning of the abuse, she had been fearful of going out at night or of trying new places and experiences. She wanted her husband to go with her to all the places she used to frequent but, with his heavy work schedule, he was unable to do so. Quite naturally, she considered asking Bob Jr. to accompany her.

She also had fantasies about discussing the abuse and her fears and pain, putting her head on her son's shoulder, and asking him to hold her. "Wait a minute," she suddenly thought. "That's not appropriate. It's one thing to let Bob Jr. know about my feelings about the abuse in order to help him cope with his; but it's quite another thing to turn him into a substitute husband since mine isn't available to me."

Mrs. Jones would have preferred to have one strong person—such as her husband—to listen to her, give her solace, and support her at this time. But this option wasn't available. She would have to make do with sharing small parts of her pain, fears, and other concerns with several people, distributing her needs among friends and relatives who could help her on a more limited basis. She also had the option of therapy. In this manner she was able to avoid the frustration of turning to an unavailable husband, and to avoid the mistake of turning to her son who, although not a young child, was still her child and not the appropriate person to fill her adult needs.

Further Reading

Your local library, child protective services agency, and social services department are all excellent sources of pamphlets and books on child sexual abuse.

In addition, you may want to check local bookstores. Because of the recent increased public awareness of child sexual abuse, there may be several pamphlets and books from which to choose.

He Told Me Not to Tell is an excellent booklet for children under twelve, available from King County Rape Relief, 305 South 43rd, Renton, WA 90855. This booklet is also available from Uniquity, Helping People Help People. You can order their catalogue from 215 4th Street, P.O. Box 6, Galt, CA 95632, (209) 745-2111 or 1-800-521-7771 (outside of California). The catalogue has an entire section on child abuse. *A Better Safe Than Sorry Book: A Family Guide for Sexual Assault Prevention* (Gordon) and *Alerting Kids to the Danger Zones—Sexual Abuse* (Berry) are a couple of the booklets available for purchase from the Uniquity catalogue.

4

The Healing Process

Regardless of the depth of your love for your child, or your knowledge of psychology, know from the outset that you cannot be your child's therapist. You will play an essential role, nonetheless, in finding appropriate help for him, and providing encouragement during the difficult times of the healing process.

The healing process is very complicated. Certain elements, however, apply to most victims: you need to be aware of these as you seek help for your child.

The first stages of sex abuse therapy involve your child in

- Remembering, not denying, the traumatic abusive incidents

- Fully recognizing, not minimizing, the effects of the abuse

- Realizing that any personal weaknesses or perceived "defects" on his part had nothing to do with the abuse or its impact, but rather that the abuser is responsible for the abuse itself, the coping mechanisms that had to be developed to survive it, and any ill effects that followed

So many children (and adults) enter therapy, then quit when the therapy begins to deal with painful material—just when the most progress can be made. More than anyone else in your child's life, you can make the difference at this crucial juncture by helping him endure the emotional upheavals that are part of healing so that he can get well. You're the one who can reassure him over and over that his pain will pass; you can explain that pain is his guide through the shadowy mountains to the sun on the other side. This is a good time to teach your child some basic coping skills, such as anger management. These skills are described in detail in Chapter 6.

How Long Does Healing Take?

You need to stay in close touch with your child's therapist about how you are supporting your child and what coping skills the two of you are working on. The therapist should welcome your involvement and may offer some ideas of her own to help you.

Sexually abused children are not all the same. Some have endured other forms of psychological and physical stress in addition to the sexual abuse. Emily was both an incest survivor and a parentified child. Her childhood was abnormal not only in that her father sexually abused her, but in that she was forced into a parent role toward both her mother and father. Healing for Emily involved overcoming the effects of the sexual abuse, as well as learning how to reclaim the child within her: as a child, she had never been allowed to play, having been burdened with adult responsibilities from an early age. Children who have been sexually abused by family members or others they trusted need a more intense and probably longer course of therapy than children who have been violated by strangers.

Parents often ask, "How long will my child's healing take?" There's no pat answer. While much depends on the skill and knowledge of the therapist in the area of trauma, equally important, if not even more important, are factors such as the duration and severity of the abuse and the amount of time between the abuse and therapy. Some studies show that adult one-time rape victims can become symptom-free after six months to one year of counseling, provided that the counseling is received soon after the rape. Incest survivors, on the other hand, who typically endure more trauma than a one-time rape experience, require a much longer period for healing.

As would be expected, Emily's healing process took more time and work than that of Jeb, the boy who had been molested by his scoutmaster. Not only was Emily abused by a family member, but she was abused more often over a longer period of time. She was also deprived of a place where she could feel safe, as the abuse occurred in the family home. Jeb at least knew that Mr. R. wouldn't come after him in his own home. Emily was abused for almost eight years before getting help. During this time her coping mechanisms—such as numbing and repression—became habits, and her growth in other areas was severely stunted.

In contrast, Jeb was abused for "only" two years and his parents sought help for him immediately. Like Emily, Jeb used numbing and repression as defenses and had trouble relating to his peers. However, Jeb had been practicing these maladaptive behaviors for only two years, whereas Emily had been using them for eight. It took Emily's therapist a proportionately longer time to help Emily undo the damage of her abuse and to teach her healthier ways of relating to herself and others.

The sooner your child receives help after the abuse, the less chance there is that his negative or self-destructive coping mechanisms will become firmly entrenched. As time goes by without your child getting help, dysfunctional coping patterns will have become part of the normal range of his behavior. When these coping mechanisms become routine habits, considerably more time may be needed for the healing to occur.

Therapeutic Goals

Your child's age will also shape the length and form of the therapy. If he or she is an infant or toddler, a medical exam may be all you can provide for the moment. A consultation with a psychotherapist or mental health professional trained in the area of sexual abuse, however, may help you identify symptoms requiring therapy which might arise as your child gets older.

For the very young child, therapeutic goals may be limited to bringing the sexual abuse out of repression, educating your child about sexual abuse in general, helping him to identify his emotional reactions to the abuse, and teaching him how to protect himself from further abuse. In some cases, the therapy may be short-term, with the possibility that your child will get additional help later if new problems arise.

With young children, and even with preadolescents who have great difficulty identifying their emotions, the therapist may use picture drawing and other nonverbal methods, such as playing cards or board games, as a means of establishing a relationship with your child and helping identify feelings and problem areas.

In contrast, therapy with an older child depends primarily on talking, and will involve more complex issues such as removing guilt and self-blame, establishing a positive self-image, socializing comfortably with peers, and reclaiming sexuality by learning how to be comfortable with and enjoy his body and physical attractiveness. Older children can be given reading material on sexual abuse.

Because there are so many factors to consider, therapy must always be individualized. Don't hesitate to bring to the therapist's attention additional information about any current or past stresses in your child's life, such as death or illness in the family, financial hardships, or recent geographical moves. You owe it to your child not to hold anything back from the therapist, even if you are embarrassed or ashamed by the disclosure. If you yourself were abused, or if you feel responsible in some way for your child's abuse, this knowledge will help the therapist understand your child's attitudes and reactions.

Preparing Your Child for Therapy

Individual Therapy

You need to communicate clearly to your child that the reason why you are taking him to see a therapist is because he was abused. "If you had been hit by a car and broken a bone, I would take you to a doctor who knows a lot about bones. Now that someone has hurt you, I am going to take you to a counselor who knows a lot about children who have been hurt like you and what they might be feeling.

"I'm not taking you to a counselor because you're 'bad' or 'sick,' or as a punishment. I'm taking you because I care about you and want you to feel better."

You also need to be very clear about what a therapist is and isn't. "A counselor is someone who is there for you. The counselor's job is to listen to whatever you have to say and to help you understand yourself better. If you have a problem with friends, or school, or with me, you can talk it over with the counselor and she will try to help you.

"The counselor is *your* counselor, not Mommy's or Daddy's. She doesn't call us up and tell us what you said—about anything. Whatever you say about me, the counselor won't tell me. I will be talking with her from time to time, so she can help me help you—but she will always tell you when I call and what we talked about.

"A counselor is not supposed to be a tattletale. She won't tell me anything you tell her without asking you first. Those are the rules. If she breaks them, we will have to tell her so. The only time she can call me without asking you first is if she is afraid you are about to hurt yourself.

"This counselor has talked to many children who were touched [abused, violated] the way you were. She will not be upset if you want to talk about what happened that day [or, between you and the man next door, or whatever]. She will not force you to talk about it, more than you are able. But she *will* try to help you understand that it wasn't your fault and that you are a good person even though somebody did something bad to you."

You may want to review these points with your child's therapist before the therapy begins to ensure that everyone is following the same ground rules—and so that the therapist understands your expectations and those of your child.

In deciding what you're going to say to your child, you should, of course, gear your vocabulary and metaphors to your child's age and level of sophistication.

Group Therapy

Group therapy with other abuse survivors, led by a qualified, caring therapist who is knowledgeable about sexual abuse, is often recommended in addition to individual therapy. Young children are usually not placed in a group. But from preadolescence on, children may profit from a combination of group and individual therapy.

Being in a group helps a child realize that he is not alone, helps reduce the stigma associated with having been abused, and helps him emerge from his social isolation. In group, he can practice his developing social skills and acquire a community of support in addition to a realistic and empathic perspective on his experiences with abuse. He may also receive honest and valuable feedback about himself, feedback that he might be willing to accept only from other abuse survivors.

You can help prepare your child for group by asking him how he feels about being in a group. Help him identify his concerns: "How do you feel about being with kids you don't know? What are you afraid someone might say or do in the group?"

Be certain that your child understands what group therapy is and isn't. "Group therapy can be fun, but it isn't a party. People don't come and go as they please. Everybody arrives at a certain time and leaves at a certain time. You can bring up any subject you want in group, but group therapy is special because there you can talk about serious things—things that make you sad, angry, scared, or mixed up. Sometimes you can't talk about those things other places. But in group you can, and nobody will think you're weird or make fun of you for how you feel. And if someone does hurt your feelings, then the group leader will make them stop.

"You may not like everybody in the group and they might not all like you, but that's okay. You'll probably find that you will come to like most of them a lot. They aren't your friends now, but they may be soon.

"I know it'll be hard the first day, walking into a room full of strangers, but soon those people won't be strangers any more. You will soon see that many of them have the same problems and feelings you have.

"Give the group a try. You may be surprised that after going a few times, you start to feel like it's 'home' because you can say whatever you want and because many of the children there have been through experiences similar to yours and have similar feelings.

"Don't be afraid. Nothing scary or bad happens there. All the kids do is talk, and if somebody gets too upset, or gets nasty, the counselor stops them. You can speak up, too, if someone is bothering you. And if you want to speak up, but can't, you can say so. You could say, 'I want to talk in here but it's hard for me.' Or, 'Something is bothering me about the group, but I can't talk about it.'

"It's always scary to do something you've never done before, isn't it? Even I get scared when I do something new. Like when I learned to drive and first went on the highway, I was really scared—but now I drive on the highway all the time, right?

"I remember when you were a little baby, how afraid you were to take your first step. But you did anyway because you wanted to walk—and now you walk all the time. If you never took that first step, you would've never learned to walk. It's the same thing with group. You might be afraid to take the first step of showing up, but you want to stop hurting, so you are willing to be very brave and do something about it. You may be surprised to find that even though you may not be sure today about whether or not you are going to like being in a group, when it comes time for the group to end, you may be sad.

"And remember this: If you find the group doesn't help you, or if things happen in group that upset you, be sure to tell the group leader and the counselor. You can tell me, too, if you want to."

At this point it's important to define the group structure: when it starts, how long it lasts, whatever you know about the other children, and so on.

Uncovering the Trauma and Reshaping It Mentally

The Trauma of Remembering

Some survivors remember the abuse all too vividly. However, others, like Emily and Jeb, have repressed the memory either entirely or in part. If your child has submerged the memory of the abuse, he needs to "uncover the trauma" so that his healing can begin. The traumatic events need to be brought out of repression and into his conscious awareness, then shared in individual or group therapy.

This process may take many months and may occur in bits and pieces. Your child may recall part of a memory during one session and remember the rest some sessions later—or even a year or so later. Some events may never be recalled in full. Some individuals cannot recall even one specific incident, but only a powerful sense of having once been abused. This may be all that is required for their healing to begin.

In general, the least traumatic memories will be recalled first. Healing is facilitated when your child can recall the core or central trauma he experienced during the abuse. Some therapists use artwork, writing exercises, dance therapy, hypnosis, or other methods to help uncover the trauma.

It's important that the therapist or group not push your child to remember more than he can handle, for every revelation of the trauma creates stress for him. It's very likely that the more your child comes to remember about the abuse, the more severe his symptoms will become, at least for a while. You may notice that therapy brings about increased thinking or dreaming about the abuse. He may have more nightmares and insomnia; eat, drink, or sleep more; or seem more irritable. He may regress to some childlike behaviors: babytalk, bedwetting, separation anxiety, clinging to stuffed animals or dolls, and so on. Some survivors feel suffocated, nauseated, or as if they are being choked when they recall particular aspects of the abuse.

Such symptoms are to be expected. The reclaimed memories bring on an onslaught of emotional pain that will probably be handled psychosomatically or through symptoms and regression first, before your child is able to cope with them more effectively. If the therapy is working, many of your child's buried emotions and memories will begin to surface. As they surface, he will experience more inner turmoil, more restlessness, and more pain. Experiencing those feelings may make him temporarily underfunction and more vulnerable psychologically. As a defense against his increased feelings of personal vulnerability, he may become more hostile and closed toward you and other members of your family.

It's important that neither you, nor the therapist, panic when your child seems to be getting worse. In sexual abuse therapy, as in other forms of therapy associated with trauma, things often get worse before they get better. An experienced therapist expects such regression and other outwardly disturbing symptoms, and should explain to you and your child that they are actually signs of progress. Rarely is the course of sexual abuse therapy—especially incest therapy—smooth or painless. You need to warn your child about this so that he doesn't panic either. (See the section in this chapter called "Feeling the Feelings.")

The memories need to unfold at a pace that your child can handle, not according to some artificial timetable established by someone else. Healing is more likely to occur if traumatic memories surface a little bit at a time as your child is ready for them. If they surface all at once or at a rate your child cannot handle, he may become severely symptomatic, extremely depressed (perhaps even suicidal); and may eventually flee from therapy or else continue in therapy superficially, either denying or discounting the abuse (as Emily did with her school counselor). In some cases, it is perfectly appropriate and acceptable for a client to stop therapy after some of the memories have surfaced, to process those memories, take a break from therapy for several months or even years, and then to return when ready to handle more of the past.

This decision should be made jointly by your child and his therapist. Taking a break from therapy is not the same as the therapist deciding that he or she can no longer work with your child; nor is it the same as your child deciding that he's tired of going for counseling. Usually such decisions are made after at least a few months of counseling and reflect the fact that the client has reached some kind of plateau in the therapy where he may need to stop and consolidate his progress without adding the stress of further introspection.

After all, the purpose of therapy is to free one to participate in life, not to become a substitute for living. At a certain point in time, it may be better for your child to read a book, develop a friendship, take an extracurricular course, go swimming, or simply have more time for himself than to be in counseling. It also may be important for your child to prove to himself that he can cope with his inner struggles and his life problems without a therapist to lean on. Managing on his own, without depending on a therapist, can help increase your child's self-esteem and self-confidence.

However, it's also important that your child know that the therapist will be there if the struggle becomes too difficult, or when he is ready (if ever) to deal with additional issues. A joint decision to stop for a while—and it may be a long while—should not feel like abandonment or rejection to your child.

If you are concerned about the decision, discuss it with your child's therapist, not your child. For example, you may feel that your child still needs counseling because he's still having frequent nightmares or anxiety attacks. If so, let the therapist know. He or she may want to reconsider the decision based on the information you provide.

In the final analysis, the decision is not yours, but that of your child and his therapist. Nevertheless, it's perfectly appropriate for you to ask what arrangements have been made for continued contact between your child and the therapist. Can your child call for an appointment as needed? Is your child supposed to "check in" with the therapist as needed? You should also ask the therapist to identify warning signs, such as increased depression and other symptoms, which indicate that therapy or some other form of intervention should be resumed. Also, if you see your child suffering too much when "on break" from regular counseling, you can always consult with the therapist and then remind your child that he can return to therapy if he desires. Perhaps all he needs is a one-session "tune up." If more sessions are needed, these can then be arranged.

Your Child's Therapy Will Affect You, Too

Your child's involvement in therapy may also create anxiety for you. Although the sexual abuse may be the focus of the therapy, it's usually not the sole focus: undoubtedly the therapist will be delving into your relationship with your child, your personality, your family dynamics, and many other things that may make you uncomfortable. Quite naturally you will wonder, "What is my child saying about me in therapy? Is the therapist blaming me for something?"

Although you want your child to feel better and be whole, you may feel threatened by the fact that he's going to change; this is only natural. You may also wonder if the therapist is going to exert more influence over your child than you do. You may even worry that the therapist will replace you in your child's affections. You might be curious about what's going on in therapy (after all, you're paying for it)—but you don't want to seem to be butting in. You might have some feelings of jealousy that your child is receiving all this help for his problems when you have had to go through this trauma alone.

Such anxieties and emotions are entirely normal. They occur whenever one member of a family enters therapy and the others do not.

Depending on the particulars of your child's case, the therapist may include you in some of the sessions and/or hold conferences with you regarding your child's progress and care. The therapist's prime loyalty, however, is to your child, not you; and he or she must not betray client confidentiality.

Establishing Trust

In all forms of therapy, a trusting, caring, supportive client-therapist relationship is essential for a positive outcome; but this is especially the case with abuse survivors whose trust in other human beings has been shattered. It's through the establishment of a trusting bond with the therapist (or with certain group members) that your child will be able to remember the trauma more fully and deal with it constructively. For example, it was by hearing others talk about their incest experiences in group therapy that Emily first began to recall the horror of her home life and then gain the courage to talk about it.

If the therapist or group is rejecting, blaming, or unresponsive to your child, he is likely to remain silent or emotionally neutral about the abuse—a position which he has probably maintained in the past and which has prevented him from healing.

Such was the case with Jeb and his first therapist. Because of this particular therapist's blaming, impatient, and angry manner, Jeb barely talked to her about any part of his life, much less the abuse. Jeb's silence only frustrated and angered the therapist more, which made Jeb retreat even further. For abuse survivors like Jeb, "bad therapy" is *not* better than no therapy at all. It is only destructive in that it reinforces the abused child's feeling that he won't ever get over the abuse and will never be "normal" again. He reasons that if a supposedly qualified therapist can't help him, then he must truly be a hopeless case doomed to suffer forever. If, in addition, his parents say something like, "All that time and money spent on that therapist and you still aren't better," he may lose all hope and feel like both a therapeutic failure and an unwanted burden to his parents. At this point it is imperative *not* to blame your child and to find another therapist as soon as possible.

Only when your child feels safe with the therapist or group can he reveal himself. In a well-run group, the leader carefully monitors the reactions of the members to one another and does not permit (and immediately rectifies) any nontherapeutic responses. In such a group, your child can benefit immensely by hearing other group members describe their experiences with abuse and how they are coping. The open sharing of others may trigger his memory and help him feel more comfortable about sharing.

Getting Over Shame

Often survivors feel ashamed for

- Not having fought the abuser
- Not having succeeded if they did fight back
- Having some physically pleasurable reactions to the sexual stimulation

In therapy or group your child will come to realize that he probably reacted as appropriately as possible, given his age and knowledge and the particulars of his situation. In the words of Ellen Bass and Laura Davis, authors of *The Courage to Heal*, your child needs to learn to "honor" rather than despise what he did in order to survive.

For example, Sandra felt guilty because after the first time she was forced to have intercourse with her uncle, she cooperated without resistance. While it was not difficult for her to recall the specific sex acts forced upon her, it took several months for her to remember that her uncle had threatened to harm, and possibly kill, her younger sister if Sandra did not comply with his demands.

In group she was able to remember one evening when she did resist her uncle: he promptly burnt her baby sister's leg with scalding water. On the way to the hospital, Sandra's uncle warned her that if she was ever "difficult" again, he would allow her sister to drown in the bathtub and tell her parents that it was an accident.

For Sandra, these threats were more terrible than the sexual abuse itself. Not only did they reinforce her feelings of helplessness and entrapment, but they made it unmistakably clear that her uncle was a truly malicious man. To endure the abuse, Sandra had told herself that her uncle really loved her, as he often said he did, and that he was basically a good man.

When these illusions were shattered, Sandra had to face the fact that she had been deluding herself all along: she was not her uncle's "special girl," but the helpless victim of a very sick man. She came to group filled with self-loathing and rage that she had "allowed" herself to be so victimized. The group disabused her of the notion that she had "allowed" anything, assuring her that she had had no real choice in the matter. Without such feedback, Sandra could easily have stayed stuck in guilt and self-loathing. With help, she realized that any person in her situation might have reacted as she did. She was neither a fool, a coward, nor a weakling.

The Impact of Sex-Role Stereotyping

Expressiveness and Instrumentality

We live in the age of women's—and men's—liberation. Yet traditional sex-role stereotypes die hard. Some boys still feel that they need to always be strong and never cry, just as some girls feel that they must always be "sweet" and never get angry. Yet the male survivor of sexual abuse needs to grieve his losses, and the female survivor needs to experience her rage. If your child's therapist adheres to gender stereotypes, the therapeutic process will be impeded.

Females are supposed to be emotional, conforming, conscientious, responsible, passive, and noncompetitive. Males are supposed to be self-controlled, intellectual, risk-taking, adventuresome, and aggressive. Women are also supposed to be oriented toward home and family, to be nurturing, dependent, obedient, supportive, and responsive to the needs of others. Males, on the other hand, are career-oriented, unemotional, self-reliant, productive, creative, and curious, rather than socially oriented. These are the gender stereotypes that children are taught from an early age.

In general, tradition assigns women an *expressive* role, while men are supposed to be *instrumental*. In their expressive roles, girls can express need, warmth, emotions, self-doubt, and sadness. In their instrumental roles, boys are able to manipulate the environment and exhibit creativity and competence through their achievements.

In order to heal, your child needs to learn to be both expressive and instrumental. All children, male and female, need to learn to express their feelings. And all children need the satisfaction of possessing social and practical skills. Both expressiveness and instrumentality can be important issues for survivors of child sexual abuse. A therapist needs to encourage growth in both areas, regardless of your child's sex.

Boys especially need to learn that expressing their emotions is not a sign of weakness or fear. Similarly, girls need to learn that being competent and assertive is not unfeminine. Therapists can help free children from traditional sex-role "shoulds" by having them examine their early learning about sex roles as well as the sex-role pressures they're experiencing now. Therapy should never reinforce traditional sex roles, but should help children move beyond stereotypes to their own individual identities.

Freeing Your Child From Gender Stereotypes

You can help with the process of freeing your child from gender stereotypes. Depending on his age, you can ask him such questions as, "Do you think boys are different from girls? How?" "Do you think it's sissy for boys to cry or bad for girls to get angry?"

Explore what your child has learned about what it means to be a boy or a girl. You might try the following series of questions, adjusting them to the age and sophistication of your child: "If somebody stabs you, would it hurt less if you were a boy or a girl? If it's okay for a girl to cry if somebody stabs her, why isn't it all right for a boy to cry?"

"If I steal some money from someone, do you think that person has a right to be angry? What if the person is a girl? Does she have to be 'nice' or can she get mad, too?"

You can then explain: "Being sexually abused is like being stabbed and robbed. It makes no difference if you're a boy or a girl. Either way, you have the right to cry because you were hurt, and to be angry because you were robbed of your privacy and your right to control your body."

Books that can help you free your child from sexist beliefs and inhibitions are available at most libraries. Ask your librarian for help.

What Are Your Own Attitudes Toward Gender Identity?

At some point in this process, you may need to examine your own attitudes toward sex roles. It's one thing to say, "Of course it's okay for boys to feel helpless and for girls to be furious"—and quite another thing to truly believe and accept this on a gut level. Very few of us have escaped traditional sex-role conditioning; and very few of us, even the most enlightened and well-meaning, are completely free of prejudice or inhibition on our gender identity.

Identify your own attitudes toward sex-role stereotypes. Take two pieces of paper. Label one page: "Women and Girls." Label the other page: "Men and Boys." Divide each piece of paper into three columns. Over the first column, write: "Women and girls should always..." on the women's sheet, and "Men and boys should always..." on the men's sheet. Then list all the "shoulds" you have ever heard or read about regarding men and women.

For example, "Women should always be modest...put their children before themselves...keep their homes in order...." On the men's sheet, you might have such entries as, "Men should always be strong...work hard for their families...take the initiative sexually," and so on.

Over the second column on each page, write: "Where I learned this." For each "should" in the lefthand column, write down where you learned that boys or girls should act or be a particular way. For example, did you learn a particular "should" from your grandparents, your mother, your father, a teacher, a book, a movie, a friend?

Label the third column on the page for your own gender: "How do I feel and how do people react to me when I don't follow this rule?" Then, for each "should," list what feelings you have and how people react when you break the rules for your sex.

Over the third column on the page for the opposite sex, write, "How do I feel when a man [or woman] doesn't follow this rule?" Then, for each "should," write down how you feel when someone from the opposite sex doesn't obey the sex-role stereotype you were taught.

While doing this exercise, you may become aware of areas where you have conflicting feelings. Given recent changes in society, it wouldn't be surprising for you to feel mixed up about several sex-role stereotypes. Many people are confused about such issues. Some of these issues may be unresolvable—but it's important for you at least to be aware of those issues about which you feel conflict and confusion as you talk to your child about gender stereotyping.

Feeling the Feelings

At the time of the abuse, your child may have had to partially or totally suppress his consciousness of the abuse in order to survive the trauma. He is also likely to have suppressed, buried, or denied his feelings about it. Healing will not only involve reformulating the trauma so as not to blame himself, but also feeling the feelings associated with the abuse—feelings that were numbed at the time the abuse occurred. Repressed grief and anger are usually the two major emotions to emerge during the therapeutic process.

As your child's rage rises to the surface, he can be helped by his therapist to learn how to redirect the powerful energy of this rage into constructive channels. Often at this point, the therapist can assist your child in making associations between the past and the present: to see how the abuse and his reactions to it are negatively influencing his life and relationships. Therapy will help your child become more aware of his emotions and to express them more effectively.

What You Can Say to Your Child

You can help, too, by assuring your child that he is making progress, not "falling apart"—and that his feelings, although intense, will not destroy him. Neither will they last forever. Remind your child that although feeling the feelings can be very painful and disorienting, in the long run he will be strengthened by facing them rather than running away.

You can say, "You're going to counseling so that you can feel better. But sometimes the things you talk about in counseling are going to make you feel worse—but only for a while, not forever. Part of your healing involves feeling your feelings, feeling the hurt, the anger, the confusion, and other feelings—and feeling those feelings isn't fun.

"I really admire you. It takes courage to go to counseling and talk about how you feel. Not everybody can do that. Do you know that some people who are so good at doing dangerous things—like chasing robbers or fighting fires—are afraid of their own feelings? They have the courage to act, but they don't have the courage to feel. They can risk their lives on their jobs, but they're scared to death of feeling sad, bad, scared, or really, really angry.

"It takes courage to feel, to feel anything, especially the kind of feelings that can happen after you've been sexually abused. Maybe you think that you're not strong enough to take it. But all you need is just enough strength to begin. You can use a little bit of courage at a time. Then you can borrow some from your counselor, the kids in your group, and people who love you—like me. You can just keep on borrowing courage from others for as long as you need to.

"If you are really talking with your counselor about abuse and other things that bother you, you can expect that you'll have many feelings and that they'll be strong. Remember—you don't have to be afraid when you get real sad, real scared, or real angry. That's how you're supposed to feel. It might feel like you are going to die, but you won't. Nobody dies from a feeling. Just tell your counselor about it—or tell me if you want to. I promise those feelings won't stay that strong. They will get better and so will you.

"You might also start dreaming or thinking more about what happened. This is normal and good. It means that you're really working on your therapy and that you're getting better. Just like the feelings you don't like, the dreams and thoughts won't last forever. When you can get past the hard part of therapy, you'll feel much better.

"Sounds funny, doesn't it? It doesn't make sense that feeling bad for a while is going to make you feel better later on. Maybe you thought when you went to counseling that you'd get better right away and that the counselor would make you feel better all the time. But think of it like this. It's the same as if you broke your arm. The doctor would put it in a cast. So now you think it's all over, right? Wrong! The arm inside the cast itches like crazy. It itches so badly that you feel like tearing off your cast and scratching until the itch goes away. But you can't, because you need the cast to help you heal. You just have to wait until your arm has mended.

"The itching is a sign of healing—a sign that the nerve endings and other parts are getting better. But while the healing is going on, so is all that itching—you feel like you can't stand it, but you have to, and eventually the itching goes away and the arm is healed.

"It's the same with counseling. Nightmares, feeling grouchy, feeling real sad, and all those things are just like itching. You don't want them, but they are signs that you are getting better.

"While you're doing your emotional itching, I want you to know that I know it's hard for you. I expect that you might be grouchier with me, or even really angry. It's okay to feel like that. I won't let you hurt me, but I can take it if you are madder than usual, or sadder, or need to talk more.

"You might also want to be alone more. I can understand that, too. Remember how when your dog's leg was hurt, she went into the corner? She didn't feel like playing and wasn't as happy as usual. You might feel like that, too. When your feelings start to hurt, you may need to go into a corner and rest. It's okay. You don't have to pretend to be happy when you don't feel like it.

"Just remember—even though you might feel like you're going crazy, you aren't. You are really getting better. Remember just to keep talking about how you feel."

This aspect of therapy was especially difficult for Jeb. In the Jones family, emotions were not generally discussed and "being emotional" was considered a sign of weakness or, for the males of the family, an indication that one was a "sissy" or a "queer." Jeb's therapist had to help Jeb overcome his fear of feeling; and also had to work with Jeb's parents to help them understand that having emotions and talking about them is part of the human condition, not a sign of inadequacy.

If you come from an emotionally constricted background where feelings were not talked about, or if you have trouble tolerating strong emotions, you may need to seek professional help so that you can send the right messages to your child. Do not be ashamed—this is a very common problem in our society. In order to help your child cope with the intense feelings that attend trauma, you will also need to learn to be comfortable with the expression of emotions.

Other Therapeutic Issues

Barbara Cavallin, in *Treatment of Sexually Abused Adolescents: View of a Psychologist*, lists the following ten issues as being central for victims of child sexual abuse:[1]

- "Damaged goods" syndrome

- Guilt

- Fear

- Depression

- Low self-esteem and poor social skills

- Repressed anger and hostility

- Impaired ability to trust

- Blurred role boundaries and role confusion

- Pseudomaturity coupled with failure to accomplish developmental tasks

- Self-mastery and control

Depending on your child's age and the nature and extent of the abuse experienced, therapy may also need to cover other issues such as:

- Fears of homosexuality (especially in the case of same-sex abuse)

- Distorted views of sexuality

- Anger towards family members, police or court officials, or mental health professionals who had blame-the-victim attitudes, or who somehow made your child feel ashamed or inferior

At some point, your child needs to be educated regarding the prevalence of sexual abuse in our society, and to be told that whenever there is sexual contact between an adult and a child, it is never the child's responsibility. A feminist perspective needs to be provided for female abuse survivors so that they can view their abuse in the context of the unequal power relations between men and women in our society.

Abuse survivors need assertiveness training and straightforward information about their bodies and sexuality, as the abuser and the abuse may have given them distorted notions about sexuality. For some abuse survivors, self-defense classes and/or an exercise program are excellent ways to build self-confidence and self-esteem, and to reestablish a sense of control over their lives and bodies.

For Jeb, courses in karate and boxing helped him overcome his longstanding feelings of inferiority about being small. His mastery of these skills also reassured him that he now had a fighting chance to fend off anyone who tried to victimize him in the future.

Education About Sexual Abuse and Therapy

Things You Can Say to Your Child

Your child has absorbed many messages that he is guilty and 'bad' and certainly alone in being a victim of sexual abuse. He needs to be reassured again and again that the victimization of children is all too common; and that whenever there is sexual contact between a child and an adult, it is never the child's fault. What you say to your child in this regard can be an important adjunct to therapy.

You can tell your child, "Nobody knows exactly how many children are sexually abused every year, but the latest report is that at least one out of every five or six girls and at least one out of every twenty boys is sexually abused before they are eighteen. And there are probably a lot more who we never even hear about.

"That's a lot of children, isn't it? Makes you wonder why we don't hear more about it. I guess people don't like to talk about sad things. Or maybe child sexual abuse scares them, because they're afraid it might happen to one of their children. Sometimes, it might be because they think if they don't talk about it, it will go away.

"Wouldn't that be wonderful? No more child sexual abuse. It would be great! But we can't make it go away by not talking about it. The only way to make it go away is to talk about it so that when it happens, kids will know it's wrong and tell on the abuser. If there was more talk about child sexual abuse, when it happened children wouldn't blame themselves and would have more courage to tell someone about it right away.

"The way it is now, most kids are afraid to tell. They're not just afraid of what the abuser might do, but they're also afraid that other people, even their own families, will blame them.

"I wouldn't be surprised if some of the kids you know have been abused. They just don't talk about it, or maybe they don't even know they were abused. Maybe the abuser told them it was a game or some kind of 'love' or 'special time' together.

"But just because nobody talks about it doesn't mean it doesn't happen. And just because it's not in the history books doesn't mean it doesn't happen either. Child abuse, hitting kids, sexually abusing them, and other cruel acts toward children have been going on for a long time all over the world.

"I don't know why some big people think that it's okay to hurt little people, but it's not okay. In fact, it's against the law. When big people hurt little people, they are committing a crime for which they can be arrested and punished.

"Always remember—you are not alone. Just think, one out of every five or six girls, and one out of every twenty boys ... that's a lot of children."

Using Empathy and Story-Telling

If you were sexually abused as a child, or suffered some other type of trauma, or if there is a close friend or relative of yours who has been abused, you may consider revealing this truth to your child. It may be unnecessary or unwise if

- You have not worked through your feelings about being abused

- You have not asked permission of the sexually abused relative or friend

- Your child is too immature or distressed to be able to profit from this information

The purpose is not to burden your child with yet more upsetting information, but to show him that he isn't alone. Before you decide, talk with your child's therapist. Think carefully about any possible negative effects on your child and your relationship, and weigh this against potential benefits.

If you do decide to confide in your child, the important concepts to communicate are that

- You were abused

- Abuse is traumatic

- Trauma causes emotional numbing, as well as physical hyper-reactivity (nervousness, inability to sleep, anxiety, nightmares, and so on)

- Healing is possible when the trauma is talked about and understood

Your child also needs to be educated explicitly about the cause and nature of his symptoms. He will feel relieved when he learns that sexual abuse survivors often suffer a range of symptoms, including periods of emotional numbing, periods of recalling or re-experiencing the trauma, nightmares, anxiety, and regression. This knowledge will help him make sense of his reactions and emotions, and will enable him to stop thinking of himself as "crazy" because of his fluctuating and conflicting feelings.

In talking to older children, the discussion earlier in this book on post-traumatic stress disorder could be paraphrased (see Chapter 1). In talking to younger children, you may want to use story-telling as a way to communicate key concepts. You might try the following:

"Once upon a time there were two cats, Kitty and Spunky. Kitty was one of the friendliest cats in town. She purred when you held her and liked to sleep next to you at night.

"Spunky was just the opposite. Every time you went near her, she'd run away. You could hardly ever pet her and if you tried to pick her up, she'd scratch you. But you knew she wanted you to love her because sometimes she'd sit in a corner and look at you with such sad eyes, you knew she wanted some attention.

"At night sometimes you'd wake up and find Spunky next to you. But the minute you moved, she'd run and hide.

"Spunky acted scared around people, but she was real bossy to Kitty. Whenever you'd put out special cat treats, Spunky would push Kitty away and eat up all the treats and not leave any for Kitty. Sometimes she'd just jump up and attack Kitty for no reason at all— no reason that you could see, anyway.

"Kitty slept a lot, like most cats. Spunky slept, too, but not as much as Kitty, and sometimes you could hear Spunky making sad meows in her sleep.

"Really loud noises would wake up both cats, but Spunky would wake up at the tiniest sound. Spunky slept more like a soldier on duty than a normal cat. Even when she was asleep she was half-awake waiting for the enemy. You would have thought that Spunky had grown up in an alley full of wild dogs, but Spunky hadn't ever even seen an alley. She was brought up in a nice, clean house.

"Why do you think Spunky acted like she did?"

After listening to and commenting on your child's response, continue: "Spunky was an abused cat. She grew up in a home where the kids hit her, poked her, burned her, locked her in closets, and played all kinds of cruel games on her. This all happened when she was a kitten. Even as a little baby cat she learned not to trust people.

"Spunky's mother saw what was happening to Spunky, but she couldn't protect Spunky from the mean people. After all, she was only a cat. But Spunky was mad at her mother anyway, just like you might be mad at me because I couldn't stop [abuser's name] from hurting you. You might be mad at other people, too, for not helping you.

"Finally Spunky's mother moved with Spunky and Kitty to another house where the people were kind. Spunky was safe at last. But Spunky didn't know that. Even when her new owners bought her special cat toys and special cat treats, Spunky ran away from them, because she was afraid they were going to be like the mean people. Only after her new owners would leave the room would Spunky come out to eat or play with the toys.

"It took a long time for Spunky to let her new owners pet her. She liked to be petted. But in her first house, when she was petted, sometimes she was hurt afterwards. So even in the new house, whenever anybody petted her, she remembered the old hitting and mean tricks, and that made her want to run away.

"But Spunky also wanted to be held and was jealous whenever the new people held Kitty. That's why she used to push Kitty away from the food bowl. Spunky was angry at the mean people, but she couldn't fight back because she was only a cat. But she *could* hurt Kitty, because Kitty was even smaller than Spunky.

"Some abused children are like Spunky. They want to be close to others, they want love, but because being close to others also meant getting hurt, they are mixed up about what to do.

"Like Spunky, they're angry, too, but don't know how to say it. They want to hit the big person who hurt them, but since they can't, they might push around somebody smaller. Or they might break things, or run away from home, or say nasty things, or hurt themselves. They act angry, but only because they're scared inside, like Spunky.

"That's why abused children sometimes can't sleep well—because they're scared. Spunky had trouble sleeping because she was afraid she would be hurt. Even though she was safe in her new house, she was always afraid that something bad would happen to her.

"Abused children are like that, too, especially if they were abused while they were sleeping or if they pretended to be asleep while the abuse was happening. Even when they know they are safe, they are afraid that the bad thing will happen again. They have trouble sleeping because they are worried, or because the memories come back.

"Spunky is better now. She likes her new owners and even trusts them. But sometimes she remembers the old owners and she goes and hides. Spunky doesn't want to remember the bad times, but she can't help it. Spunky especially remembers the bad times whenever the new owners eat pizza. Can you guess why?

"The old owners—the mean ones—used to eat a lot of pizza and Spunky used to smell the pizza when she was being hurt. So now she remembers bad things when she smells that smell. But there's nothing wrong with pizza, is there? Most cats love pizza because of the cheese on it. Kitty likes pizza so much she jumps on the table to get some. But Spunky runs into the closet.

"Maybe you have some things like Spunky's pizza that remind you of the time you were hurt. Things that aren't bad by themselves but make you feel bad because they make you remember. You want to get away from those things because they might make you feel sick to your stomach, or like punching somebody, or like dying. You might think you're crazy for feeling that way. But do you think Spunky was crazy for not liking the smell of pizza? Of course not!

"Well, it's not crazy for you to react the way you do to things that remind you of the abuse. For example, is there something horrible about the color green? No. But if green was the color of the shirt the person who hurt you was wearing, it would be the most normal thing in the world for you to hate the color green.

"But, guess what? For three years now Spunky has smelled pizza at the new people's house and hasn't been hit by anybody. After all those times of hiding in the closet every time the pizza man came, Spunky has learned that pizza isn't going to hurt her. Pizza isn't her favorite smell, but she doesn't go running to the closet anymore. She even lets her new owners hold her.

"How about that? Spunky has gotten better. Isn't that wonderful? Spunky got better, and she couldn't even talk to tell anyone what was the matter. You can not only talk, but you can listen and you can get help, too. You don't have to stay afraid the way Spunky did. And Dad and I [or Mom and I] aren't like Spunky's mom and dad. We can help you. Spunky got better and so will you."

You may want to introduce some of the particulars of your child's situation and symptoms into this story, or use another animal to make the story more relevant. Be sure to change Spunky from a cat to a loved animal if your child is afraid of cats.

If Your Child Abuses Food, Alcohol, or Drugs

The abuse of food, alcohol, or drugs is a common response to the pain and stress experienced by a sexually abused child. Food, alcohol, and drugs are all capable of inducing the numbness he prefers to the sharpness of his pain. All three are also capable of stimulating your child when he feels downcast and dejected; of giving him courage in situations where he lacks confidence; and of quelling the conflicts he undoubtedly has about his interpersonal relationships, his sexuality, and his anger.

Eating disorders such as *bulimia nervosa* or *anorexia nervosa*, exist among both male and female abuse survivors. Body image and conflicts about sexuality and anger are usually central issues for abuse survivors with these eating disorders, as well as those who compulsively overeat. Another central issue for all substance abusers, whether that substance is alcohol, food, or drugs, is powerlessness and control.

Addictions or eating disorders often begin soon after the abuse, or at the onset of puberty, when children develop a keen interest in their own sexual development. It's at this time that the abuse can emerge or resurface as an important issue. Many survivors—and their parents—fail to make the association between the experience of sexual abuse and the child's addiction. While substance abuse or eating disorders may have many origins, the importance of abuse as a cause should not be discounted. Sadly, many abuse survivors view their addictions as further "proof" that they are worthless, immoral, and irredeemable human beings.

If your child is currently anorectic or bulimic, his therapist may want to defer intensive insight therapy until the eating disorder is under control. Your child will not be able to concentrate during the sessions if his mind is half-starved or if he is exhausted from binge-vomiting the night before.

At this point, therapy should focus on establishing normal eating patterns and eliminating the self-starvation, binge-vomiting, or both. If your child does not respond to the suggestions made by the therapist—especially if the symptoms seem to be increasing in frequency or intensity—hospitalization may be required.

If your child is binge-vomiting once a week, there may be no reason for hospitalization. However, if the bulimia escalates to three or four times a day, with the result that your child is missing school (or work) and is unable to maintain a social or family life, hospitalization may by needed. In the case of anorexia, the therapist should be in contact with a physician to determine the weight below which your child's life will be in danger. If your child's weight drops below this point, then hospitalization is almost a must.

Once in the hospital in an eating disorders unit, or in a psychiatric unit where there are staff with special training in eating disorders, the initial focus will be on symptom control, and therapy will be primarily supportive. Then, as your child makes progress, more and more insight therapy can be introduced.

However, your child cannot stay symptom-free until the sexual abuse issue is addressed directly. If the feelings associated with the abuse (or with any other major life problem your child is experiencing) are not dealt with, he will have difficulty *not* returning to his eating disorder as a coping mechanism.

The same general principle applies to alcohol and drug addictions. Eliminating the addiction is only the first step. In order for your child to stay alcohol- or drug-free, he must learn to deal with reality—the reality of the abuse and its aftereffects, the reality of his emotions, and the reality of the demands the external world places upon him—without turning to a substance for courage, sedation, excitement, or other forms of comfort.

Twelve-year-old Amelia was able to hide her anorexia by wearing baggy clothes. But when the five-foot-five girl weighed in at eighty pounds at the doctor's office, her parents had her hospitalized. She spent five months on an eating disorders ward learning to eat three meals a day, and attended group therapy three times a week.

Upon discharge, Amelia's weight was normal and she had gained a lot of insight about her relationship to her parents, siblings, and peers. In the hospital's family therapy program, she and her parents were able to improve their communication with each other and to resolve some of their differences. But the fact never emerged that Amelia had been sexually abused for years by an older cousin—primarily because nobody asked her about possible abuse, and she was too ashamed to bring it up. For months at a time, she was able to block the abuse out of her awareness.

At fifteen, several years after being released from the hospital, Amelia became anorectic again. She needed to be readmitted to an eating disorders ward; but this time her parents found one that had specialized groups for sex abuse survivors. Her mother had become suspicious when she observed Amelia's cousin George making sexual overtures to an eight-year-old at a family Thanksgiving dinner. In the supportive atmosphere of the therapy group, hearing other children's stories of having been abused, Amelia was able to publicly admit her own experience—and to place her anger where it belonged, on her cousin. When she was discharged from the hospital, she was able with the help of her therapist and her parents to maintain her healthy eating habits.

Good therapy has a double focus: controlling the addiction and addressing the feelings and conflicts underlying it.

Your child also needs to learn new ways of coping with feelings and problems. You can help him practice some of these coping mechanisms, which are described in Chapter 6.

However, when the addiction reaches life-threatening proportions—as when a child spends five or six hours a day involved with food or vomiting, an entire weekend high on drugs or alcohol, begins to steal to support his addiction, has repeated car accidents or other mishaps due to alcoholic blackouts, or develops an inability to concentrate due to drugs or food abuse—the addiction needs to be taken care of first.

Never forget that substance abuse and eating disorders are progressive problems that have the potential to do more than just cripple your child emotionally, socially, and intellectually. Addiction kills. What begins as "one small drink" to handle anxiety or anger can lead to drunk driving, injury, or death. A "social snort" at a party can quickly lead to selling sex to support a cocaine habit and venturing into dangerous parts of town to "get a hit."

Do not discount the warning signs. If your child is seriously abusing food, drugs, or alcohol, get help for him immediately. On the other hand, one drink at a party or an experimental puff on a marijuana cigarette does not warrant putting your teenager into an alcohol or drug abuse program. Your job is to use your common sense, tempered with the knowledge that parents have a natural tendency to deny self-destructive behavior on the part of their children. If your child is regularly using drugs or alcohol as a way of coping, he has a problem and needs help. If he is severely overweight or undernourished, he is also crying out for help. Observe your child and talk with him—and if you doubt your ability to be objective, get the advice of a knowledgeable professional.

Medication

If your child suffers from a clinical depression, or if his nightmares, anxiety attacks, or hypervigilance are particularly severe, his psychiatrist may recommend medication. Although medication alone cannot heal the wounds of sexual abuse, medication can make it easier for your child to function. Only a psychiatrist can prescribe medication for mood disorders. If your child has been seeing a therapist who does not have an M.D., the therapist will have to ask a consulting psychiatrist to prescribe medication. All medication needs to be carefully monitored by you, your child, and his doctor.

You also have the right to question the psychiatrist or psychopharmacologist about the particular medication prescribed for your child. If the medication is being taken as prescribed and has had sufficient time to take effect, but is still not helping or is creating too many negative side effects, neither you nor your child should hesitate to speak up.

Assume that the doctor wants to know how the drug is working and would be more than happy to consider alternatives. As is well known in the field of psychopharmacology, the effects of a drug can be highly individual: what helps one person with a certain problem may not work at all with another. One client may react to an antidepressant with constipation, grogginess, or weight gain, while there may be no reaction whatsoever from another client. There are medications that act as depressants for some people and stimulants for others. Medication, after all, is a matter of chemistry: the chemistry of the drug itself, and the chemistry of its interaction within a particular individual's body. Choice of medication and dosage are rarely textbook matters, but require some trial and error and close observation of effects on the part of the prescribing doctor. As someone who is with your child for many hours every day, you can help significantly in observing and recording side effects and reactions.

The child who is clinically depressed, or whose functioning is severely impaired by anxiety, nightmares, insomnia, or hyper-vigilance, may benefit from a carefully monitored course of medica-tion therapy. The medication can help regulate your child's nervous system so that his life is less disrupted by his symptoms. However, medication alone—without some form of therapy that addresses the abuse and any other relevant issues—is not sufficient.

Eighteen-year-old Dennis had been infatuated with alcohol since the age of fourteen. Because of their cultural background, which con-doned the heavy use of alcohol, his family viewed his drinking as a natural part of his growing up. After Dennis was arrested for drunk driving, he was court-ordered into an alcohol rehabilitation program, where he attended Alcoholics Anonymous meetings and other group sessions for several months.

Dennis sobered up, but after a few months began having minor "slips." No more drunk driving—just blackouts at parties and little "pick-me-ups" to get him started in the morning. At one party he got aggressive and was arrested.

Dennis was sent through the same alcohol rehabilitation program he had gone through before. Once again he became sober and, humbled by his previous relapse, he made a commitment to attend AA meetings faithfully. At one of those meetings, a speaker shared about being sexually abused by his father. Dennis left the meeting and went out and got roaring drunk. This "slip" lasted several months and he had to be institutionalized once more.

When his therapist questioned him about his drinking binge, Dennis had to admit that he'd been upset by the speaker at the AA meeting who had talked about being abused. The other boy's ex-perience had brought out of repression Dennis's memory of being sexually abused by his uncle. The feelings associated with the abuse were intolerable to Dennis, and he tried to drown them in alcohol.

With the help of his therapist—in combination with the alcohol rehabilitation program—Dennis learned to see the relationship be-tween his drinking and the sexual abuse.

A battery of tests at the hospital also determined that Dennis suf-fered from clinical depression. In combination with the other aspects of the treatment program, an antidepressant was prescribed which significantly aided Dennis in maintaining his sobriety. Depression often occurs in cycles and, as research has shown, drinking binges—like eating binges—often precede major depressive episodes. For Dennis, as for many other alcoholics, alcohol was a form of self-medication, not only for the sexual abuse, but for the clinical depres-sion as well.

See Chapter 6 for further discussion of the issues surrounding medication and a brief description of various drugs prescribed for mood. disorders.

Empowerment and Self-Help Groups

There are many forms of group therapy for sexual abuse survivors: groups led by mental health professionals; groups sponsored by survivor organizations such as Victims of Incest Can Emerge Survivors (VOICES) in Action and Incest Resources; and self-help groups based on the twelve steps of Alcoholics Anonymous such as Incest Survivors Anonymous (ISA). Some county and city governments have sexual assault centers or hospital programs which offer outpatient group therapy.

The full range of these groups may not exist in your area; fees also may vary widely from one area to another. Twelve-step groups are free, but others may charge anything from a nominal fee to the full hourly rate for a therapist. Some groups—especially those conducted by mental health professionals—may be time-limited and require regular attendance. Others are open-ended and clients can drop in. You will need to inquire about the leadership, structure, and fees for the groups that exist in your area.

In general, I highly recommend some form of group therapy for sexual abuse survivors. A group experience helps reduce the stigma and sense of isolation associated with being a survivor of sexual abuse, and provides invaluable peer support and interaction. In most groups—but especially in self-help groups where there is no professional leadership—participants are able to give as well as receive. Your child's self-esteem can increase by leaps and bounds as he sees the ways in which he is able to help other survivors of sexual abuse.

However, some children may not be ready for a group experience until they have first received some individual therapy, and have not only intellectually but on a gut level accepted the reality of the abuse and the seriousness of its consequences. Your child should not be forced into a group until he is ready. Group is not suitable either for children who are suicidal or homicidal, who are extremely dependent or overly susceptible to the suggestions of others, or whose health is severely handicapped by their addiction.

Most twelve-step programs offer tremendous support and encouragement to those who are struggling to overcome addiction. However, if your child is abusing alcohol, drugs, or food to such an extent that he is physically ill, unable to take care of himself, or a danger to himself or others, he may need hospitalization. Chapters 8 and 9 deal with the choices and issues attending hospitalization.

Even though twelve-step groups are not professionally led, thousands of people have benefitted immensely from them. You should be aware, however, that all groups are not the same and that there is a wide variability in the nature of the meeting, its leadership, and membership. Some groups, for example, encourage family reconciliation to the extent of discouraging the expression of anger. This might be inappropriate for your child, particularly if he is an incest survivor. By reading the group's literature, and talking to other members if possible, you and your child's therapist can help your child decide whether or not a particular self-help group is right for him.

The purpose of any therapy is to provide support for your child and help him regain his self-esteem, confidence, and trust in himself and others. If participation in a group experience fails to approach these goals, you and your child need to reevaluate his options.

A Note of Caution

Blame-the-victim attitudes and misunderstandings about the nature of trauma and abuse exist in twelve-step programs just as they do in the general public. Some sponsors and program members, just like some therapists and members of your family and community, may be uncomfortable with the intensity of your child's feelings and experiences, and may give him negative feedback when he speaks up. Your child needs to be cautioned that not everybody will understand or feel comfortable listening to his accounts of his traumatic experiences.

"Take what you want and leave the rest" is an often-heard slogan in AA, Overeaters Anonymous, Narcotics Anonymous, and other twelve-step programs. Your child needs to remember that slogan in terms of what he hears at meetings, as well as in terms of the people he meets. He should always be selective about whom he talks to about his deepest feelings—because not everybody will be able to tolerate or understand them.

Another legitimate concern is that twelve-step programs stress critical self-examination. Members are asked to take inventories of their past mistakes and to come to acknowledge, and deal with, their character defects. The goal is spiritual progress, not spiritual perfection. This goal may be admirable; and self-awareness, even of one's defects, is invaluable and necessary for psychological, as well as spiritual growth. But it's especially important for abuse survivors to build their self-esteem and acknowledge and deal with their rage at their abuser. Your child needs a program that recognizes and honors those needs.

Participation in a twelve-step program should ultimately build your child's self-confidence and help him vent his rage outward in appropriate ways rather than inward toward himself or other inappropriate victims. If this is not the case—for example, if your child has an overly critical and controlling sponsor within the group—discuss your concerns with your child and your child's therapist.

For example, Joshua attended a Narcotics Anonymous meeting near his home for over three months before he decided that it wasn't helping him. Although there were other abuse survivors in the meetings, they rarely shared their experiences. When Joshua shared, he felt like an "outsider"; his intense feelings of rage and sorrow were misinterpreted as "emotional binges" or "character defects." Also, there were many individuals at the meeting who were court-ordered to attend NA and who were not dedicated to recovery. Some of them acted as if the meeting were a joke: afterwards they swapped not only drugs, but stories about how they had beaten up or raped others.

Since twelve-step meetings tend to differ in focus and membership, Joshua was advised by his therapist to try and attend other NA meetings until he found one in which he felt comfortable. Unfortunately, none of the other NA meetings in his city was geographically convenient.

Bonnie, on the other hand, had an extremely positive experience with Overeater's Anonymous (OA). After the first meeting she attended, she no longer felt alone. She found a sponsor, whom she telephoned every day with her food plan for that day and whom she contacted whenever she felt hungry, angry, lonely, tired, or afraid (the usual times when she tended to become obsessed with food or to binge). When her sponsor was unavailable, she had the phone numbers of at least two dozen other OA members to call and talk to.

Over time, Bonnie learned to turn to her OA sponsor and friends rather than to food for support. Although there were other abuse survivors in Bonnie's OA group, they tended not to talk about being abused in the meetings. Such sharing did occur on the telephone, however, and eventually Bonnie began to attend meetings of Incest Survivors Anonymous (ISA) with some of her OA friends. At ISA meetings, Bonnie developed even more friendships. Because she had the benefit of individual counseling and some experience in OA, she was able to be helpful to quite a few incest survivors who were just beginning to look at their abuse experience or who did not have the financial means or emotional willingness to be involved with individual counseling. As her ability to make friends and give to others grew, so did Bonnie's self-esteem.

The beauty of twelve-step programs is precisely this: participants find that the most humiliating and shameful moments of their lives can forge connections to other people rather than be causes for isolation. Experiences of humiliation and shame are redeemed as reasons for giving and receiving support from others.

The Meaning of Recovery for Sexual Abuse Survivors

You may be disappointed when therapy does not heal your child as rapidly as you desire: the process of healing can be painfully slow. Therapy for sexual abuse survivors usually requires at least one year. Depending on the individual and the nature and duration of the abuse, healing may take even longer. Complete healing requires that your child attend sessions regularly for the duration of the therapy, not just during periods of crisis.

Of course you hope that therapy will erase all the psychological scars of the abuse, that you will no longer have to be saddened by your child's sadness, or tortured by his feelings, behavior, and bitterness. Therapy *can* help restore your child to a normal level of functioning; but you should recognize from the outset that no therapy can remove the abuse from your child's memory.

The trauma of sexual abuse can leave permanent psychological scars; and your child's feelings about the abuse are bound to return from time to time. Amnesia is not the goal of therapy. Recovery for your child lies not in "feeling better all the time," or in never thinking about or being hurt by the abuse again, but rather in being able to find comfort in interpersonal relationships—especially intimate ones—and being able to function in society. Recovery also entails being able to focus on the positive in life and to experience a wider range of feelings than fear, anger, and self-hatred.

If your child is an incest survivor, healing does not necessarily mean that he will "forgive and forget" and have a friendly relationship with the abusive family member. You and your child both need to let go of any expectations that the abuser will repent or provide compensation for the abuse; and it is up to each of you whether you choose to feel compassion for the abuser. In some cases, healing may mean that a child needs to cut himself off entirely from the abuser and his supporters. The essential thing is that your child feels free of the power of the abuser and can still function despite his memory of the trauma.

Therapy cannot take away pain, or rage, or numbness, but it can bring these emotions under your child's control by increasing his emotional connectedness to himself and others. With help, your child can grow beyond his abuse experience and learn to invest his energy in his present life and his future. He may still suffer from intrusive thoughts, but these will be less frequent and less intense than before. He may still have periods of numbing, rage, or grief—but these periods will be shorter in duration, better understood, and less feared.

One female survivor explained, "After the rape, I never thought I would be able to be close to a man again. I had no problem sleeping with men, but in therapy I learned that going to bed with men too quickly was my way of putting myself down and not having to face the real issue: intimacy. After I became more selective about who I slept with, I then had to deal with the issue of emotional closeness.

"Sometimes I'd look at the man's face and see my abuser's face instead. Or I would expect my partner to start yelling and screaming and cursing at me like the man who abused me did. I've come to realize that whenever I start a new relationship, at the beginning I'm going to be afraid that the man is going to violate me and betray my trust—and I want to end the relationship right that minute. In therapy I learned to give the relationship a little time, to tolerate my fears and wait and see if in fact they're justified or just ghosts of the past.

"Whenever I start a new relationship and go through the fear period, I get some of my old symptoms back—the negative thinking, the binging, the drinking, making little cuts on my arm. Then I get scared, like I'm going back to those days when I was almost totally self-destructive. But my therapist taught me to tell myself, 'You're just having a little attack of post-traumatic stress disorder. Pick up the phone and talk about it, or pick up your pen and write about it. It will pass. It is part of your life, but no longer needs to dominate your life. Because you were abused, you must expect to go backwards sometimes; sometimes you'll feel like you're stuck in the past again. But you aren't going to stay there in that old pain. In twenty minutes, an hour, or two hours, you will be back in today.'"

Further Reading

Courtois, Christine. *Healing the Incest Wound: Adult Survivors in Therapy*, New York: W.W. Norton and Company. 1988.

Bass, Ellen, and Laura Davis. *The Courage to Heal*, New York: Harper and Row. 1988.

Lew, Mike. *Victims No Longer*, New York: Neuraumont Publishing Co. 1988.

5

Guidelines for Finding a Therapist

(and Appropriate Behavior as Therapy Progresses)

One of the most important tasks you will be faced with in helping your child to heal is the selection of the therapy or program that will best meet her needs. This chapter is devoted to helping you decide which interventions are right for your child. Unfortunately, there are many therapists and programs that should be avoided. In choosing, you have the right to "shop around" and make a selection based on your child's needs as well as yours.

Criteria for Effective Therapy

Effective therapists or therapeutic programs must

- See the sexual abuse as real and important in itself

- View the child as a survivor capable of being healed—not as a willing participant in the abuse or a hopeless psychiatric case

- Educate the survivor about child sexual abuse and the nature of the therapeutic process

- Teach the child coping skills such as anger management, assertiveness, and stress management

- Utilize medication and behavioral management techniques when appropriate, but not to the exclusion of insight therapy (if appropriate to your child's age)

- Be aware of the effects of sex-role stereotyping on the healing process

The Selection Process

Compile a list of names from the recommendations of friends, doctors, or sexual abuse survivors who have had positive therapy experiences, and hospitals with specialized programs for sexual abuse survivors. (You can also compile a list of people or programs *not* to call.) Names are also available from local rape crisis centers, battered women's shelters, and women's organizations, such as the National Organization of Women. Look in the phone book under city or county social service agencies for the phone numbers of these organizations.

When you've come up with the names of four or five good prospects, call and interview each of them by phone. Before going into their qualifications, find out how much they charge, if they have any openings, and whether the time slots they have available would be workable for you and your child. Eliminate therapists who are geographically inaccessible, who seem to know little about sexual abuse, or whose fees are prohibitive. When discussing fees, remember to ask about the possibility of a sliding scale, how payments are to be made, and what happens if your child misses an appointment.

If the therapist meets your needs for the above criteria, inquire about his or her training and experience. While you needn't sound hostile, don't avoid asking the hard questions for fear of seeming impolite. Remember—your child's mental and physical health are at stake. Consider asking questions such as the ones that follow. You can preface your questions by telling the therapist that you are faced with a bewildering array of alternatives now, and you want to make the best choice possible for your child.

- "What is your background in the area of child sexual abuse? What experience have you had in treating children suffering from depression/eating disorders/alcoholism?" (Gear your questions to your child's particular problems.)

- "How much and what kind of training have you had in these areas? What, in your view, constitutes the healing process for a victim of sexual abuse?"

- "What approaches would you take towards healing an eating disorder (alcoholism/suicidal behavior/depression)? In the case of an eating disorder, would you work with a nutritionist or dietitian? In the case of clinical depression, do you have a psychiatrist with whom you consult on issues of medication?"

- "What is your view on self-help groups or other group therapy?"

- "What is your format for communicating with your client's parents? What limits do you impose on contact with parents? Do you also conduct family therapy?"

- "How long have you been in practice?"

- "How many sexual abuse survivors have you seen in therapy?"

- "What other types of patients do you counsel?"

- "What would you do if my child became suicidal?"

- "Are you associated with any particular hospital or therapists' group?"

- "Are you a member of any professional organizations?"

Narrow your list down to a final two or three therapists and take your child with you to visit them. In the past, many therapists gave an initial consultation free of charge or at a reduced rate. Today most therapists charge a full fee for their time at the initial consultation. Despite the cost, it's essential that you and your child meet with the therapist face to face before making your selection. Does the therapist seem warm and supportive? Is he or she respectful toward you and your child? Do you feel as if you could talk with this therapist about your child?

More importantly, how does your child feel about the therapist? Qualifications are important—and you should only be considering qualified therapists at this point. But the final decision may be a matter of finding the best emotional match for your child.

Pay attention to your own gut feelings, as well as to those of your child. If your child doesn't like a particular therapist after the first interview, you can ask her in what ways the therapist was unappealing.

For example, fifteen-year-old Tom didn't like Dr. Y. because on the first interview Dr. Y. asked him why he couldn't just make up his mind to stop drinking and do it. Tom, who had been in Alcoholics Anonymous for a year, had learned that alcoholism is an addiction and that giving it up is more than a matter of willpower.

"I wish giving up drinking was that simple," Tom told his mother. "We have to find a therapist who knows about AA."

Tom's objection to Dr. Y. was perfectly rational. However, not all children will be able to articulate why they feel uncomfortable with a particular therapist, or their reason may seem completely irrational. Ten-year-old Susan, for example, vehemently stated, "I don't like

Dr. X. She's yucky!" Don't dismiss such comments as totally irrelevant. Dr. X. may be a very qualified and caring therapist, but may
be a poor emotional match for your child. Or your child may sense,
for reasons she cannot identify, that she won't be able to share openly with a particular therapist.

Emotional factors, as well as nonemotional ones, need to be taken
into consideration in making your selection. Of course, if your child
finds every therapist "yucky" or otherwise unacceptable, she may
simply be expressing a general resistance to therapy—and you may
be stuck with making a decision based on your own knowledge and
instincts about your child.

Even if you like the first therapist you interview very much, go
ahead and meet with at least two others so you have a basis for
comparison. Even though this process may be costly, the initial in-
vestment will be well-spent if it puts your child on course with the
right therapist right away. If no one from your first group of prospects meets your needs, enlarge your list. But if you can't find the
right therapist after having seen six or seven, reexamine your criteria
and consider the possibility that you might be expecting too much.

Evaluating the Course of Therapy

Once you've selected a therapist, you can start your child's therapy
on a trial basis. Make a commitment to have your child work with
the therapist for a month, six weeks, or some other limited time period; then reassess your choice. How does your child seem to be
faring? How effective has the therapist been in addressing your
child's secondary symptoms (such as alcoholism or an eating disorder)? What is the therapist's assessment of your child's progress and
prospect for healing? If the therapist you've selected turns out to
have been a poor choice, use the knowledge you've gained to make
a better one. As in Jeb's case, the wrong therapist can do more harm
than good. As you make your decision, bear in mind that the course
of therapy is not always smooth: backsliding, regression, and hostility on your child's part may all be part of her healing. Dump a
therapist only if you believe that he or she is doing your child
harm—or if you feel that your child's prospects for progress with
this individual are very slim.

It may seem self-evident to you that such a traumatic event as
sexual abuse would be seen as both important and real by any professional. Yet there are schools of thought in the mental health field
that regard sexual abuse as a figment of the child's imagination or
a projection of the child's sexual impulses. Still others recognize that

child sexual abuse occurs, but believe it to be relatively harmless. (These are the therapists to avoid!)

Since coursework on sexual abuse and resulting psychological problems is not required to become a licensed social worker, psychologist, or psychiatrist, it is critical that you inquire about the training and background of any potential therapist or the staff in any therapeutic program. Don't be afraid to ask how many workshops the therapist and staff have attended or how many books they have read on sexual abuse and related subjects.

You can also ask how they keep up with the latest developments in the field of abuse. Are they reading any books or articles now or planning to attend any workshops in the near future? Do they have colleagues available for consultation who are experts in sexual abuse? The same questions can be asked regarding the specific symptoms that are troubling your child.

Therapists who haven't taken it upon themselves to learn about sexual abuse can be easily fooled by a child's insistence that the abuse did not really occur or that, if it did, it "meant nothing" or didn't affect the child "all that much." Unaware that abuse survivors frequently deny or discount the abuse and its psychological consequences, these therapists may limit their efforts to helping with superficial problems or the secondary symptoms associated with the abuse. However, your child will never be healed unless the issue of the abuse is confronted directly.

A Case Study

Jennie was sexually abused by her next-door neighbor beginning when she was eight years old. At first she didn't understand the meaning of his actions. By the time she was eleven or twelve, though, she knew that what he was doing was "bad" and concluded that she was "bad," too, because of her involvement with him.

The neighbor gave Jennie the usual abuser lines—that she "provoked" him into it because she was so pretty, that she must like it, that she would be put in jail or an insane asylum if she told, and so on. By age fourteen, Jennie felt inferior to other girls and ran away from any boy who tried to talk to her. She avoided her peers; yet, in her mind, others were avoiding her. Unconsciously she felt that the sexual abuse "showed" and caused others to reject her.

Jennie sought therapy, hoping it would help her become more popular at school. At one point in the therapy, Jennie mentioned the abuse—but since she didn't elaborate on it, and seemed to have little emotional reaction to it, the therapist didn't pursue the subject in greater detail. Instead the therapist gave Jennie suggestions on how to improve her relationships with her peers, not realizing that Jennie's intense anxieties and fears about relating were rooted in the low self-esteem and patterns of social isolation that are so common in survivors of sexual abuse. Even when Jennie began to express suicidal thoughts and mutilate herself, the therapist bought into Jennie's explanation that her self-destructiveness was due to problems with her peers. A well-informed therapist would have known that suicidal thoughts and self-mutilation are frequent symptoms of sexual abuse.

Several months after beginning therapy, Jennie overdosed on sleeping pills. The psychiatric resident on call in the emergency room, who knew nothing about Jennie's case but who had done some reading on sexual abuse, told Jennie's mother that suicide attempts combined with self-mutilation often, but not always, suggested a history of physical and/or sexual abuse.

"But the therapist says it's because Jennie isn't getting along with her girlfriends at school," Jennie's mother said.

"Kids don't o.d. on sleeping pills and scratch their skin off because of friends, Mrs. X. Usually it's a problem with the parents or, like I said, abuse."

When Jennie's mother confronted the therapist, the therapist shrugged. "Yes, she mentioned something about the neighbor fondling her, but she didn't indicate that it caused her any real problems. Besides, he stopped doing it about a year ago."

As Jennie's case illustrates, a license and a plaque on the door are no guarantee of either insightfulness or sensitivity.

Supportive Behavior While Your Child Is in Therapy

Interacting With the Therapist

As a parent you have the right to know what general methods or approaches your child's therapist is using, the focus of therapy, and the therapist's view of your child's progress. You do not, however, have the right to a blow-by-blow description of your child's therapy sessions or to know what your child has said about you or anyone else.

It's perfectly acceptable for you to "check in" with the therapist every few months for a progress report; or more frequently if your child is in a crisis situation. Do not phone every week and expect a recap of the last session. The therapist needs to be informed if your child's behavior changes; you can do this by leaving a phone message. It's only necessary to talk directly with the therapist when you're getting a progress report—one every few months—or if your child is displaying self-mutilating or suicidal behavior. Under such conditions, the therapist should be in touch with you within four to six hours. Under emergency conditions, however, you should not wait for the therapist to call. Take your child to the emergency room of a hospital that has a psychiatric ward, and have her admitted immediately.

If the therapist wishes to use such procedures as hypnosis, medication, or hospitalization, you have the right to hear the therapist's rationale.

Interacting With Your Child

Even though the therapist is not *your* therapist, it's perfectly appropriate to ask how you can best help your child. Perhaps you are having trouble straightening out some parent-child difficulties. If you feel stuck about how to handle a particular situation with your child, you should feel free to call the therapist and ask for guidance. A skilled therapist will be able to give you a perspective on your child's needs without betraying client confidentiality.

You might be uncertain about how hard to push your child to attend an important family function. While you do not want to be dictatorial, you also want your child to feel included and you want to help free her from her isolation.

You may feel unclear about how much freedom to give your child. Perhaps she's now in recovery from an addiction. In the initial stages of recovery, she may have decided to stay away from places or gatherings where her addictive substance would be in plentiful supply—but now she feels stronger and wants to go to parties or events where others may be indulging. Should you let her go, and possibly slip; or should you protect her from herself until she's stronger? Your child's therapist may have a suggestion or, if this is an important or recurring issue, perhaps the therapist will make this the subject of a therapy session.

You can phone the therapist in such situations—but it's important that you tell your child beforehand. She needs to know that the therapist is *her* special resource, and not yours.

If you do speak with the therapist, he or she may be able to guide you in phrasing your concerns so that your child can receive them as words of love rather than as a series of demands.

The following example can serve as a model for supportive behavior on your part. (You are trying to convince your child to attend a family gathering.)

"I know you have a lot on your mind and that you've been hurting a lot lately, but I just want to remind you that Grandma and Grandpa's fiftieth anniversary party is coming up at the end of the month. All the relatives will be there and they'll want to see you. I'd love for you to come, but I don't want to pressure you either. I know sometimes you get depressed and need to be alone, or sometimes you need to do your artwork instead of being with people. I also know that you can't predict when you're going to need to have time for yourself.

"Sometimes I get mixed up about how to handle these invitations for you. As you know, I talked to your therapist about it, about how I want you to know how welcome you are to come, but also how I don't want to put more pressures on you than you already have. The therapist told me just to be honest.

"I also need to be honest about two other matters: the first is that a lot of times you don't want to go to family functions, but once you get there you have a good time. I don't want you to stay away from family things because you feel bad about the abuse. I don't want to let you isolate yourself. On the other hand, I realize that you can get overloaded and need to be alone.

"I'm afraid that if I don't press you you'll think I don't care if you come with us or not. I'm also afraid that if I keep reminding you about it, you'll feel hassled. I know you like to decide things at the last minute, but I have to make airline reservations at least seven days in advance in order to get a good rate."

You can then invite your child to discuss the issue with you. Ask her how she would like you to handle it and listen to her feedback. But don't put her in the parent role of making the decision by herself. For example, you could say, "I'm thinking of this plan: I'll remind you one more time about the party, and I'll ask you a week before we leave whether or not you're going. If you *are* going, I'll buy the tickets for all of us. If you plan to stay home, then I'll arrange for Mrs. T. [a neighbor, another relative, a babysitter—whatever is appropriate] to spend the weekend here so you won't be alone. If you stay behind, I want you to call me at an agreed-upon time so that I can feel reassured that you're okay. Do you have some ideas about other options that would make us feel more comfortable? Let's talk."

Some therapists may not want to talk to you directly except under emergency conditions, and may not want to conduct family therapy or joint sessions with you and your child. This probably is in the interest of establishing strict and clear boundaries between your needs and those of your child. The therapist may also want to reassure your child that the therapist's loyalties are not mixed.

If this is the case, your child's therapist may work in conjunction with a family therapist who can see both of you and/or other members of your family. If you do end up seeing a family therapist, you can ask your child's therapist how often the two professionals will confer about her progress. This is important: the family therapist needs to know of your child's progress in individual therapy, since her needs will change as she heals. Similarly, if there are other problems in the family, or if you and your child are in conflict, your child's therapist needs to know: these problems also will affect the course of your child's healing.

If the Therapist Excludes You

If the therapist refuses to deal with you at all or calls you intrusive whenever you ask questions, ask directly what he or she would consider to be appropriate behavior on your part, and under what conditions there can be communication between you.

You can expect that the therapist will not want to talk to you about your personal problems, your problems with your spouse or other children, your problems at work, and so on. You must also expect that he or she will not talk to you every day or spend hours on the phone with you. If your child is in such a fragile psychological condition that you need to keep in daily contact with her therapist, it may be time to consider hospitalization.

However, if the therapist will only talk to you under emergency conditions, is not available to discuss your concerns about your child, and has not provided a family therapist or liaison to address your concerns, you have every reason to feel frustrated. You can feel justified in considering a change to another therapist who is more open to communicating with you, or who provides the means of communicating through a family therapist. Since the support of parents is so crucial to a child's recovery, it's essential that you be kept abreast of major developments or setbacks in your child's healing; and that your questions about how best to support your child receive the attention they deserve.

Blame-the-Parent Therapists

You don't need more guilt, blame, or shame than you feel already. Even if you had nothing to do with your child's abuse and could have done nothing to prevent it, on some level as a parent you feel guilty because you are responsible for your child's well-being. You may spend many sleepless hours wondering if there wasn't perhaps something you could have done, some action you could have taken. But it's time now to focus on what you *can* do to promote your child's emotional, mental, and physical health.

Unless you're the mother of an incest survivor, or you permitted the abuse of your child because you were being abused or threatened yourself, your child's therapist is unlikely to blame you even indirectly for your child's pain. However, you may be judged a "deficient parent" if the therapist subscribes to one of the following three theories:

- Good parenting can make a child relatively resilient and strong in the face of stress.

- Your child somehow sought the sexual abuse in order to meet needs that were not being met by you at home.

- The actual event of the sexual abuse plays a relatively minor role in your child's difficulties compared to the mistakes you've made as a parent.

Each of these theories has logical inconsistencies of which you should be aware.

Myth 1: Good parenting can make a child resilient to the stress of sexual abuse.

The experience of combat veterans in World War II, Korea, and Vietnam, prisoners of war from a variety of cultures, and victims of refugee and concentration camps has shown that, given sufficient stress, even the "strongest" and "best" of men and women will "crack." Study after study has demonstrated that even the most psychologically healthy individuals from stable families will develop symptoms of post-traumatic stress disorder when subject to trauma, especially repeated trauma. Sexual abuse entails betrayal, powerlessness, traumatic sexualization, and stigmatization: it is an extremely traumatic form of victimization. Even if you were a perfect parent (if such a creature existed!), you could not have prevented your child from suffering the after-effects of sexual abuse.

Myth 2: Your child sought the abuse in order to meet needs that were not being met by you at home.

No parent is perfect. There is not a human being alive who had a childhood during which all of his or her emotional needs were met. It's not even desirable that all of a child's needs be met all the time: in preparation for adulthood, a child needs to learn to some extent to deal with frustration. If all her needs were met at home, she would have no need for friendships and relationships outside the family. Extra-familial relationships are essential to fostering the basis for an independent life as an adult.

Even if your child was "needy," this does not mean that she sought out the abuse. Perhaps, like Jeb, she sought affection and attention—but not sexual activity or abuse. It was the abuser who perverted your child's natural and normal needs for tenderness, touch, or acceptance. Nothing you did or didn't do as a parent caused the attacker to abuse your child: the impetus for the abuse came from the abuser himself.

Myth 3: The event of the abuse itself plays a relatively minor role in your child's difficulties compared to the mistakes you've made as a parent.

Freud and his followers believed that personality is shaped by early childhood conflicts. This perspective—that childhood issues shape one's entire life—has dominated psychology and psychiatry for decades. In recent years, however, there has been increasing recognition that events at any time in the lifecycle—in adolescence, mid-life, and even in old age—can also shape the personality. Sexual abuse is no less traumatic for taking place outside the context of the family or early childhood experiences, no matter what Freud says.

Since you're human, you probably have made some errors in raising your child. But where is it written that every parent must strive for perfection? And who has taught us to feel guilty and inadequate if we fall anywhere short of this goal? Regardless of what you did or didn't do in rearing your child, the sexual abuse had its negative impact independent of your influence on your child.

It is certainly possible for your child's therapist to help you better understand your child's needs and personality; as a result, you may change some of your attitudes and behaviors as a parent. Perhaps the therapist also can help you examine some of the consequences for your child of your actions and decisions as a parent. But this should always be done in a manner that respects your dignity and good intentions. It is not only humiliating, but ineffective in the long run, for a therapist to try to change a parent's behavior through tactics of guilt or shame.

Cherchez la Mère

Although both mothers and fathers have been blamed by mental health professionals for the problems of children, there is a long tradition of assigning most of this blame to the mother. The tendency both of lay people and professionals to blame mothers for whatever goes wrong with their offspring is well-documented, beginning with Freud. In a unique survey completed in 1985, two researchers reviewed over a hundred recent articles in clinical journals and found that mothers were more often blamed for problems in children than were fathers. In fact, mothers were blamed for seventy-two kinds of psychopathology in children, including aggressiveness, anxiety, arson, bad dreams, behavior problems, failure to mourn, frigidity, homosexuality, the need to be anally penetrated, success conflict, truancy, and incest.[1]

In the articles surveyed, three times as many words were used to describe mothers as opposed to fathers, and the word "mother" was used 200 times more frequently that the word "father." Five times as many articles used the mother, as opposed to the father, to illustrate the cause of a child's problems. Furthermore, "in no article was the mother's relationship described as simply healthy, nor was the mother ever described in only positive terms."

Although the father's absence of involvement was noted in some of the articles, this factor, along with the subsequent strain on the mother, was never correlated with the child's problems. In 82 percent of the articles, from every angle, mothers emerged as far more blameworthy, although it was usually they who had sought help for their children.

There are many influences on a child's development. Certainly an experience with sexual abuse can negatively affect a child as much as, if not more than, a less-than-perfect mother. Parents of either gender who are guiding a child through the healing process should be aware of this almost unconscious bias among some helping professionals and, in fact, throughout our society. Shouldering guilt and blame will do nothing to help your child get over the trauma of sexual abuse.

Attitudes on the Part of the Therapist That Can Help or Harm Your Child

Therapists need to view your child both as a victim (someone who was unjustly violated in a situation where she was rendered powerless), and as a survivor (someone who found the resources to bear the unbearable). If, instead, the therapist or program tends to see your child and her abuser as both being responsible for the abuse, or views your child as having "seduced" the abuser, then you should search for professionals with a more supportive and informed outlook.

Avoid therapists who view the child and the abuser as being "equally victimized," as well as those who, in the case of incest, blame the abuse on the collusive, passive, frigid, or otherwise "sick" or ungiving mother. The role of the mother either in encouraging, or more usually, in ignoring the incest needs to be clarified in therapy. Perhaps the mother was being abused herself or had a condition that limited her ability to mother her children. While no mother is perfect and the mother's predicament needs to be explored in therapy, the therapist must also validate the abused child's anger toward her mother and her grief regarding any ways in which her mother failed her.

But no matter how directly or indirectly the mother supported the incest, she must not be used as a scapegoat for the abuser's behavior. For your child to heal, the therapist needs to continually put the responsibility for the abuse on the abuser, not on your child or other family members. While family dynamics and personalities may have contributed to the development of the abuse, it was the abuser who committed the crime, not somebody else.

The therapist also needs to understand the mind-set of a victim/survivor. The typical survivor feels defective, damaged, and undeserving of love, care, and protection. The therapist must also view your child's maladaptive or negative behavior patterns and attitudes in light of the abuse. Your child may have more than one psychological problem; but her problems can be better understood in terms of the ways in which they have helped her cope with the abuse—not as signs of inherent and intractable "sickness" or instability.

The therapist should not view your child as being beyond help; rather, he or she should hold a firm view that healing is possible, and be able to transmit that optimism to your child.

The therapist needs to address your child's victimization on three levels:

- The actual incident

- How the incident was reacted to by others (police, the courts, social service agencies, your family, and so on)

- To what extent your child has labeled herself a victim and behaves that way (passive, placating, self-abasing in sexual or nonsexual situations)

If the therapist understands the psychology of victimization, he or she will not chastise your child for trying to run from or sabotage therapy or other positive experiences. The therapist will also understand that he or she is dealing with a client who is escaping her pain by numbing her feelings and who therefore needs an active and caring therapist, not a silent or authoritarian one.

Your Relationship With Your Child's Therapist or Group

Your relationship with your child's therapist and other psychological support providers depends a great deal on your child's age. If she is under twelve, you and her therapist will probably be communicating frequently, and the therapist will be asking you for reports on your child's behavior. If she is under eight, communication will be even more frequent.

Once children become teenagers, however, issues of confidentiality become more crucial. Teenagers typically want to assert themselves as independent individuals. Your teenager will want reassurance from her therapist that you are not "butting in" or somehow trying to control her therapy. The therapist must be discreet about information or observations to be shared with you. He or she may suggest family therapy sessions in favor of dealing with your concerns about your child over the telephone or in parent-therapist conferences.

Regardless of your child's age, however, your relationship with her therapist should include mutual respect and a spirit of cooperation. You and the therapist share the same goal: the attainment of emotional and physical well-being for your child. In a sense, you are a team—but like members of any team, you each have different jobs, and you may have to deal with differences, jealousies, and misunderstandings.

From the start, it's important for you to realize that therapy is not a cure-all: therapists are not gods whose magic utterances can make your child healthy, happy, and whole after a certain number of sessions. It's unfair and unrealistic to expect the therapist to effect any magic cures. However, you can expect him or her to be dedicated, sincere, and supportive of your child's welfare.

It's not unreasonable to expect evaluation conferences with the therapist every three to four months, to call the therapist when you notice new or increased negative behavior on the part of your child, or to ask for guidance in handling certain situations. The therapist must, however, respect the confidentiality of your child's therapy sessions. Professional ethics demand that the therapist not reveal to you specifics of the therapy unless your child poses a danger to herself or others.

You and the therapist should see yourselves as a team, not competitors. If you feel that the therapist views you as a nuisance, or if he or she calls you names, throws psychological labels at you in a hostile manner, or otherwise verbally abuses you, it may be time to consider getting another therapist.

As a parent, you have the ultimate responsibility for the welfare of your child. If, over time, you do not see improvement, you need to ask for the therapist's view of your child's progress. It may be that she is progressing in areas that are not visible to you, but which are still significant. For example, she may be working through her denial of the abuse, even though her schoolwork hasn't improved.

Dealing With Your Own Feeling About Your Child

Your child's relationship with you and her feelings about your family can profit from being examined in therapy. Inevitably, your relationship with your child will be scrutinized; some of your shortcomings will be analyzed and discussed. Since you are doing so much for your child and have her best interests at heart, knowing that you are going to be talked about in therapy may feel like a betrayal. You may be angry, both at the therapist and your child.

You may have the all-too-human desire to know what they're saying about you. It's important to acknowledge this feeling—then tell yourself that your child's therapy will best proceed if you resist the impulse to get involved, or impose on it your own desires and needs. Remember that your child must bring up her own issues with you as they emerge. Don't force any confrontations on her just because these issues have surfaced on your own agenda. When and if she's ready to talk with you, she'll talk. Keep yourself open and available for any discussions she may wish to have; but stay out of her private discussions with her therapist. Resign yourself to the fact that you may not know for years—if ever—what comments were made in therapy.

You may resent this in light of the fact that you love your child more than the therapist does, and have obviously sacrificed more for her than the therapist (who is, after all, getting paid). You may also be feeling somehow inadequate because your child needs an outsider to help her. You may even feel that you're being replaced. Perhaps your child used to confide in you and now is doing more and more of her sharing with her therapist. This hurts. You feel left out and it's easy for this hurt to translate itself into anger and suspicion directed toward your child's group or counselor.

"Well, what did that therapist say about me today?" you may wonder as your child stands up to you or defies you after her weekly session. It's at this point that you must realize that the therapist is not all-powerful, just as you are not. You cannot justifiably blame every difficult situation with your child on the influence of her therapist. However, if your child says, "Mr. X told me you're really sick," or "Mrs. W thinks you should allow me to stay out past midnight on weekends," it's time to pick up the phone and check the accuracy of your child's statements.

At all times, there needs to be an open line of communication between you and the therapist (within the guidelines suggested earlier in this chapter). Your feelings of anger, jealousy, competitiveness, or whatever need to be aired—but not to your child. Use a therapist of your own, or a good friend, to help you sort out which of your concerns about the therapist stem from your own insecurities and the normal parental anxieties about "letting go," and which stem from the limitations of the therapist.

You may feel the same conflicts in regard to your child's involvement in a support group. You may have wanted nothing more than for your child to emerge from her isolation and begin to relate to others. Yet you may find yourself feeling jealous of the time the support group takes away from the time the two of you once shared. You may feel "replaced." Again, it's important for you to acknowledge your feelings without acting on them. The last thing you want to do is to discourage your child's involvement in the group by making her feel guilty about "abandoning" you. Find an outlet for your feelings apart from your child. You might try to look at your child's involvement with others as a positive experience for her and a chance for more freedom for yourself.

Whenever you find yourself resenting your child's involvement with a therapist or group, remember that this represents a healthy step in her recovery. This is one way in which she's separating herself from her trauma and moving toward recovery.

What To Do If Your Child Is Misdiagnosed

The purpose of a diagnosis is not to label or stigmatize your child but to help determine an appropriate treatment plan. Without a proper diagnosis, your child runs the risk not only of being given the wrong medication, but of being subjected to an incomplete or ineffective psychotherapeutic approach.

A common problem that afflicts sexual abuse survivors is that often they are diagnosed as having a personality disorder (such as borderline personality, dependent personality disorder, obsessive-compulsive personality disorder, avoidant personality disorder, and so on). Your child's behavior and emotional patterns may fit well into one of these categories. However, such a diagnosis ignores the likelihood that the apparent disorder may be part of your child's coping strategy in reaction to the trauma of the sexual abuse. As such, it may be inappropriate to paste this stigmatizing label on her.

Unless a therapist is well-informed about, and sensitive to, issues pertaining to sexual abuse, he or she may easily fail to see how some of your child's symptoms originated as coping mechanisms.

Although it is not your place to make the diagnosis, your child's therapist may choose Post Traumatic Stress Disorder (PTSD) as the most appropriate diagnosis for your child. PTSD is an anxiety disorder, not a personality disorder, and clearly attributes symptoms to trauma. Such a diagnosis keeps helping professionals—and your child—focused on the main cause of your child's pain: the abuse itself.

Some mental health professionals tend to view clients with personality disorders—especially borderline personalities—as being very difficult to treat and capable of making only limited progress in therapy. When a therapist holds limited hope or expectations for your child because he or she views your child as having a personality disorder, the therapist may not work as hard toward your child's recovery. In this situation, if your child fails to make progress, the therapist can blame the persistence of symptoms on the personality disorder. Your child may actually be responding to the therapist's negative or limited expectations of her; or may fail to progress because of the lack of attention being paid to the issue of sexual abuse.

If your child has been given a diagnosis of personality disorder, don't panic. It's possible for such a label to be applied without creating a self-fulfilling prophecy of failure. In some cases the label may be necessary to secure a particular medication or treatment for your child. Nevertheless, you should be on guard for any attitude on the part of the therapist that your child is a "hopeless case."

In truth, many of the symptoms of borderline personality overlap the symptoms of PTSD. Some preliminary small-scale studies have shown that a high percentage (over 74 percent) of hospitalized patients with a diagnosis of borderline personality were sexually abused as children. The importance of differentiating the abused from the unabused patient lies in helping direct the therapist to the right cause of the problems and a more effective solution.

What is needed is a diagnosis called Postsexual Abuse Syndrome. Such a diagnosis has actually been proposed, but has not yet been officially recognized. Until it *is* recognized, it will be critical for therapists to correlate symptoms with trauma rather than viewing the symptoms as expressions of a seemingly permanent disability. Similarly, if your child is addicted to alcohol, drugs, or food, the effects of the addiction as a response to the abuse or as a means of coping with life's stresses should not be mistaken for a major personality or character disorder.

Bulimics are sometimes labeled as "borderline personalities" because some of their behavioral patterns, mood swings, and psychological problems closely resemble those of the borderline personality. Yet for some bulimics, when the bulimia stops or comes under control, the borderline personality characteristics diminish or even disappear. Unless a therapist is aware of this possibility, he or she may prematurely or inaccurately diagnose your child.

The purpose of this section is not to make you an expert on psychiatric disgnoses, but to give you permission to inquire about and challenge, if necessary, the diagnosis given to your child. Even the experts sometimes disagree on the proper diagnosis for a particular client. You can learn about the various diagnoses from the *Diagnostic and Statistical Manual III, Revised*, which is available at most libraries. If, after doing as much research as you can on your own, you feel that your child may have been misdiagnosed, you should speak up at once.

Don't be afraid to ask the therapist or psychiatrist for a full definition of the diagnosis and an explanation as to why he or she feels that your child fits a particular category. As a responsible parent you have every right to know how and why your child has received a certain diagnosis which—once in the records—may be with her for life. It's especially important to speak up if you feel that the diagnosis is having a negative effect on your child's therapy. For some therapists, the label means nothing; but for others, as noted above, the diagnosis can create a negative, self-fulfilling prophecy.

It may well be that the therapist or psychiatrist has made a correct assessment, however much you would prefer it not to be true. You may not have fully understood the diagnostic category; or, for one reason or another, you may be unaware of certain aspects of your child's emotional life and behavioral patterns. It's common for children, especially preadolescents and adolescents, to conceal "secrets" from their parents which they might reveal in therapy. While the therapist cannot betray a child's confidence, he or she can speak in generalities or otherwise indicate reasons why your child falls primarily in one category (such as clinical depression), but exhibits elements from other categories as well.

Your child, like all human beings, is complex. Although one diagnosis may describe much of her behavior and emotional life, it's very likely that her personality will also contain elements of other psychological types. She may be given a dual diagnosis; or two different professionals, both perfectly competant, may disagree on which diagnosis is primary.

Regardless of your child's label, it's essential that the therapist acknowledge the crucial role of the abuse in creating your child's problems. There may indeed be problems in addition to those that were caused by the abuse; however, the sexual abuse needs to receive serious attention for your child to progress in her healing.

Changing Therapists or Programs

Even harder than selecting a certain program or therapist is the decision to change either of these. Since you have already invested considerable time and money in making your first selection, you may hesitate to take on the task of calling and visiting various facilities and therapists all over again. You may not have a choice, though. If your child is not responding well to her present treatment—after giving it enough time to see its potential—or if she informs you of some therapeutic abuses or questionable practices, you may have no choice but to begin your search all over again.

Some situations obviously require action—for example, if the therapist or a staff member at the hospital makes a sexual advance toward your child, or physically or verbally abuses her. She should not be subjected to such a situation; and you may want to consider pressing charges.

Another situation that justifies changing is if the therapist is frequently late—not just a few minutes but significantly late—or does not give your child her full treatment time as scheduled.

In most cases, however, the decision is not so clear-cut. Perhaps you feel that your child is being given too many sedatives and not enough therapy. Or, when you voice your concerns, you are ignored or humiliated by the therapist. There may be other factors that make you feel as if you and your child are being neglected or improperly cared for. Perhaps your child's program restricts her excessively, or the professional in charge ignores your requests for explanations and doesn't return your phone calls.

The first step in this type of situation is to discuss your concerns with the therapist. There may be reasonable explanations for what troubles you. However, if you are not satisfied, get a second opinion from another therapist. Go as far as you must to get the answers you need.

Before deciding to change therapists, ask your child how she feels about the treatment she's getting. You definitely don't want to give your child the impression that the minute she's uncomfortable in therapy, or when some slight problem arises, she can simply drop out. Therapy is painful, and she understandably may want to avoid it at times. Keep that in mind when you ask her how she feels she's doing. Her views are important, but should not be the only reason for making a change (except in the case of flagrant abuses, as described above).

Often a child's view of the therapist or program is colored by her desire to avoid painful issues, her resistance to change, or other such motives. Some of this resistance to therapy may disappear after a few sessions. In the meantime, your child's discomfort and her fear of her feelings may emerge as anger or extreme criticism of the therapist or treatment program.

Don't take your child out of her program with the first complaint. Give the therapist or the program some time. Children, especially adolescents, hate restrictions and may naturally rebel. If your child is also an addict and is being deprived of her fix, she may be feeling the effects of withdrawal and be angry that she has to go through this additional discomfort. Realize, too, that as an abuse survivor your child may have some inital problems in developing trust toward the therapist or program.

When she voices aversion to the therapist, don't take sides unless your child discloses abuse, malpractice, or gross ignorance on the part of the therapist. Listen carefully to what she says, repeat it back to her to be sure you've understood it accurately, then encourage her to share her feelings with the therapist.

Your child may be in the right—but you and she need to give the therapist or program leaders a chance to explain their point of view. It takes some time for a good therapeutic relationship to develop. However, if your child's complaints persist, and if you see little or no improvement in her symptoms, it may well be time for you to make the first step toward considering a change. The very first step is to make an appointment to speak directly with the therapist about your child's concerns. Ask for an evaluation appointment to see how the therapy is going.

During this session, you can inquire about your child's progress, bringing up specific areas that are troubling her (or you). If the therapist listens carefully and sympathetically, this is a good sign. On the other hand, if the therapist begins to attack you, reminds you that he or she knows more than you do about psychology or psychiatry, or becomes overly defensive, realize that this might very well be the wrong therapist for your child.

The basic question to ask is if the therapy is dealing with the abuse and your child's other core issues. Perhaps only peripheral issues are being discussed. If so, why? If the therapist says that your child seems unwilling or unable to deal with the abuse, ask how the therapist plans to help your child move closer to self-disclosure.

Since your child is probably numbing her feelings away, she does not need a passive therapist. Neither does she need an overly aggressive or intrusive one. She needs a therapist who can gently, but actively, move her toward confronting the abuse and the many issues it has raised in her life.

The decision to change therapists or treatment programs is an unusually difficult one. You'll need all the information you can get, which may include making trips to the library and having discussions with other mental health professionals or parents whose children have gone through therapy, too. You must also take your child's feelings into consideration.

You may feel overwhelmed—that would only be natural. But be sure that you persist long enough to get all the information you need to make the right decision.

If your child feels helped and likes her therapist (even if you don't), you may decide not to change but rather to wait and then reevaluate the situation. Even though there may be a more qualified therapist available, the bond your child has developed with her present therapist is valuable, despite the therapist's limitations. Trust is a tremendously important issue with abuse survivors: you do not want to destroy any trusting relationship your child has developed (unless it is abusive or otherwise obviously destructive). On the other hand, if you believe that the therapist or program is unethical or incompetent, you may have to take matters into your own hands despite your child's positive feelings.

Finding a therapist or program can be a complicated procedure, as you have just read; but it is the next vital step in your child's recovery. Remember always to keep in mind what is best for your child, and your family, as you look for the right therapist or program. Don't be afraid to follow your instincts about which therapist or program will best suit your child (after you have done your research!). Often your gut feeling will prove to be right.

6

Tools for Healing

Therapy is more than just discussing feelings; it is also a process of education. Your child, like any other person in therapy, needs information—not only about sexual abuse, but about how to deal with life more effectively. A good therapist will provide your child with this information. However, unless your child is in an inpatient unit, his therapist probably only sees him for one or two hours a week. You, on the other hand, spend a great deal of time with your child, during which you can reinforce the therapist's teaching. This chapter provides you with guidance in helping your child to better manage anger and stress, learn to relax, and effectively assert his needs—all tools that will accelerate his healing and equip him for a happier life.

Discuss your intention to assist your child with these skills with his therapist or the people in charge of his counseling program. Since your child has been abused, he probably has some special needs or problems. His therapist will be able to advise you about how best to proceed with your efforts or which efforts to avoid entirely.

For example, if your child has been extremely traumatized, relaxation therapy—which is usually beneficial for most people—may not be advisable. Under particular circumstances, relaxation therapy can cause flashbacks, nightmares, or other anxiety reactions. If this occurs, the technique needs to be discontinued, at least until your child has more effectively dealt with his trauma.

To varying degrees, sexual abuse retards the emotional and developmental growth of a child. Because so much psychic energy is involved in coping with the abuse, there is less energy available for acquiring social and other skills. Abused children often have trouble managing their anger and stress in healthy ways and in learning to be assertive. In general, the abused child has learned to manage his emotions by suppressing them or by expressing them indirectly via an addiction, self-mutilation, or other self-destructive patterns. It is not enough for therapy to help your child get in touch with his feelings: he must also learn how to manage them.

The suggestions given in this chapter are just that: suggestions, not prescriptions or psychotherapy. If your child is exhibiting extreme or extremely troubling symptoms, he should be under the care of a qualified mental health professional. Also, certain cautions must be observed in using any of the suggested coping mechanisms. These cautions are clearly outlined at the end of each section, and should be read carefully and discussed with your child's counselor.

Anger

Typically an abused child displaces his anger about having been abused, either onto himself, others, or both. For example, Jeb allowed himself to be picked on at school, yet at home he victimized his younger sister. In therapy Jeb learned to recognize the various degrees of his anger and how to discharge it without hurting himself or others.

Sexually abused children can be taught specific skills, such as speaking or writing about anger rather than acting it out, or using a punching bag or an exercise program to discharge hostile and angry emotions. Your child's therapist or group program may offer such techniques to your child; you, however, are in the important position of being able to encourage and reinforce them. If your child doesn't learn coping strategies for anger from his therapist, you can use this chapter as a guide for teaching these techniques yourself. The important point is that coping strategies need to be taught and practiced so that your child no longer punishes himself or someone else with his anger.

Anger is a problem in many homes. Expressions of anger may be forbidden; or anger may be expressed through verbal abuse or physical violence. A child will tend to model himself after his parents. In the Jones household, where anger was taboo, Jeb learned to suppress his angry feelings. This suppression didn't create a significant psychological problem for him until he had to suppress the massive rage he felt at being abused. Since he had no model for expressing it, he took his anger out on himself, in the form of self-mutilation and depression, and on his sister, in the form of hitting and verbal abuse.

Since Jeb's parents weren't comfortable with anger and had provided no model for its expression, Jeb's therapist had to start from square one in teaching Jeb about anger. She had to convey to Jeb that anger is a normal and acceptable human emotion, and that there are ways to deal with anger constructively.

Self-Evaluation About Anger

The first step toward helping your child with anger is to examine how you deal with it yourself. Anger is a problem emotion for most people. It would be quite surprising if you had no conflicts surrounding anger and were able to mange your anger perfectly at all times. If you feel that your problems with anger are significant enough, you may want to seek help—not only for your own sake, but for the sake of your child.

Ask yourself the following questions and jot down a few thoughts. Your own life experiences with anger will provide powerful examples which you can use as you try to help your child.

"How did my mother deal with her anger? How did my father deal with his? What was I taught by my parents, my grandparents, my teachers, my schoolmates, my siblings, and others about anger? What does my religious faith say about anger? Did I receive any contradictory messages about anger? What were they? How did I deal with the contradictions?

"How did I deal with my anger as a child? As a preteen? As an adolescent? As a young adult? What happened as a result (at each age level)? How do I deal with anger today with respect to my spouse (or partner), my child, my employers, members of my family, friends, strangers? What are my major problem areas when it comes to anger?

"What messages have I given my child about anger, verbally and by my actions?"

If you tend to "stuff" your anger and never show it; if you tend to store up anger and frustration until you reach the explosion point; or if you're prone to outbursts of rage, realize that you model these behaviors for your child. Regardless of what you try to teach him about the "right" way to deal with anger, you're also teaching him—and much more powerfully—by the ways in which you deal with anger yourself.

The suggestions that follow are intended as guidelines for helping you help your child to manage his anger. As you teach your child how to use his anger effectively, you may also be teaching yourself.

Responding to Your Child's Anger

In trying to help your child with anger management, as with the other coping skills to be described, communication skills are essential. Whenever you talk in depth to your child, stop several times to ask if he understands what you're talking about, how he feels about the topic, or if he has any questions. When he expresses his feelings, acknowledge them—don't deny or discount them. Then ask him if he'd be willing to tell you more about how he feels.

Some parents are afraid to acknowledge their child's anger for fear they are condoning it or some aggressive act that might result from it. This is not the case. You can acknowledge anger, or any other feeling, without necessarily judging it as "right" or "wrong." Two books which can help you improve your communication skills are *How to Talk So Kids Will Listen and Listen So Kids Will Talk*, by Adele Faber and Elaine Mazlish (Avon Books, New York, 1980) and *Coping with Teenage Depression: A Parent's Guide*, by Kathleen McCoy (Signet Books, New American Library, New York, 1982).

In *How to Talk So Kids Will Listen and Listen So Kids Will Talk*, the authors identify eight different ways in which parents respond to their children's anger. These include:

- Denial of feelings

- Philosophical responses

- Advice

- Questions

- Defense of the other person involved (if another person is involved)

- Pity

- Amateur psychoanalysis

- Empathy$_1$

"It's nothing to be upset about. Why don't you talk about happy things instead?" is a denial response. Such responses are unproductive, as they reinforce your child's own tendency not to deal with his emotions directly.

Responding philosophically—by saying. "Life is hard, kid" or some such thing—not only belittles his pain, but also fails to provide your child with any practical means of dealing with his anger, apart from sweeping it under the rug.

No doubt you have excellent advice to give to your child—but it's better to help him discover his own responses and come up with his own solutions. Instead of offering him a solution right away, sit down with him and help him outline his options. "Let's think now. What are all the things you could have done to help yourself in that situation? Let's write down all your ideas."

Encourage your child to include all possible solutions at this point without censoring any of them as unreasonable. You can introduce some of your own ideas as well. "Have you ever considered this ..." or "Do you think it would make sense to ..." are good lead-ins.

After compiling a list of alternatives, say, "Now let's go through these one by one and eliminate the ones that don't seem practical to you. Then we can go through the ones that are left and you can pick the solution that seems like it would work best."

Check out your perceptions by asking him if you're correct in your understanding. "I think you feel this way. Am I right—or are you feeling some other way?"

You can then ask open-ended, neutral questions: "Tell me more about it. What happened?"

Responses that defend the other person involved ("He was right to do that to you. He was busy and you were being overly demanding of his time.") will probably make your child feel guilty and angry at *you,* and will tend to cut off your communication. While it's important that your child learn to assess how someone with whom he's in conflict feels and thinks, this is best saved until his own angry feelings are fully aired.

Pity responses, such as "Poor baby. Go lie down. You must be sick about this!" may convey concern, but they don't do anything toward helping your child manage his anger better in the future.

Resist the impulse to be an amateur psychoanalyst. Saying, "You're probably angry at your friend because of your secret jealousy toward your brother that you feel would make me angry. ..." may be clever—and may even be accurate; but this can be experienced by your child as a humiliation and still doesn't provide him with any practical tools for dealing with his feelings.

When your child tells you he's angry, try to respond right away with empathy. For example, you might say, "Gosh, you must be mad," or "That would have made almost anybody mad," or "Some people might not have been upset, but knowing what I know about you, I can see how that would make you furious."

When you respond with empathy, you show your child not only that you care, but that you can listen and understand. Your best approach is the empathic response, followed by exploratory, nonjudgmental questions and your support in helping him find workable solutions.

Anger Management

Try to communicate the following ideas about anger to your child:

- Anger is a normal and acceptable human emotion.

- Anger is a feeling, not an action; an emotion, not an aggressive act.

- Anger makes most people feel like committing acts of aggression—but there are other ways of coping with the natural desire to lash out.

- It's perfectly normal to want to act on anger right away—but usually it's wisest to wait and think about the incident before taking action. Acting on anger immediately without reflection can often hurt you and make you feel more frustrated, unhappy, and angry in the end.

- Anger can be used to make things better if, and only if, the situation that sparked the anger is thought through and discussed.

- It's possible to talk about your anger—especially to counselors, parents, and other people you trust—without being punished or put down.

- Anger seldom appears in pure form. Usually it's mixed in with hurt feelings, rejection, or some sort of loss and sadness. You must acknowledge these other feelings that go along with the anger if you are to be able to deal with it productively. In some cases, anger is not the main emotion, but only a defense against hurt feelings and sadness.

Talk to your child about anger at a time when he's not angry, tired, or otherwise distressed. He'll be able to pay better attention if he's not distracted by his own emotions. You'll need to talk about anger many times—not just once. As incidents involving anger arise in your family life, use these times as points of discussion.

You can talk about anger when you yourself are angry, but only if you feel in control of your anger and can use the ways you are dealing with it in the present moment to illustrate anger management.

Talking to Your Child About Anger

"I want to spend some time with you today talking about a very important subject: anger. Even though all people feel angry at times, no one talks much about anger, and most people feel mixed up about it. The first thing I want you to know is that it's normal to get angry sometimes. Everybody in the world gets angry. Even priests, ministers, rabbis, and people who try to be saints and good all the time get mad.

"So many things that happen in life are frustrating or annoying, and sometimes we get hurt or aren't treated fairly. These are times when almost anybody would get angry."

You may want to insert one or two examples of times you became angry, clearly differentiating between anger caused by frustration and annoyance, and anger caused by abuse or other forms of unjust treatment. Also bring up instances where anger was the result of fatigue, illness, or other physical discomforts, as well as instances where the anger was a cover-up for hurt or grief.

"Tell me what makes you angry. Did something, or someone, make you angry today?" Wait for his response. Help your child identify what part of his anger was caused by frustrations and irritations, what might have been caused by injustice or unfair treatment, and what was the result of fatigue or other physical problems. These are not at all easy distinctions to make. The main thing is to get your child in the habit of analyzing his anger.

Remember to ask your child if he was also sad. "Sometimes we're not only mad, but sad. I remember when my dog died, I was so mad I wanted to punch a hole in the wall. I was sad, too, but I didn't like to think about the sad part. It was easier to be mad because when I was mad I felt strong, like I could do something. But when I felt sad, I felt weak—because then I knew that nothing I could do could bring back my dog. Do you remember ever feeling like that?"

Help your child understand that during any emotionally intense experience, he's probably going to have more than one feeling at a time. The following analogy might be helpful: "Have you ever gone to an ice cream shop and asked for a chocolate cone, but when you got it back you could taste some strawberry and vanilla on it, too? Or maybe there were even hunks of other flavors you didn't order.

"Feelings can be like that, too. You can be mainly angry, but also have a little taste of other feelings like sadness or hopelessness. Or you can mainly feel one way, but also have some other strong feelings—maybe you feel *really* angry and *really* rejected all at the same time."

Point out that there are four basic feelings: sad, mad, glad, and scared. Then ask your child to examine a situation in which he was upset, and have him distinguish between the various emotions he felt. You can then ask him to differentiate various intensities of emotion.

For example, you can say, "Chocolate is chocolate, but dark chocolate fudge tastes different than milk chocolate. When you are sad, mad, glad, or angry, sometimes you feel that way a lot, sometimes a little, sometimes just in between." Then take an instance and ask your child to rate the intensity of his emotion.

Because your child has been abused, he may experience anger at events that remind him of the abuse situation. Seemingly minor, almost trivial, events may trigger a major reaction in him, just the way Spunky reacted to pizza. You may feel puzzled by the intensity of your child's reaction.

At this point, it would be easy to invalidate his feelings by saying, "I think you're overreacting. I don't see why that should make you mad," or "That's ridiculous. Why would anybody get upset over something like that?" Instead, try asking exploratory questions, such as, "Help me understand how you feel. Are you willing to tell me what made you so mad about what happened? Is there anybody else or anything else you're mad at, too? I'm wondering if what happened reminds you of the time that you were hurt." (Refer to specifics of the abuse incident if, and only if, the child is at a point where he has discussed it with you, and has indicated that he's able to talk about it without undue pain. In general, it's best to refer to the incident in terms of "the time you were hurt, or violated, or abused, or made to suffer, or had your will taken away from you," rather than bringing up particular details.)

Teach your child about the physiology of anger. Ask, "What did your body feel like when you were angry? What did you think in your head? What did you do? What did you want to do, but kept yourself from doing?" Wait for the child's response.

Now for the mini-lecture: "Anger affects our bodies. Sometimes we feel hot, we start breathing hard, we feel tight and tense and want to do something. We can get so mad we can't think and sometimes we say or do things we don't want to do and are sorry for later."

With older children, you can describe the rush of adrenaline, the increases in heart rate, blood pressure, blood sugar, and the other physiological changes due to anger which energize one to "act."

Emphasize the difference between *feeling* angry and *acting* angry.

"Anger is a feeling, not an action. Being angry is not the same as doing something angry. You can be so angry you feel like punching. But you don't have to punch. You don't have to say nasty things, hit people, tear up their belongings, or do anything else either, like [cut yourself, binge eat, binge drink, take drugs, or whatever your child's problem behavior is]. All you have to do when you're angry is to feel it.

"Keep telling yourself, 'I'm okay. All that's happening to me is that I'm feeling angry and all I have to do with my anger today is feel it. I can figure out later what to do about it. All I have to do now is ride with it.'

"Then promise yourself that you'll do something about it later, after you've had a chance to think it over. When you're really mad, you can't think very well. So it's best to wait before taking action.

"But if you feel you're going to burst, do something safe, like [mention any activity that involves physical exertion and is safe for your particular child, such as going for a walk, swimming, shooting baskets, or some other exercise]. You can also bang on your drum, hit a punching bag, hit some pillows, get an empty plastic soda bottle and hit a couch or pillow with it, stomp your feet, or even yell and scream."

An Exercise for Releasing Angry Feelings

Demonstrate the safe physical release of anger for your child by hitting some pillows or a couch with an empty plastic bottle or using your fist, a shoe, or some other safe object. At the same time, demonstrate that you can talk about anger by speaking about something that has made you really mad.

For example, while you're banging an old shoe on a pillow, say something like, "I'm so mad at you, Mrs. C. You kept me waiting two whole hours. I missed my favorite TV show because of you and was late for my doctor's appointment, too. You selfish person. You ruined my day. I hate you for it. I'm so mad I feel like hitting you, but I don't want to go to jail, so I'll hit this pillow again and again, as many times as I need to until I calm down."

You can now mention other instances of being angry, showing how anger about one matter often brings up anger from the past. Keep beating the pillow and say, "Ooh, I don't know why this happens, but everytime I get mad about one thing I remember other things I'm mad about, too. Right now I'm so mad at Mrs. C., but I'm mad at Mrs. X., too. She had a party a few months ago and invited me at the last minute. After all I've done for her, she almost forgot me, her best friend. How could she do that to me? I'm so hurt. So mad. I don't ever want to see you again, Mrs. X. Go away and don't bother me. I wish you knew how mad I am. You'd be sorry." Use examples that are emotionally relevant and age-appropriate for your child.

Then ask your child to take a plastic bottle, hit the pillows, and talk about something *he's* angry at. Reinforce and encourage him to express as much anger as he can. "The person you're angry at isn't here. So you can say whatever you want and you won't hurt anybody." If your child seems to be patting the pillows instead of hitting them, ask, "Are you sure you aren't angrier than that? Remember, you can't hurt the pillow."

If he still can't seem to talk about or express any anger, ask him to imitate you. "I know this might seem strange because you haven't done it before, but try copying me for a while. Maybe you aren't mad about anything now, but imagine you *are* mad. Think of something that made you so mad you could pop. Can you show me by hitting the pillow or with words how angry you are?"

If your child still can't imitate you or seems reluctant to participate in this exercise, ask him why, without chastisement in your voice or implying that he has "failed" because he hasn't been able to follow your direction. Say: "You're having problems doing this, aren't you? I hope I haven't made you uncomfortable by showing you how to do something you don't want to do. I'm just trying to show you a safe way of acting when you're feeling angry. Do you know why it's hard for you?" This could lead to a discussion of your child's fears and reservations about having and expressing anger or about the anger he may have seen expressed by his abuser. He may also resent your trying to "force" him to do something, just like his abuser did.

Reinforcing the Expression of Angry Feelings

The next time your child is angry and tells you about it, reinforce him by saying, "I'm so glad you're telling me how mad you are. I would much rather you tell me how mad you are than have you do something you'll be sorry for later, like hit your sister [the cat, the wall] or hurt yourself by [binging, drinking, drugging, and so on]."

Then hand him a plastic soda bottle and a pillow (or direct him to the physical but safe activity that he seems to respond to best) and ask him if he can remember to do what you practiced together.

You can offer other alternatives to your child. "If you're really mad, you can always come home and tell me about it, or tell somebody else who loves you. Or you can write down what's making you mad on a piece of paper. Say whatever you want. You don't have to show it to anybody. You can even throw away the paper when you're done."

If your child believes in God or a higher power, you can suggest that he talk to God or his higher power about how angry he is. At any time when he wants to talk to you, or to his therapist, but neither is available, you can suggest that your child "pretend" to talk to you or the counselor.

Always reinforce your child for being in touch with his anger. "It's good that you know when you're angry. You used to be angry, but instead of expressing it, you'd hide in your room [or whatever other negative behavior was practiced]. I used to worry about you a lot then. So when you tell me about being angry now, it makes me feel that you're doing a good job at feeling your feelings. I'm glad you aren't running away from your anger any more. I'm really proud of you—it takes a lot of courage to face your own feelings.

"Maybe somebody told you that anger is bad, but it isn't. It's only bad when you do bad things to other people, yourself, or animals, or other people's property. In fact, anger can be good in that it tells you that something is wrong. Maybe you're too tired and need to sleep more. Maybe you're working too hard and need to slow down. Maybe somebody is taking advantage of you or hurting your feelings all the time, and you don't know how to stop it."

Choose a particular incident when your child was angry, and help him think it through. Ask him, "What actually happened? What were you thinking or feeling? What do you think the other person was thinking or feeling? What did you want that you didn't get? How can you get what you want from this person [or situation] next time?"

You can practice the problem-solving aspect of anger management by using an instance when your child is angry with *you*. Encourage him to tell you when he's angry at you, then discuss his anger with him. "I want to know what's making you mad at me so we can talk about it. Maybe we can change things so they'll be better for you, maybe not. But if you talk to me, there's hope we can change things. If you don't talk, nothing can change at all."

You should prepare your child for the fact that not everybody is going to be as receptive to listening to his anger as you and his therapist are. "Anger scares a lot of people. You can talk to me and [name of therapist or others who are supportive] about your anger, but not everybody is able to deal with the subject. So don't be surprised if you try and talk to some people the way you're talking to me, and they tell you to be quiet, or that you're bad or selfish for feeling angry.

"That doesn't mean that you *are* bad or wrong to feel the way you feel—only that these people may not have had anybody to help them with their own anger when they were kids. When this happens, you can talk about it with me or [name of therapist] and we can help you figure out what, if anything, can be done."

Cautions in Teaching Anger Management Techniques

If your child is angry almost all the time; if his anger is extremely intense; if the only emotions he seems to express are anger and depression; if he is physically injuring others (or pets) or mutilating himself, then the above anger management techniques are clearly insufficient. Professional help is needed immediately. Your child may still profit from the techniques described here, but if his aggression or self-mutilation are extreme, hospitalization may be warranted.

Another danger is that the pillow-hitting and other exercises suggested for safely releasing anger may sometimes release homicidal, sadistic, or otherwise aggressive fantasies toward the abuser or some other individual. Your child may feel considerable guilt about these fantasies, even though they are perfectly "normal." When he is unable to follow your suggestions about anger management, his difficulty concentrating, apparent disinterest, or other forms of resistance may be rooted in his anxiety about these fantasies.

"Does talking about anger make you think about scary things?" you might ask. If he reveals any of his fantasies to you, try not to act horrified (even if you are). Remember, your child was abused and it's normal for him to want to retaliate. Encourage him to share these fantasies with his therapist. Use your common sense about sharing them with the therapist yourself. It's especially important to be in communication with the therapist if your child's homicidal or sadistic fantasies are elaborate, particularly bizarre, persistent, or have delusional qualities, all of which suggest that he may be in serious need of professional help.

Your child may have difficulty with the anger management suggestions in this chapter for three additional reasons. First, if the sexual abuse just occurred, your child may be in an acute reaction state in which he is so distraught, anxious, and confused that he can't concentrate on learning anything new. At this time, it would be best merely to be supportive of him, rather than trying to teach him new skills.

A second possibility is that your child is clinically depressed. Suppressed anger often underlies clinical depression: your child may not be able to get in touch with his feelings. Or he may have so much repressed anger that getting in touch with even a little of it holds the terror of being flooded with all the rage he has stored up over the years. This prospect may simply be overwhelming.

Discuss the situation with your child's therapist and inquire about whether he or she would support you in addressing your child's fears in the following manner: "You're probably angry about so many things that you're afraid of exploding if you start talking about any of them. Maybe you're worried that if you start expressing your anger, you won't be able to control yourself. If you want to, you can try talking about what makes you angry one thing at a time. I won't let you explode—we can make a deal where you can just end the conversation when you feel uncomfortable or that you're about to burst."

If your child was severely traumatized, or if he suffered repeated or prolonged victimization, he may be suffering from certain chemical imbalances as a result of the trauma.[2] These imbalances, common to a wide variety of trauma survivors, can lead to "all-or-nothing" or "fight-flight-freeze" reactions. An individual this traumatized reacts either with intense rage or with its opposite—an almost complete emotional shutdown or numbing. The depletion of dopamine, catecholamine, serotonin, and other neurotransmitters can cause irritability and aggressive outbursts, intense moods, and mood swings. Fearing his lack of control over his anger, which in this instance may be biologically based, your child may "shut down" as a physical and emotional defense.

The anger management strategies suggested in this chapter will be especially difficult for your child to implement if he suffers from one or more of these chemical imbalances. Medication may be needed to help restore balance.[3] An exercise program may also be advisable, as exercise itself can produce needed chemical reactions. Consider purchasing an exercise bike, a treadmill, or some other exercise equipment for your child if some other vigorous form of exercise is not readily available to him year-round.

Relaxation Training

It's important that your child learn to relax himself through muscle relaxation techniques or some other wholesome method, rather than seeking relaxation through isolation, alcohol, drugs, food, or other destructive means.

Relaxation plays a central role in anger and stress management. Once your child masters some of the relaxation techniques suggested here, he can use them whenever he's angry or stressed to calm himself down. Some of the most useful knowledge you can impart to your child is that when he's feeling angry or stressed, he has the power to change his mood and soothe himself through some form of relaxation. Relaxation techniques can also be useful in alleviating some of the symptoms that are common to abused children, including panic attacks, extreme anxiety, insomnia, and other sleep problems.

Each child is unique, however. Your child may become more relaxed by playing a game of soccer or basketball than by going through deep breathing and muscle relaxation exercises. Or your child may do best with a combination of both. As folk wisdom has taught us through the ages, relaxation is aided by hot baths, warm milk, and soothing music.

The advantage of progressive muscle relaxation is that it can be practiced at any place or time—at school, on a date, in the car, standing up, sitting down, alone, or with others. Once your child has mastered this skill, he will be able to comfort himself under almost any circumstances. This ability will provide a tremendous advantage as your child deals with the anger and stress brought about in the healing process.

There are many self-help relaxation tapes available on the market. However, the technique is a gift that you can give your child yourself. In this way your child's learning of the technique will be paired with, and empowered by, your loving presence. You can also make an instructional tape in your own voice so that your child can practice on his own. At the beginning, though, it's best if you do the exercises with your child at least several times.

Have him either sit or lie down in a quiet place. He should be wearing comfortable clothing and not be overly hungry or otherwise physically uncomfortable. In a soothing and natural voice, give the following instructions:4

"Close your eyes. Try to clear your mind of other thoughts and concentrate on what I'm saying. As much as you try to clear your mind, stray thoughts will enter. Don't worry about them. They'll soon fade away.

"Don't be afraid. I'm not going to hypnotize you or make you do anything you don't want to do. We can stop whenever you want. Just lift your hand in the air and we'll stop.

"I'm going to teach you how to relax yourself. You deserve to feel relaxed. There will be many times when you feel stressed, angry, tired, or overwhelmed. You might not realize it, but at those times your muscles get tight and that makes you feel more stressed, more angry, more tired, and more overwhelmed.

"You can't control the people, places, and things around you, but you *can* learn how to relax yourself, how to comfort yourself, when life hurts or is hard.

"First take a few deep breaths. Breathe in, hold it, that's good. Now breathe out... slowly. That's good. You're doing great. Now let's do it again. [Repeat three times.]

"Now we're going to take each muscle group in your body and make it tight, then relax it. Let's start with your right arm. Hold it out straight and make a fist. Feel the muscles tighten. That's good. Now make it tighter, tighter. That's good—now relax it. Relax it a bit more. Let it stay that way a while and just enjoy the relaxation.

"Let's relax your arm one more time. Hold your arm out straight and make a fist. Feel the muscles tighten. Now let go and relax.

"Notice how good it feels to be relaxed. Notice if there's any part of your arm that isn't relaxed. Try to relax it."

The same instructions should then be repeated for each major muscle grouping: each arm, the shoulders, the legs, the toes, the abdomen, the buttocks, the chest, the eyebrows, the jaw. The instructions for the abdomen are to hold it in, then let it out; for the buttocks, to squeeze them together, then let them relax; for the eyebrows, to furrow them together, then let them relax; for the toes, to curl them, then relax them; for the legs, to lift them in the air, then let them drop slowly; for the chest, to clench the breast muscles, then let go; for the jaw, to push the back teeth together and let go.

Each time, instruct your child to hold in the muscle group (for about 10-20 seconds) then relax it. Each time say, "Notice the relaxation and enjoy it." Be generous with reinforcing comments, such as, "You're doing great. That's good. Continue as you're going. You're doing a wonderful job," and so on.

After you've relaxed all the muscle groupings, ask your child to take two or three more deep breaths. "Each time you breathe in and out slowly you are becoming more and more relaxed. Notice how wonderfully relaxed you are and how you don't want anything to disturb this wonderful state of peace.

"When you're ready, take another deep breath and open your eyes. You will be wide awake and alert, but relaxed." After the first session, ask your child for feedback. How did it feel to be relaxed? Are there certain muscle areas that gave him problems or that were harder to relax than others? Perhaps those could be given extra attention during the next session. Did he have any disturbing thoughts or fantasies during the exercise? If so, how frightening or upsetting were they?

Relaxation training should be practiced at least once a day, preferably two times a day, for at least two weeks, until the ability to relax becomes almost automatic.

The next step is to have your child make a list of situations that usually make him tense and anxious; and to rank these from the least stressful to the most stressful situation. He should then try to practice his relaxation techniques during the least stressful situation and report back to you about how it went. You can discuss with him any problems he had relaxing during the situation as well as the benefits he might have gained by relaxing—perhaps he was able to think better because he wasn't so tense.

Caution

Do not teach your child relaxation without consulting with your child's therapist first. Be specific with the therapist about the techniques you are planning to use. This exercise must be used with caution for any traumatized person, because relaxation can bring traumatic material out of repression. You cannot emphasize enough to your child that if he starts to become afraid or have bad memories during the exercise, he needs to signal you so that you can stop the session immediately.

While some therapists use relaxation techniques to uncover repressed memories, you should never, *ever*, under any circumstances, attempt to do the same. Furthermore, if your child's therapist is using relaxation or hypnosis and you have any doubts about the advisability of these techniques, do not hesitate to discuss your concerns with the therapist.

Assertiveness Training

Much anger, and depression, results from a lack of assertiveness. Your child may not know how to ask that his needs be met—and, deep down, he may believe that he doesn't deserve to have his needs met. This is a common legacy of sexual abuse. Your child may be continuing in the role of the victim even in situations where he, in fact, has some degree of control.

In teaching your child how to be assertive, you need to distinguish between three types of behavior: assertiveness, passivity, and aggression. "Being assertive is not the same thing as being bossy (or aggressive). To be assertive means that you stand up for yourself firmly and that you're able to express what you want or need openly and honestly, without denying the rights of other people. When you're passive, you let others take advantage of you without protest. When you need something from someone and don't ask for it, that's being passive, too. On the other hand, aggression means that you push around or hurt others to get what you want, or you deny others their rights in order to get what you need."

You must also stress that assertiveness does not mean telling other people what you think is wrong with them. "If you tell your teacher, 'I think you're a no-good liar,' of course, you're entitled to your opinion, but you'll get better results if you tell the teacher how her behavior makes you feel; you'll do best if you can point out to her exactly what she's doing that's upsetting you so much.

"For example, you might tell the teacher, 'Sometimes you tell me to do one thing, and then you tell me to do the opposite. This makes me feel very confused. Could you please clearly tell me what you expect of me? It would really help me if you could put it in writing, just to make sure I've understood you correctly.' Speaking to your teacher this way would be being very assertive. Can you see how it's also much more fair than calling her a liar? Your assertive behavior gives the other person the opportunity to change whatever it is that's upsetting you. It's constructive."

Provide some examples of your own and ask your child to identify whether the behavior you've described is assertive, passive, or aggressive. You'll need to find examples that are relevant to your child's age and experience. If your child is five or six, the following example might be helpful.

"Pretend you're at a birthday party and the father is passing around pieces of cake. You don't get a piece, but you say nothing. Are you being assertive, aggressive, or passive?

"Now let's pretend you don't get a piece and you take a piece of cake away from the child sitting next to you without asking. Are you being assertive, aggressive, or passive?

"Now pretend you don't get a piece, and you go up to the father and say, 'I would like a piece of cake.' How are you acting now?"

Generate a few examples until you feel that your child understands what assertiveness means. Remember to add that assertiveness means more than asking for what you want or need. It also means stating your feelings, giving yourself permission to change your mind, allowing yourself to make mistakes (and be responsible for them), and giving yourself the right to say "no" to unnecessary requests and demands.

Then ask your child for examples of times when he was assertive, aggressive, or passive. Ask what he could have done differently in those situations. You can help him generate assertive responses to situations in which he'd usually respond either passively or aggressively. Ask him about times when he felt put down. How did he react? How could he behave differently the next time he's in that situation?

Speaking in "I" statements is essential to assertiveness. Teach your child to express his needs and feelings directly: "I need more time to finish this project," "I feel anxious when you raise your voice at me," "I'm afraid to go on this trip—I want to stay home," and so on.

Another area which must be discussed is how your child feels about being assertive. Have him try being assertive in a situation in which he would usually be passive or aggressive. Then ask, "How did it feel to be assertive? Was it positive or negative? Did it make you anxious? How do you think others reacted? Did it make you feel differently about yourself?" Reassure him that it's normal to feel anxious when trying out a new behavior, but that the anxiety will pass as he learns the benefits of asking assertively that his needs be met.

If your child is old enough, he may be able to profit from any number of popular books on the subject, for example, Manuel J.

Smith's book, *When I Say No I Feel Guilty* (Bantam Books, New York, 1975).

Stress Management

Because your child endured the stress of sexual abuse, and perhaps physical abuse as well, he may be hypersensitive to stress in general. In many cases, his first response to a stressful situation may be similar to his response to the abuse—fight, flight, numbing, self-abuse, or whatever. He may even react to present and future pressures as if they were the original trauma: even relatively mild stressful events may seem overwhelmingly intense to him.

To be able to manage the challenges that life inevitably brings—especially those involved in accepting responsibilities—your child needs help in learning how to

- Differentiate clearly between present stressful situations and the original trauma

- Manage stress more effectively than he has in the past

With help, your child will no longer need to run from life's problems, because he'll no longer need to feel that he's powerless or ineffective. The anger management, relaxation, and assertiveness techniques already described can considerably reduce the stress in your child's life. Other helpful techniques are breath control, positive self-talk or thought stoppage (for negative thoughts), goal setting, and time management.

Breath Control

Your breathing mirrors your emotional state. When you're anxious or afraid, you tend to breathe in a rapid and shallow manner. This sends a signal to the rest of your body that danger is at hand. The danger may be either physical or psychological.

If the danger facing you is physical, then the "emergency state" in your body should be maintained, and you should flee—or do whatever is appropriate to save your life. However, if the danger is psychological, then you have time to take some deep breaths. This will help send out the message to the rest of your body, "I am not in mortal danger. I have choices."

Deep breathing also affords the opportunity for your cognitive or mental processes to kick in. When a person, or any organism, feels threatened, the resulting physiological arousal (rapid breathing, increased heart rate and blood pressure) militates against rational thinking. When your child says, "I was so scared (or nervous) I couldn't think," he's reconfirming a physiological fact: you can become so anxious that you literally can't think.

Teach your child that he can restore his capacity to think by changing his physiological state to one of relative calm. He can combat panic and anxiety by practicing the deep-breathing exercises described below in conjunction with techniques you've already taught him.

Most people are not aware of how they are breathing at any given moment. The first step towards helping your child learn the technique of breath control is to have him observe how he breathes. Tell him, "Breathing is such a part of us that we hardly even notice it.

"How are you breathing now? Do you remember how you breathe when you're running or walking fast? How about when you're sitting, resting, or sleeping? What about when you're afraid or anxious?"

"When we're resting or sleeping, we tend to take slow, deep breaths, like this. [Demonstrate deep abdominal breathing.] See how the breath goes all the way in, filling up my lungs, see how I'm breathing from deep down in my abdomen? Now you try it.

"When we exercise, or when we're excited or afraid, we tend to take shallow, fast breaths, like this. [Demonstrate shallow chest breathing.] See how I seem to be breathing in and out of my mouth and not so much in and out of my lungs? Now you try it."

Practice the different types of breathing several times with your child.

"When you were abused you didn't have much power. You were forced to go along with what the abuser wanted.

"There's something that happens very often to sexual abuse survivors: because they were in a situation where they were powerless, they come to feel that all of life might be like this; that they don't have choices, that they can't say 'no', or can't tell people what they need.

"Because you were so frightened when you were abused, it would be very normal for you to become easily frightened by other situations. You can tell when you're feeling frightened by how you're breathing.

"Rapid, shallow breathing tells your body and your brain that there's an emergency—once this happens, you may start to panic. Once panic sets in, it's very hard to think sensibly about what to do next. Now here's the trick. If you change your breathing pattern to the slow, deep breaths we practiced before, you can calm yourself down. This tells your brain and your body that you're in control. Because you panic less, or maybe hardly at all, you can think clearly about what you want to do. Isn't that amazing? Most people think that they don't have any choice about feeling scared or feeling calm—but you do. If you can remember to make yourself breathe slowly and deeply, your body and brain will work for you, instead of against you. This will be a tool that you can use throughout the rest of your life.

"Now let's practice those deep breaths again. As you breathe in and out deeply and slowly, tell yourself, 'One step at a time, I can handle this situation. Maybe I am anxious and afraid, but I can calm myself down by breathing deeply. As I continue breathing deeply, I'll be *less* anxious and afraid. This situation is difficult for me, but it's not the abuse situation. I have control now. I know how to calm myself down so that I can think clearly about my options. After I calm down, I can think about what I want to do.'"

Ask your child to practice breath control in situations which he thinks might be stressful for him. You can also role-play some hypothetical situations. For example, a teacher's purse is stolen and your child is falsely accused. A friend is suddenly rejecting. An adult starts yelling and screaming at your child for no reason at all.

Positive Self-Talk or Thought Stoppage (for Negative Thoughts)

Sexually abused children or teenagers should examine their abuse experience on three levels: first, the incident; second, how they as well as others (family members, friends, social agencies, and so on) reacted to the incident; and third, the effects on their self-image and self-esteem. It's in the third category that your child can now exert some mastery and control.

The abuse experience may have made him feel powerless, weak, incompetent, deficient, and inadequate. Subsequent experiences may have reinforced these feelings. As a result, he may have acquired a victim mentality, or at least a self-concept of being incapable, ineffectual, and weak. Although he's no longer being victimized by the abuser (or by nonsupportive family members, friends, social agencies, and so on) your child may be victimizing himself if he has internalized society's negative labels for him, and if he sees himself in weak or negative terms.

He still will have to fight to see himself in a positive light. You can help him in that fight by saying, "Your abuser robbed you of your dignity and damaged your self-esteem. We cannot let him (or her) continue to rob you of your peace of mind and the other satisfactions that life has to offer. I want you to take some time to think for a while and tell me what kind of bad names you call yourself when things go wrong or when you feel you can't handle a situation."

Your child should then list some negative labels. If he can't come up with any, suggest the following: "Do you ever call yourself a weakling, a dummy, a failure, a reject?"

"When you hear yourself calling yourself these words, say to yourself, 'Stop. I'm not going to think like that about myself any more. I love myself too much to call myself bad names. I call myself these bad names when I feel afraid, when there is a situation that's difficult to handle. I am not [fill in negative labels]. I am a person who can think. I have a good brain and if I stop calling myself these ridiculous names I can figure out what I need to do. I can ask for help, too.'

"Ask yourself, 'What is it I have to do?' Then tell yourself, 'I can handle this situation. After all, I handled being abused. Not much could be harder to handle than that. I'm a survivor. I'm strong. If I relax and take some deep breaths, I can think about what to do next.

" 'If I'm upset [angry, afraid, anxious], that's okay. These are only feelings. I won't let the feelings control what I do. I'm at my worst when I'm angry, anxious, and afraid. I'm at my best when I'm calm and have had a chance to think about how I feel and what I need to do.

" 'If the feelings hurt, I can talk about them with my counselor [mother, father, etc.] later. I don't have to act on them now.'"

Have your child repeat after you the following positive self-talk messages: "One step at a time, I can handle the situation. I may be afraid and anxious and want to run away, punch somebody, drink or drug [substitute the relevant negative behavior], but I can take a few deep breaths, relax my muscles, and then deal with the situation. My fear and anxiety might not disappear entirely, but they won't paralyze me [control me, make me do things I don't want to do, including avoiding the situation].

" 'This is not the abuse situation. I have choices. I've come a long way since I was abused. If I stop beating myself up with negative labels, I can relax enough to think about what would be best to do. I have the support and love of many people who can help me with this problem. I do not need to panic.'"

Goal Setting

Say to your child, "You are entitled to have goals of your own. There are certain expectations of you at home, at school, and in society. But it's important to have goals of your own, too. It doesn't matter what kind of goals they are: they can have to do with school, sports, recreation, art, religion, or whatever. The main thing is that they be *your* goals, not somebody else's.

"Having goals of your own is a way of taking charge of your life. Taking charge of your life is important for all people, but especially for abuse survivors. Some abuse survivors don't feel they deserve to be living at all, much less be successful. And some of them have been so crushed and twisted by the abuse that they can't imagine themselves taking control over anything, especially their own lives.

"Of course you can't control your entire life. Nobody can do that. But you can set goals for yourself and try to achieve them.

"Being abused used to absorb your life. Just surviving the abuse was your goal. But now the abuser is gone and you're slowly getting over this. You are now free to do things that are good for you, free to develop your talents and abilities, free to set goals for yourself and enjoy the satisfaction of reaching them.

"What are some of your goals?"

If your child can't seem to identify any goals for himself, say, "One way of finding out what your goals are is to say to yourself, 'I want ...' —then fill in the blanks. Let's try that. Say 'I want ...' "

Write the goals on paper. (Either you or your child can do this.)

Next examine each goal from different aspects, such as achievability, meaningfulness, and concreteness. Have your child ask himself the following questions:

- Is this goal achievable? Do I have the time, energy, and talent to achieve it?

- Is this goal desirable to me? Is this my goal, or is it somebody else's goal for me?

- Is this goal concrete and measurable? Are there ways I will be able to see if I'm reaching my goal?

- Can I break this goal down into smaller goals so that I can enjoy a sense of accomplishment when I've completed each stage?

- Is this goal safe for me to pursue? Will it be safe and nondisruptive for people around me?

- Can I achieve this goal on my own, or will I be dependent on the help of others or other factors, such as financial assistance, the weather, someone's approval?

Discuss with your child which goals he wants to keep and which he might want to reconsider. For example, if a goal is heavily dependent on others, it's riskier to pursue than a goal he can accomplish on his own. Similarly, if a goal requires an enormous amount of time which he doesn't have at the present, he may want to postpone that goal for a later time. Also, he may want to reject goals that do not flow from his inner needs and talents, but which have been imposed on him by the expectations of others.

Your next task is to teach your child about priority-setting: to rank his goals in their order of importance to him. Ask "Can you rank-order the goals? Put an A by the goals that are most important to you; B by the goals that are important but not as pressing; C by the goals that may be important but you don't mind putting on the back burner; and D by the goals that are least important to you.

"The way you spend your time should reflect your priorities. Some people work better on their goals in the morning; some in the afternoon; some in the evening. You need to spend your best work time on your A goals first, then on your B. The C and D goals should be done last or as breaks from working on your A and B goals."

You can then help your child with some time management skills.

Time Management

If your child is a teenager, he may profit from a time-management seminar or course, where skills such as priority-setting and time analysis are taught. However, you can teach your child the fundamentals of time management by having him list his daily activities and the time he typically spends on each one.

Then ask him the following questions, giving him plenty of time to think about his answers. "What are your goals for the day? Which goals are more important than others? How much time do you typically give to each goal? How could you restructure your day so that you can give your priority goals priority time? What obstacles do you anticipate in taking control over your time? How can some of these obstacles be overcome?"

Tell you child, "Having goals is a way of loving yourself. When you set goals, you are promising yourself that you are going to do something which is important to you. If the goal is meaningful to you, you will feel very good about yourself when you reach your goal, or when you see yourself making progress toward it. Even if nothing else goes right in a day, if you have taken steps toward meeting your goals you will feel as if you have accomplished something and that the day wasn't a waste.

"It's your right to plan your day so that you can meet your goals. You don't have control over all your time, but let's look at the time you *can* control. Maybe I can help you decide how you can best use your free time to meet your goals."

Help your child make a time commitment to each of his goals. Take care that he doesn't reenact the trauma in which he was overwhelmed by planning a schedule that taxes him beyond his ability or strength. Tell him, "It's important to plan time to work on your goals and to stick to your schedule. But part of the schedule should include breaks, rest, and fun. Don't schedule too tightly, and always leave at least an hour for the unexpected every day.

"Now let's make a list of all you plan to do today [or for the weekend]. How do you usually go about doing these things? Are there ways you might schedule the activities better so that you get more done in less time?"

Stress to your child the importance of making a plan for the day (or week). "Having a plan is important. You may not be able to stick to it exactly or achieve everything that is on your plan, but you'll have the plan to fall back on when you don't know what to do next."

Procrastination

Another area that needs to be examined is procrastination. Ask your child, "Do you ever plan to do something, then find a lot of little excuses not to do it? You think that doing these other little things is going to make it easier for you, but it makes it harder for you because you end up disappointing yourself by not achieving your main goal. That is called procrastination, or putting off working on the A and B goals in life.

"If you procrastinate sometimes, this doesn't mean that you're lazy and won't ever amount to much. You need to look at why you are procrastinating. For example, are you procrastinating because you feel that the A goal is too much for you? In that case, you can break the A goal down into smaller steps. Or are you procrastinating because you have planned a schedule with too little fun or rest and are rebelling against it? It's important to plan a reward for yourself after working on a goal.

"Or you may be procrastinating because you don't feel you deserve to be a success.

"You do deserve success, but my telling you this over and over again won't necessarily convince you of it. This might be a good topic to discuss with your counselor.

"You can succeed in reaching your goal, if you don't procrastinate too much. What are some ways in which you procrastinate?"

Have your child identify ways he might procrastinate, such as by taking two-hour breaks, not saying 'no' to friends who call or other interruptions, or by working on C and D goals rather than focusing on A an B goals.

Coping With Phobias and Anxieties

Simple Phobias

Phobia means fear and, according to the Bible, "fear hath torment." A phobia, however, is not one of the passing fears that are common to all of us. Children frequently fear animals, blood, the dark, water, and so on. Rather, a phobia is a persistent, recurring fear of a certain object, person, or situation (generally called a "stimulus") which significantly affects one's life. In addition, the person with the phobia usually experiences intense anxiety when exposed to the phobic stimulus and a sense that the intensity of the fear is somewhat unreasonable.

Sexual abuse survivors sometimes develop phobias or exaggerated fears of certain people or situations. Although your child's fears might seem "irrational," they may be extremely "rational" in terms of his emotional life, especially if they developed as a result of conscious or unconscious associations made during the trauma or its aftermath.

For example, if your child is black and his offender was white, your child could easily develop a phobia about white people. Similarly, if the offender was male, a fear of men could develop.

Six-year-old Bobby had an intense fear of green vegetables. The evening before he was abused, his parents had been urging him to eat his spinach so he would grow up to be strong. "If you don't eat your vegetables, you're going to be a weakling and the 'bad man' is going to get you."

That night, the "bad man" got Bobby. He was sexually abused by an adult neighbor. Bobby tried to fight off the offender, but was unsuccessful. He attributed his failure to not having eaten his spinach. The spinach came to symbolize Bobby's "badness" in not obeying his father, his "badness" in being "weak," and his fears of his own passivity. He projected his self-hatred onto the spinach and then generalized the fear onto all green vegetables.

Sometimes the association between a phobia and trauma is less direct. For example, ten-year-old Anne developed a fear of cars and highways, not because she was abducted in a car, but because the numerous court interviews which followed the disclosure of her abuse were held in a nearby town. Anne and her parents had to travel nearly an hour each way to press charges against the offender.

In some cases, phobias represent fears of feelings and impulses that are deemed "unacceptable." The individual tries to disown and disavow these impulses by projecting them onto inanimate objects or animals. Aggressiveness and sexuality are two of the most common unacceptable or hard-to-handle feelings which underlie the fear of a certain stimulus. The stimulus becomes an object of dread; however, what is really dreaded is the problem feeling.

For example, a child's fear of "lions eating me up" and other animal fears can be interpreted as symbolizing fears that his aggressiveness or sexuality will "consume" or "destroy" him. These fears exist in the general population; but they can be especially strong among sexual abuse survivors because they have been directly confronted with aggression and sexuality, their own as well as their abuser's.

In some cases phobias can be severely crippling. There are many instances of adult female incest survivors who suffer from agoraphobia. In psychology, agoraphobia refers to a fear of being trapped or being somewhere from which there is no escape. A child with agoraphobia may be afraid to go to shopping malls, ride in vehicles, be on a bridge, stand in a line, or be in other situations where he feels shut in. He prefers to stay at home, where he feels safe. The housewife who finds grocery shopping traumatic, as well as the child who hates to go on vacations or to parties, may be suffering from agoraphobia.

You need to determine whether or not your child is suffering from a genuine phobia or simply a passing fear which may be normal for his age group. A qualified psychotherapist can help you with this. If (a) the fear is persistent and intense; (b) the fear causes your child to consistently avoid certain situations or endure them only with great anxiety; and if (c) your child on some level recognizes that there is "no reason" to be so afraid, yet (d) continues to suffer from anxiety symptoms (such as increased heart rate, perspiration, and so on) due to the phobia, there is a good possibility that he would be diagnosed as having a genuine phobia.5

If your child is phobic, you can help him best at first by respecting the phobia. Don't call him "stupid" or "silly" for having a phobia. On some level, he knows that his fear is "unreasonable," and he already feels ashamed and deficient about it. Remember that for children, as well as adults, phobias have a magical quality. Your child may feel that if he avoids certain situations, or people, he will be protected from harm and can prevent a repeat of the abuse situation.

Try an empathic approach: "Getting in the car [or whatever the dreaded stimulus is] really frightens you, doesn't it? It must be so hard for you when we have to go places. I never realized how afraid you were of cars until today."

The next step is to ask open-ended questions, such as, "What does it feel like for you to be in the car? Can you describe what you are feeling, or are you too nervous [scared, anxious, whatever word your child understands] even to know?

"What are you thinking when you're in the car, or are you too scared even to think at all? How does your body feel when you're in the car? Do you get hot and sweaty? Do you feel your heart beat fast? Do you get a stomach ache, a headache?"

Let your child talk without judging what he's saying as "right" or "wrong," "justifiable," or unjustifiable." Watch your facial expressions. Even though you may not say anything judgmental, if you look at your child as if he is deranged or nonsensical, you'll communicate that message to him. All children are sensitive to adult moods and feelings; however, abused children tend to be more sensitive and attuned than others.

You need to get as much information about the nature of your child's phobias as possible. A judgmental attitude, or look, will not encourage him to share openly with you. This information is valuable, not only to you, but to your child's counselor.

If your child's phobias seem to be controlling his life, inhibiting his social and educational development, or otherwise severe, he needs professional attention. However, you can help him handle situations that frighten him by instructing him to use deep breathing or relaxation exercises. For example: "Before you get into the car today, I want you to do your relaxation exercises and tell yourself, 'It's going to be hard for me, but I can handle it.' Then when you get in the car, do the exercises again, being sure to do your deep breathing. While we're driving, you can talk to me about how you are feeling.

"I know this reminds you of [the abuse, the court trial, or whatever the stressful event was that is associated with the phobia]. I know it feels like the time you were so scared [helpless, trapped]. But this time is different. We are not going to court [or, this white man is not the abuser, or, having spinach doesn't mean you are going to be abused tonight, or whatever]. We're going to a party [or, this white man is very kind, or spinach has nothing to do with abuse, and so on].

"You're probably saying, 'I know that, Mom [Dad]. Why do you keep telling me this over and over again?'

"I know your brain understands that you're safe now, but sometimes it takes a while for feelings to catch up. In your head, you know you're safe. But in your heart you may still be afraid, and that's okay. That's normal after what you've been through. It will take time for you to learn to not be afraid, but it will happen.

"Now can you promise me something? Promise that you'll try to stop calling yourself 'crazy,' or 'bad,' or 'sissy,' or whatever other negative word you are calling yourself for being afraid.

"You didn't choose to have this fear and having it is no fun. This fear is causing you a lot of pain and aggravation, and you would give anything in the world to be free of it, wouldn't you?

"You will get over it someday and you are working toward that. Just the fact that we can talk about it will help you be less afraid. One day at a time, one car trip at a time [or, one green vegetable at a time, etc.], you will get better.

"I admire you for being able to get in a car at all, given how scared you are of it. I also admire you for facing your fears, rather than running from them. That takes courage.

"It's hard, I know. But it won't always be this hard and I and [list other supportive people] are here to support you as you struggle. Together we'll chip away at this fear, a little bit at a time. Each time we try together you'll be a little less afraid, until someday you will hardly be afraid at all."

A very helpful resource for you and your child can be found in *The Anxiety and Phobia Workbook* by Edmund J. Bourne (Oakland, CA: New Harbinger Publications, Inc., 1990). Consult with your child's therapist for additional suggestions.

Social Phobias

Sex abuse survivors are vulnerable to developing social phobias. Such individuals commonly suffer from self-esteem problems and often have problems relating to others because they feel "deviant," "tarnished," "deficient," or otherwise inferior because of the abuse. Social phobias also exist among the general population. Like simple phobias and panic disorders, they are highly amenable to treatment.

A social phobia is an intense fear of situations where one will be observed by others. With a social phobia, unlike the abuse situation, your child does not fear that he will be attacked or trapped, but rather that he will "make a mistake" and humiliate himself.[6]

For example, your child may be afraid of speaking in public because he anticipates saying or doing something inappropriate which will embarrass or humiliate him. Or perhaps he fears other performance or social situations. He may even feel that the abuse "shows."

Professional help is needed with social phobias, as with the simple phobias. Medication can help alleviate the anxiety associated with social situations and provide your child with a few "success" experiences in situations that were formerly feared.

With medication controlling his excessive anxiety, your child may be able to function better and unlearn the idea that he "can't handle" a given situation. After a few success experiences, he will begin to acquire confidence and truly believe that he can be effective or competent in the situation he formerly feared. At this point, depending on the particulars of the case, the medication may be discontinued.

As with simple or nonsocial phobias, the best way you can help your child is to listen to his anxieties and fears without judging them as signs of personal deficiency. After listening you can ask questions, such as, "What do you think people are thinking about you when you [mention the situation—for example, public speaking]? What's the worst mistake you think you will make? Have you ever made that mistake? What happened then?

"If you did make this mistake, what do you think would happen next? How would you feel and what would you think? How do you think others would feel? Why do you think others wouldn't understand—[for example, it's normal to be nervous while giving a talk and for the nervousness to show]? If someone doesn't understand why you made a mistake [or whatever the feared behavior is], what does that say about him or her as a person? Why do you think you have to be perfect in everything you do? Do you expect others to be perfect?"

You can help reduce anxiety about a specific event (for example, giving a talk at school) by asking: "What would make you less nervous [anxious, or whatever word your child understands] about doing this? How can I help you prepare for this?"

You can then help your child reduce his anxiety by reminding him to do his breathing and relaxation exercises before that event and suggesting that he can practice relaxation during the event as well. Don't imply, though, that by following all of your (and his therapist's) suggestions he can be anxiety-free. "Just because you might still have anxiety after practicing the relaxation techniques doesn't mean that you've failed. It's natural to have a little anxiety when you [give a talk, go to a party, or whatever the event is]. Most people do. Relaxation helps reduce your anxiety, but it may not eliminate it entirely."

Panic Attacks

Like simple phobias and social phobias, panic attacks are a form of anxiety disorder. Typically they last for a few minutes, but sometimes they can last far longer. With simple phobias and social phobias, fear and anxiety are expected. For example, the black girl who was attacked by a white person expects to feel afraid around white people; the little boy who has a social phobia expects to feel extreme tension prior to a school debate.

In contrast, panic attacks are unexpected and unpredictable. According to the *DSM-IIIR*, in order for your child to be classified as having a panic disorder, at least four of the following symptoms must accompany the attack:

- Shortness of breath or smothering sensations, dizziness, unsteady feeling or faintness
- Palpitations or accelerated heart rate
- Trembling, shaking, sweating, choking
- Nausea or abdominal distress
- Depersonalization or derealization
- Numbness or tingling sensations
- Hot flashes or chills
- Chest pain
- Fear of dying
- Fear of going crazy or being out of control[7]

In addition, there must be at least four attacks within a four-week period, or one or more attacks followed by at least four weeks of intense fear of having a subsequent attack.

Some of the physical symptoms that attend panic disorders occur as a result of medical problems, such as hyperthyroidism; as a result of caffeine or amphetamine intoxication or withdrawal; or as the result of other psychotropic drugs. It's imperative that your child receive a full medical exam in order to rule out the possibility that the panic attacks are being caused by hypoglycemia, heart problems (especially mitral valve prolapse), hypertension, asthma, thyroid, or other medical problems. It's possible that your child has both a medical problem and a panic disorder, and that they exacerbate each other—but only a qualified physician and mental health professional can determine if a dual diagnosis is warranted.

Taking your child to a physician is a "must." It is also a "must" to take your child to a mental health professional with expertise in panic disorders. Recent studies show a high correlation between panic disorders and suicide attempts, especially if depression is also present.[8] If your child does not get the help he needs he is not only at risk for a suicide attempt, but for the development of an addiction, especially alcoholism.

You need to find a physician and a mental health professional who are knowledgeable about panic disorders. Although anxiety disorders, which include panic disorders, affect more than 1.5 million Americans and are a common psychological problem, many physicians and mental health professionals are not as familiar with the syndromes as they should be.₉ You need to inquire about the doctor's and therapist's background in this area.

The Anxiety Disorders Association of America (6000 Executive Boulevard, Suite 200, Rockville, MD 29852-3801) can provide you with names of doctors and therapists in your area with expertise in panic disorders; as well as with information about self-help groups for individuals with panic disorders and/or phobias, including social phobias. According to the Anxiety Disorders Association, over 75 percent of individuals with panic or phobic disorders can improve significantly when the treatment is appropriate. You may want to purchase a copy of Dr. Reid Wilson's booklet, *Breaking the Panic Cycle—Self-Help for People with Phobias*, published by the Anxiety Disorders Association of America. In this booklet, Dr. Wilson outlines seven steps toward overcoming phobias and panic attacks and shows how once a panic attack occurs, it can create a vicious cycle of panic at having a panic attack, withdrawal, isolation, self-hatred, and self-disparagement. His suggestions include the use of many of the stress management and relaxation therapy techniques already discussed, as well as the ideas of approaching goals through small increments and facing tasks one at a time.

Truancy and Other Problems With School

Acting Out

When therapists say that a child or teen is "acting out," they are referring to the process whereby the child or teen is attempting to express and draw attention to his feelings indirectly, with problem behaviors, rather than directly, with words. The more you can teach your child the language of feelings and create a climate in your home where feelings are respected and talked about, the more you can avert "acting out" behaviors such as truancy and other school problems.

When your child runs away from home, stays away from school, hits other children at recess, or challenges the teacher in a nasty manner, he is trying to say something to somebody—either to you, the abuser, or someone else. With his action he is making a statement about his feelings about himself, and about his life—a statement that reflects his anger, fear, anxiety, and low self-esteem.

Some children "act out" at home, not at school. Before Jeb went into treatment, he displaced his anger at his abuser onto his sister, not his classmates or teacher. There are other children, however, who are angels at home, but "act out" at school. Some children "act out" at both places, and some don't "act out" at all—on others, that is. Emily, the well-mannered, super-responsible incest survivor, never raised her voice at anyone, either at home or at school. She did not "act out" externally on others, but internally, by venting her pain and fury on herself in the form of depression, self-mutilation, and suicidal behavior.

Underachievement

Another problem some sexual abuse survivors have is under-achievement in school. They simply cannot apply themselves fully to their academic work because their emotional turmoil interferes with their ability to concentrate and discipline themselves. If they suffer from nightmares or other sleep disorders, they may be too tired to be fully attentive during class. Or they may have trouble concentrating because of the numbing and anxiety which often attend post-traumatic stress disorder.

Your child's underachievement may be a highly charged emotional problem for you, especially if you and your family put a high value on academic achievement. It may also be an emotionally laden problem for your child if he has internalized your high value on academic performance or if he prides himself on his academic achievements for other reasons. If your child is getting help, however, the underachievement probably is temporary.

You can say, "I know you're capable of doing much better in school than you're doing now—but, don't forget, you were emotionally hurt, and going through what you went through does take its toll.

"You know I want you to make good grades, but more important than the grades, I want you to be healed of the terrible experience you had. Your main 'homework' now is to heal your emotions. You can always catch up in school later. It will do you, and me, no good for you to be a top A student and miserable inside. Also, you won't be able to make an A in the other parts of life—like playing, having friends, and loving yourself—unless you heal from the abuse."

If the major source of your child's underachievement is the emotional drain caused by the abuse, consider with your child, the school, and your child's therapist, the possibility of your child assuming a lighter school load or taking incompletes in some courses.

Talking With Your Child

When your child is truant or has other school problems, your first task (in conjunction with teachers, school counselors, and other school officials) is to try to find out what he is trying to say with his behavior. You should realize that he himself may not know. He's mixed up, not only because of the abuse, but because being a child or teen in this rapidly mobile, ever-changing society is an extremely difficult proposition. If your child already knew what his feelings and problems were, he would not be asking for help (indirectly) by expressing his feelings and problems (indirectly) through problem behaviors at school.

Before you approach your child, take some time to examine your emotional responses to his problem behavior. Ask yourself, "How do I feel about this? Am I furious, embarrassed, saddened, confused? Do I also feel betrayed by my child?

"Am I interpreting his behavior as a lack of gratitude on his part for all I've done for him? As a sign that I've failed as a parent? Am I worried that I'll be blamed for his behavior by my parents [spouse, in-laws, neighbors, friends, and so on]? How did my parents treat me when I misbehaved? Am I treating my child the same way? Do I want to treat my child the same way? How could I improve on how my parents handled me?"

You may also be afraid, thinking that perhaps you cannot handle yet another major problem. "Oh, no—first the abuse, now this. I can't take any more."

You need to know how you feel, not only for yourself, but so that your feelings do not interfere with getting as complete a picture as possible of the reality of your child's school, social, and family life; you want to understand the meaning of his truancy. Quite possibly, once you better understand the reasons for your child's behavior, your feelings about the situation may change. Probably you will become less angry, less upset, and less frightened.

In talking with your child and with school officials, you need to determine the following:

- Is your child's truancy or other acting-out behavior a pattern, or is it a rare occurrence?

- Is the behavior in any way a response to some provocation— such as ridicule by a teacher or classmate, a sexual advance, or threats?

- Is the behavior a response to an anniversary date reminiscent of the abuse or the anniversary of another major loss—the death of a loved one, or another major life event? For example, if the abuse or other loss is associated with the month of November, is your child suddenly acting out in that month as an indirect way of dealing with his feelings about the event?

- Is your child being truant because of a phobia about school, a social phobia, or an underlying panic disorder? (In these instances, refer to the suggestions in the previous sections of this chapter.)

- Is your child having flashbacks, fugue states (times of amnesia), or difficulty concentrating and/or memory problems at school due to PTSD from the abuse?

Information Gathering—Other Contributing Causes

You will need to talk to your child, but you will also need to ask the school principal, the teachers, and others for their concrete observations and subjective perceptions of your child's emotional state, social interaction skills, and academic performance. Ask if they have observed any changes in your child in recent months; if there have been any changes in school rules or policies, or if some event occurred that may have triggered the truancy—such as a gang fight in the school playground, a school fire, the death of a teacher, a confrontation between your child and one of the teachers, and so on.

At the same time, ask what the rules are regarding truancy and other problem behaviors and—very important—what educational, tutoring, social, and psychological resources the school system has to offer you. For example, most school systems have a psychologist who can provide psychological testing for your child. Such testing can reveal if your child suffers from a learning disability or memory deficit, as well as if he harbors deep-seated angers or fears.

Don't exclude the possibility that a medical or physical problem is contributing to your child's school problems. He may be having problems at school because he can't keep up with the other children due to a vision or hearing problem. Inquire about the last time his eyes and ears were checked, and request that he be tested again if seeing or hearing seems as if it might be part of the problem. Or perhaps he has hypoglycemia and can't concentrate or control his aggressiveness when his blood sugar is low. There are other medical problems that can contribute to problems at school. If you have any doubts, a medical checkup is warranted.

Confronting the Problem Behavior

When you approach your child to discuss the truancy (or other problem), approach him with an open mind and with love—as an information-gatherer and loving parent, not as a stern or punishing judge.

"Your school called and, according to [name official(s)], you have [name behavior]. Is this true?

"I also spoke with [...], who is concerned about your [relay any other information you have].

"It sounds to me like you're trying to say something by [name infraction], something to the teacher(s), your friends, me, or somebody. Maybe you don't know how to say how upset you are with words, so you're expressing your feelings through your action.

"As far as I see it, your [problem behavior] is a cry for help and I'm here to help you. But you need to remember that the school policy is [explain policy on the behavior] and that there will be consequences if you continue to [name behavior]."

At this point, don't make dire threats or spell out the worst consequences—for example, police action or reform school—right away. Begin with the most minor consequence and simply state, "and there are worse consequences after that." There is no need to frighten your child. If you threaten with the consequences, you may be inviting him to retaliate with an 'I don't care. Put me in jail!' attitude. At some point, you may need to spell out all the possible consequences, but it's to be hoped that the problem can be nipped in the bud.

"If you continue to [...], eventually the school will have to intervene. I want to help you so this doesn't have to happen. But you have to help me help you by telling me what the problem is, or else there's no way that we can solve it. The teachers want to help you, too, especially [name teachers who have shown their willingness to help]." Also mention any positive feedback the teachers had about your child—for example, "Mrs. So-and-So thinks you are so gifted in [...]. She wants to do all she can for you."

"I hope you will open up to me, or one of the teachers, because there may be ways to solve the problem that you haven't thought of. For example, if someone is picking on you, that child could be counseled, made to stop, and/or moved to a different class. If you have trouble hearing the teacher, we can get you a hearing aid. If you're having trouble completing your lessons, we can get you a tutor. If the problem is that you just aren't interested, there are options like work-study programs or early graduation [list whatever other options are relevant].

"Maybe the problem has to do with school, or maybe the problem has to do with your feelings about something like the abuse or [state other possiblilities]. If you're trying to tell me you are mad at me by staying away from school, I wish you'd tell me directly how mad you are at me rather than endanger your future. I promise to listen carefully and not punish you. If you aren't mad at me, but at somebody else, let's talk about it. Maybe something can be done.

"So what do you think the problem is?"

Compromises and Solutions

It's to be hoped that the above introductory remarks will encourage your child to talk openly and begin to participate in what will probably be the first of many talks.

Once you determine the nature of the underlying problem, you will need to go back to the school system and commence a thorough search for the service alternatives which might be available for your child. Depending on the school system, this might entail several phone calls to different departments. Do not assume that the receptionist at one department knows what is available in all other departments. Make as many phone calls as needed and keep a notebook on who says what, because you may receive conflicting information.

Some school systems have work-study programs, school furlough programs, special classes for children with disturbances or learning disabilities, or other special programs. One of these might better meet your child's needs, at least in the short term, than the regular school program.

In some cases, a change in schools might be warranted. For example, sixteen-year-old Joan, a sex abuse survivor turned alcoholic, blacked out in the girl's room one day after a night of partying. She was in treatment for alcoholism, but had been "slipping" because it was the anniversary month of being abused. Joan was utterly humiliated at having her problem with alcohol made known at school, but she also felt (irrationally) that her experiences with sexual abuse were also exposed.

Joan's best girlfriends assured her that had said nothing while intoxicated about being abused, but Joan was positive that now everybody in the school knew about the abuse. She became truant because she felt she could no longer "show her face" at "that school"; she projected all her hatred at being abused onto the school. She developed such an intense hatred of the school that she was adamant that the only way she would ever return to any school would be to go to a different one.

Joan's parents were not opposed to a school transfer—however, the only other school close to their home was of an inferior quality. They saw that their daughter's fears were "irrational," but respected the intensity of her shame enough to permit her to transfer to the new school, even though it was not best for her academically. They reasoned that she was sure to fail at the old school because of her attitude; so she had a better chance for success at a new school, even if it didn't offer the same academic excellence as the old one.

It's always wise to consider your child's strong feelings, no matter how irrational they may seem to you.

The key word in talking to your child about school problems is "options." Say, "You can continue to [underachieve, act out] and perhaps such and such will happen as a result. Here are some other options you have...."

Other suggestions for dealing with school problems can be found in Kathleen McCoy's book, *Coping with Teenage Depression: A Parent's Guide* (Signet Books, New York: New American Library, 1982).

Depression

Coping with a depressed child is painful, frustrating, and exceedingly draining. When all of your best efforts to infuse your child with the joy of living and the spirit of hope do not seem to result in a permanent improvement, you might feel like giving up.

Remember that feeling. That is how your child feels all the time, or almost all the time—hopeless and exhausted.

You might also feel angry—at yourself for not being more effective in helping lift your child's depression, and at your child for causing you so much emotional strain. Remember those feelings, too. Your child might feel the same way toward himself: frustrated in his attempts to "feel better" and mad at himself for being depressed.

As explained in Chapter 2, depressions can be mild, moderate, or severe. They can also be cyclical: your child's mood may plunge when he is about to begin another cycle. Review the symptoms of depression listed in Chapter 2, keeping in mind that the following symptoms might also indicate depression:

- An apathetic attitude
- An inability to experience pleasure
- Mood swings
- Underactivity or overactivity
- Physical complaints with little or no medical basis
- School problems
- Persistent feelings of worthlessness and guilt
- Strings of "accidents"
- Addictions
- Self-mutilation
- Sexual or aggressive "acting out" behavior

Although the wildly aggressive child is not usually thought of as "depressed," it's quite possible that the hostility is a cover-up for depression and low self-esteem. "He's too ornery to ever commit suicide," you might think. However, more than one such hostile child or teen has killed himself.

Keep in mind also the close relationship between depression and alcoholism, drug abuse, and eating disorders. Not only can the various types of substance abuse be forms of self-medication for depression, but substance abuse can in itself create symptoms of depression. In cases of prolonged abuse, a genuine biochemical depression can evolve. Perhaps you suspect that your child suffers from depression, but he also suffers from alcoholism, drug addiction, or an eating disorder. It cannot be determined whether or not he truly suffers from depression until he becomes sober, drug-free, or establishes healthy eating patterns.

For example, since alcoholism can create many symptoms of depression, mental health professionals usually wait until an alcoholic client is alcohol-free over the course of two or three weeks before they consider making a diagnosis of depression. If the depressive symptoms remit in two or three weeks, the depression was caused by the alcohol abuse. If the symptoms persist, or worsen, then the client is diagnosed as having two problems: depression and alcoholism. Similarly, if a client is a cocaine addict, he needs to endure his withdrawal symptoms, which often have depressive features, before a diagnosis of depression can be made.

You also need to be on guard for the depressions which might follow giving up a substance abuse problem. One reason why many alcoholics, drug addicts, and eating disordered individuals have difficulty giving up their drug of choice is that when they do, they frequently suffer intense anxiety or intense depression. They are disappointed, and perhaps shocked, because they thought that they were supposed to feel better when in treatment. Instead, they are feeling worse. Consequently, their immediate temptation is to turn to drugs again to deal with the depression (the same process can occur with eating disorders).

If your child suffers from a true depression—not one induced by an alcohol, drug, or food addiction—he may well need medication in addition to counseling (see the section in this chapter on *Medication*).

Unfortunately, a social stigma founded on ignorance surrounds depression, as it does sexual abuse. The National Institutes of Health is currently conducting a public awareness campaign about depression. The goal is to inform the public that depression is a widespread illness (not a sign of personal inadequacy) affecting millions of Americans, and it's also highly treatable. Like so many disorders, depression has both a psychological and a biochemical component and may need to be treated on both levels.

Because of this stigma, in many cases children and teens try to hide their depression. They want to act "normal" and "happy" so they can "fit in." "Nobody would love me if they knew how bad I feel all the time" is their underlying thought.

If your child is truly depressed, your first response may well be to want to "fix him"—to liven him up and bring him joy by buying him gifts, taking him to the movies, or telling him jokes. These efforts are helpful in that they show your love and help stimulate your child both psychologically and physiologically. However, these efforts will not "cure" the depression on a permanent basis.

In some cases, your peppy attitude may even make things worse. If your child is severely depressed, he may wonder what is wrong with him that he can't respond positively to your many loving efforts, or that he can't sustain any positive feelings he acquired as a result of your efforts.

This does not mean that you should discontinue your verbal reinforcements, hugs, kisses, or any forms of special attention you're giving your child. Above all, keep talking about hope, which is the antithesis of the dominant feature of depression, hopelessness.

Never forget: your efforts may help make the difference between life and death for your child. If he has isolated himself from others because of his complaining, irritability, and so on, he may be very alone in the world. (Chapter 7 gives example of how to talk to a child who is depressed to the point of having suicidal thoughts.)

However, you cannot be your child's life support system forever. If he has depression, he needs and deserves additional help. He will still need you as a source of encouragement and attention, and also as someone who can simply acknowledge the reality of his depression in a world that makes him want to treat his condition like a "dirty secret" similar to sexual abuse.

Given the stigma and shame that shroud depression, simply acknowledging your child's condition and the pain he must feel can be of utmost importance on his road to recovery. Continually let your child know that

- It's okay for him to be depressed

- You know depression hurts

- He doesn't have to pretend to be happier than he is around you

- With the help he's getting, he'll overcome the depression—but it will take time, and struggle

You do not want to make the mistake made by Karen's mother. Karen, age eighteen, had been sexually abused between the ages of eight and twelve by a neighbor. She subsequently became alcoholic, drug-addicted, and promiscuous; but she denied her problems until, one evening, high on drugs, she was gang-raped. Soon afterwards, she sought help.

Six months in an alcohol and drug rehabilitation program and two years of faithful attendance at AA and NA meetings stopped the alcohol and substance abuse, and two years of psychotherapy helped Karen deal with her childhood sexual abuse and the rape. However, what Karen and her parents didn't know was that she had an underlying clinical depression.

She thought that her tendencies to isolation and negative thoughts were part of her addiction to alcohol and drugs, for she learned in AA and NA that alcoholism and drug addiction were "diseases of isolation and negative thinking." She also felt ashamed because, even though she was working the twelve steps of AA and NA to the best of her ability, she still did not feel "joyous, happy, and free" as these twelve-step programs promised. Yet she hesitated to tell her AA and NA sponsors, as well as her parents, how negative, listless, and unhappy she felt, because they had all already overextended themselves on her behalf for many months.

"I should be cured by now. What's wrong with me?" she wondered.

When one of Karen's cousins was getting married out of town, Karen's parents decided to attend the wedding. Karen didn't want to go. She felt inferior to her cousin, who she felt was not only more beautiful than she, but untainted with a history of sexual abuse and multiple addictions. "No one is ever going to marry me," was Karen's thought. She wanted to stay home, where she felt safe. Also, she hated traveling because of being confined in vehicles, which reminded her of being constrained and tied up by her abuser.

"You have to go," her parents insisted. "This is a major family event."

Reluctantly, Karen packed a suitcase. The airplaine trip was traumatic for her because of the confinement, but she managed to endure. Once the family reached the hotel, however, Karen broke down into tears.

"What's wrong with you? Aren't you happy for your cousin?" her mother asked.

Karen's pain was so bad that she finally revealed the truth. "Mom, I'm so depressed. I cry like this a lot, but I hide it from you. I'm afraid to be here, and I'm so tired I don't know if I have the energy to put on my dress and stand up during the wedding.

"I'm so unhappy, Mama, I feel like dying all the time. I feel so worthless and so ugly. I walk around pretending all the time, pretending to be okay, but inside I'm crying a lot, crying about the abuse, the rape, crying because I ruined my health with my drinking and drugging, because I'm so scared that nobody will ever marry me."

At this point, Karen began to sob so hard that she could no longer talk. Her mother just looked at her and walked out of the room.

Her mother was not heartless. She just did not understand. Sexual abuse, alcoholism, and drug addiction—she knew something about these problems. But these feelings of despair in her daughter, what were they about? Did they mean that her daughter was a "hopeless case"? Would she and her husband be saddled with an "emotional cripple" for the rest of their lives?

On some level, Karen's mother was also threatened by the depth of her daughter's pain. "What do I do now?" she wondered. "Better to do nothing than to make a mistake and make my daughter feel even worse."

If Karen's mother had known about depression, she might have responded like this: "I feel so sad for you. Oh, how I wish you had told me sooner! To think you've felt this bad for so long and kept it all inside. How hard it must have been to bear all that pain all alone. Such pain is hard to bear, even when it's shared with others. But to bear it alone—what a burden! How lonely you must have felt.

"This wedding must be torture for you. You always did feel that Suzie was prettier than you, and now she's getting married and you're not. This wedding must bring up all your issues about the abuse and the rape and it doesn't help that everybody will be drinking and you can't.

"I am so glad you spoke up, Karen, and I want you to promise me that in the future you will always tell me when you feel so bad. I don't care if you feel bad thirty-five more times before I die. I am your mother and I am here to help you.

"As you were talking, I heard your pain. But I also heard some depression talking. Depression is an illness. Millions of people have it. In fact, it's one of the most common psychiatric problems in the United States. Depression is a horrible illness. It makes people feel hopeless, worthless, fatigued, and sad all the time. But there is help for it. Good help.

"As soon as we get back home, I'm going to take you to be evaluated for depression by a psychiatrist. I don't want to play psychiatrist with you, but can you tell me how long you've had these crying jags? Feelings of fatigue? Feelings of hopelessness? Have you ever felt like killing yourself? Have you ever come close but not told me or your father?

"You probably think you are a weak person, but I think you are a strong person. You've been handling this depression without any help all this time, and without alcohol or drugs, either. That's quite an achievement. So many people with alcohol and drug problems go right back into their addiction the minute they feel depressed.

"But you didn't. You stayed clean and sober. That's a lot to be proud of. In fact, it's almost a miracle. It takes a lot of determination and strength to go on with life without your old addiction when you feel that bad.

"Now let's see what we can do about getting you through this wedding, which, as it turns out, is going to be quite an ordeal for you.

"How about this? When you get too tired, come back into the room and rest. I can come with you if you want. If you feel like drinking or going for drugs, come to me instead and we can go for a walk.

"You don't have to tell anybody how bad you feel. But when we get back home, I want you to tell the doctor all about it.

"Depression hurts, Karen, but there's a lot of help available and you can feel better soon. For today, use one of those AA slogans— 'One day at a time'—and use me and your dad for support. Call your AA and NA sponsors if you want and don't worry about the cost of the long-distance phone calls. It takes what it takes and if you're so depressed, you need to allow yourself all the help you can get."

You may also want to refer to Kathleen McCoy's book, *Coping with Teenage Depression* (cited in the previous section) for further information about helping a depressed child.

Nightmares and Sleep Disorders

Nightmares, insomnia, night terrors, and other sleep disorders are inherent to the PTSD born of sexual abuse. Insomnia, early morning awakening, and other sleep problems are also also common features of depression. Even if your child does not have PTSD or depression, sleeping problems may exist if he was abused at night, while sleeping, or in a bed. Any of these associations can create anxiety or bring forth memories that prevent a good night's sleep. In addition, it's not uncommon for trauma survivors to be flooded with memories of the trauma when not diverted by activities and other people— such as at bedtime.

Psychotherapy can help your child deal with the experiences and feelings that underly the sleep problems. And medication, if warranted, can help reduce any biochemical imbalances which might contribute to sleep problems. However, even if your child is in therapy and/or has an appropriate medication program, it's very likely that you will be called upon more than once to soothe him so he can sleep, comfort him during nightmares or night terrors, and help him deal with his fears about his sleep problems.

You will undoubtedly be called upon to help your child many times. It's common for sleeping problems to increase, despite psychotherapy and medication

- At anniversary times associated with the abuse, such as the birthday of the abuser, holidays associated with the abuse, and so on

- In response to stimuli associated with the trauma, such as a media program on sexual abuse, the sexual abuse of a friend, meeting a person who resembles the abuser, and so on

- In response to current losses like the death of a pet, a car accident, or rejection by a friend

Furthermore, therapy itself can increase, rather than decrease, nightmares, insomnia, and other PTSD symptoms—at least initially, as well as whenever major memories or feelings emerge from repression. In addition, medication is rarely one hundred percent effective.

Talking About Sleep Problems

Your first step is to gather information about your child's sleep problems. How many dreams/nightmares does he have, and how often? Are they the same dream or different dreams? What are his other sleep problems? How does he think or feel about his sleep problems? Is he interpreting them as signs that he's crazy? Has he developed considerable anxiety about not being able to sleep, having nightmares, waking up in the night? Such anxiety can perpetuate sleep problems.

Your second step is to educate your child about nightmares and sleep problems. In doing so, you will help diffuse the anxiety and fears that surround them. Say, "The sleep problems you are having are normal. Many people have sleep problems, but abuse survivors tend to have more sleep problems than most people because of what they have been through. Having been abused makes people restless and nervous. Often they're afraid to relax or sleep because they are afraid that if they let their guard down the abuse might happen again. Or maybe they start thinking about the abuse and other sad or scary things when they are alone in bed, trying to relax, and not involved in doing something.

"Is any of what I am saying true for you?"

If your child talks about being afraid to sleep, you can continue as follows: "I know you know you are safe here at home. Your head knows that very well. But your body is still scared, and that's okay. Remember Spunky the cat? It took her a long time to feel safe, didn't it? It might take you a while, too, but it will happen and there will be a day when you'll be able to sleep better.

"Do you ever think, 'Gosh, it was bad enough that I had to be abused. Now I have to have these nightmares [insomnia, or whatever], too'? Did you ever wonder why you're having these nightmares?"

Find out what your child thinks about the origin of dreams and nightmares and correct any of his obvious misconceptions—for example, that dreams and nightmares are "punishments" from God, that they fortell the future, that they are "real" in some way.

Then explain the function of dreams.

"Think of your dreams as messages from one part of yourself to another part of yourself. They may be signs that you are not finished dealing with the abuse. Your nightmares are horrible, but there is something positive about them: you can use them to finally put the abuse to rest and feel better. In fact, one of the reasons you have nightmares is to help yourself feel better. Sounds strange, doesn't it? Let me explain.

"Have you ever eaten greasy or spicy food and kept burping it up for hours? Sometimes if the food is really greasy or spicy, you might even burp it up for days afterwards. It's hard to digest that kind of food, isn't it? It takes time, doesn't it?

"The same thing happens with a traumatic experience like the one you had when you were abused. You can't digest it right away. It sort of stays 'stuck' inside you, but you try to get rid of it by burping it up in your nightmares. Your dreams are a way of trying to digest it and make it go away.

"Or you can think of the abuse like food poisoning. If you have food poisoning, sometimes you end up vomiting several times until the poisoned food is all out of your system. Nightmares and bad dreams can be ways of getting rid of the poison of the abuse.

"Unfortunately, bad dreams aren't like bad food. It takes a lot longer for bad dreams to go away than bad food. But you can help get rid of the nightmares by talking about them—to your counselor, to me if you want, or [list other trusted connections]. Some children like to write them down, draw pictures about them, or talk about them into a tape recorder."

If your child is amenable, buy him a notebook, a drawing pad, or even a special "dream diary" or tape recorder to put by his bed. Explain that dreams are easily forgotten: he should write, draw, or record the dream as soon as he can.

"Don't be surprised if for a while when you start to talk about your dreams or nightmares or anything else associated with the abuse, you have more bad dreams. Don't be afraid. All it means is that you're trying really hard to 'burp' out the abuse. Someday you might not have them at all."

If your child relates a dream to you, jot it down. You cannot be a dream analyst, but you can help teach your child to start thinking about his dreams analytically. You can ask, "How did you feel in the dream? Did you change in the dream? Where did the dream occur? Who else was in it? What were they thinking or feeling?"

Ask your child what he thinks the dream is saying.

Tools for Reducing Anxiety and Inducing Sleep

You can help reduce your child's anxiety about insomnia or other difficulties falling or staying asleep by saying, "It's okay if you can't get to sleep right away [or can't sleep through the night]. It makes you tired and cranky, doesn't it? But it won't last forever. Now let's see what we can do to help you sleep."

To help your child sleep, you may want to try some of the following suggestions:

- Go through the relaxation exercises with him

- Give him a gentle massage (if he finds this soothing, rather than reminiscent of the abuse—and if *you* feel comfortable doing this)

- Talk to him at bedtime about his day, his thoughts, his feelings, and his fears

- Play soothing music

- Have him avoid foods with caffeine (such as chocolates, cola drinks, coffee, certain medication) and foods that tend to stimulate the nervous system—such as protein foods (with the exception of warm milk)—before bedtime

- Avoid any heavy meals before bedtime; but a snack that contains calcium and/or carbohydrates—such as cereal, oatmeal, warm milk, or bran muffins—can have a calming effect

- If you are a family with religious faith, you could pray with your child and read comforting scriptures
- Give your child a hot bath (or, if he's older, draw a hot bath for him)
- Bathe your child in your love—tell him how valuable he is to you, what qualities in him you especially appreciate, and so on
- Be certain that the room temperature is comfortable
- Try to establish a regular sleeping schedule for him
- Help your child avoid taking naps (or, if they must be taken, have him take them at the same time every day)
- Have your child exercise on a regular basis, but not just prior to bedtime

If your child is older, suggest that he read a boring book or do a boring task until he falls asleep.

Medication

Recent research on a variety of psychiatric problems (depression, manic depressive illness, obsessive compulsive disorder, PTSD, schizophrenia, and others) is revealing that these are not just emotional problems, but biological ones as well. Biochemical imbalances, as well as genetic predispositions, often play significant roles in creating, and perpetuating, these disorders.

We have all heard horror stories about clients who are so over-medicated that they become virtual zombies. Not only does the medication cure them of their symptoms, but it "cures" them of their personality, their emotions, and their sexuality, too. There are also horror stories about permanent neurological damage suffered by clients who are prescribed the wrong medications or who are administered inappropriate doses of the correct medications.

As a result, some of us shun the thought of medication. "Oh no. They aren't going to turn my child into a robot!" you may say to yourself when the doctor recommends medication. At the other extreme are people who expect medication to fix everything. They fail to realize that while some psychiatric problems have a biochemical basis, psychiatric problems are not like strep throats. Emotional work, as well as medication, is needed.

An abuse survivor who also sufffers from depression and alcoholism explains: "I need my antidepressants, but I have to help the pills work. My job is not only to take the pills as prescribed (which is hard because I always want to play games with them), but to keep going to my therapy sessions and my AA meetings and to keep talking about my feelings to people. I also have to keep doing positive things for myself, like eat right, exercise a little, and make time for friends and relaxation.

"The pills can't cure me by themselves, but they help me do the things that *will* cure me. For example, before I was on anti-depressants, I didn't have the energy or the motivation to go to therapy and AA meetings. I felt so hopeless because of my depression I didn't think that therapy or AA could help me. So why go? Also I was so tired all the time, I couldn't bear the thought of dragging myself here and there." Consider taking your child to a psychiatrist for a consultation about medication when

- Your child feels suicidal

- His anxiety level or panic disorder prohibits him from going out of the house, going to school, seeing friends, or otherwise engaging in minimum routine activities

- He suffers from extreme sleeping problems, such as two or three nights of insomnia, night terrors, or nightmares every night

- He's unable to stop drinking, drugging, or compulsively over-eating despite his best efforts to stop

- He has visual or auditory hallucinations

- He frequently expresses homicidal, sadistic, or otherwise aggressive wishes, and/or acts on them

The above conditions suggest that medication might be helpful. They do not automatically imply that medication is needed. You may want to discuss your concerns with your family doctor—however, your general practitioner, regardless of his or her concern for your child, is not necessarily an expert in psychiatric medication. You need to find a doctor, preferably a psychiatrist, with expertise in psychopharmacology as well as familiarity with your child's problem area.

For example, if your child has PTSD and depression, you need to inquire whether there is a specialist in depression who has also worked with trauma survivors. Similarly, if your child is alcoholic and drug-addicted, you need a psychiatrist who has worked with substance abusers and who is familiar with the many possible interactions between the substance being abused and the medications available. If your child has a panic disorder or extreme anxiety symptoms, you need a psychiatrist who is familiar with panic disorders and PTSD. Such specialists tend to be expensive, but it is also costly to receive the wrong medication or the wrong dosage.

Questions To Ask About Medications

When you go to a psychopharmacological psychiatrist, he or she will probably do a complete medical and psychiatric work-up. You should be prepared to list your child's symptoms, their duration and frequency, and any other observations you have. After the work-up is completed, you can ask the doctor the following questions:

- What is his or her psychiatric diagnosis?

- What are the various types of medications that have been found useful for this diagnosis?

- What are the potential benefits and the possible negative side effects of each of these medications?

- Are there any initial side effects which should disappear in time (for example, "jitters" or extreme fatigue)? If so, how much time will it take (how long should you wait for the initial symptoms to disappear before you call the office)?

- Why is one particular medication being selected over another?

- How much research has been done on this particular medication, and what is the probability that it will be helpful?

- How long does it typically take for this medication to have an effect?

- If your child overdoses on these medications, will he die?

- Should you give him the daily medication or should he be given the responsibility of administering it to himself?

- What if he forgets to take the medication at the prescribed time? Should he take it later in the day, or wait until the next day? If he skips a day, should he double the dosage the next day or not?

- If he is bulimic or throws up for some other reason, what should be done if he vomits up the pill?

- If he's alcoholic and/or drug-addicted, what should be done if he "slips" and uses his drug of choice while on the medication? Will the effect be harmful? Will it be fatal?

- Will the drug be administered in ever-increasing doses?

- How will the psychiatrist determine if the dosage needs to be changed? Will blood tests be required? If so, how often?

- Does the psychiatrist have any literature on the medication that you can read?

- Can your child become "addicted" to this medication?

- What will happen to him, physically and psychologically, if he suddenly stops the medication on his own? What are the signs you can look for that will tell you that he has? What should you do to help him if this situation comes up?

- At what point can the medication be discontinued? Or is there a point in time after which the body becomes "immune" to the effects of the medication and it ceases to be effective? How long does it take for the effects of the drug to leave the body? How long after the drug is discontinued should any dietary or alcohol restraints be observed?

- If this medication doesn't work, what other medications might be available?

You have the right to expect the psychiatrist to explain your child's medication in detail. Furthermore, medication needs constant monitoring. Until the right dosage is established, you may need to telephone the psychiatrist several times. You will also need to call if the hardships caused by negative side effects seem to outweigh the positive effects of the drug.

For example, if your child is sluggish, extremely tired all the time, unable to concentrate; or if he or she has physical symptoms such as bleeding, muscle tremors, seizures, dizzy spells, hyperventilating, dark or discolored urine, rashes, inability to urinate, constipation, loss of menstrual period, severe headaches, vomiting or nausea, loss of sex drive, or other bodily difficulties, call the psychiatrist right away. Similarly, if your child still feels suicidal, homicidal, or self-mutilating, or develops hallucinations or delusions, or begins to act in an out-of-control manner, call the psychiatrist immediately.[10]

If your call is not returned promptly, call again. Don't let these side effects go unattended. Be wary of any psychiatrist who does not seem familiar with the medication, who seems to discount your concerns, or who does not return your phone calls regarding questions about or problems with the medication. If contacting the psychiatrist is always a problem, consider changing doctors.

Common Psychotropic Medications

The section below lists some of the common psychotropic medications, their possible benefits, and side effects.[11] These descriptions
are very general. For more specific information about each drug,
consult your psychiatrist or the *Physician's Desk Reference* (available
in any library).

Tricyclic Antidepressants

The tricyclic antidepressants are useful for depression. They also
have an anti-panic effect and are useful for panic disorders and some
of the anxiety symptoms of PTSD.

The three tricyclic antidepressants that have the most extensive
research base are imipramine (brand name *Tofranil*), desipramine
(brand name *Norpramin*), and nortriptyline (brand name *Pamelor*). In
general, these drugs reduce the anxiety underlying the depression
and also function, in time, to reduce anxiety and panic attacks. Individuals with low blood pressure or a history of heart disease
should receive a complete medical examination before taking imipramine.

The tricyclic antidepressant called amitriptyline has been found
to be effective in the treatment of nightmares and other intrusive recollections of traumatic memories.

Monoamine Oxidase Inhibitors (MAOIs)

These drugs are useful both for anxiety disorders and depression.
The more common MAOIs are phenelzine (brand name *Nardil*),
Isocarboxazid (brand name *Marplan*), and tranylcypromine (brand
name *Parnate*).

The problem with these drugs is that there are dietary restrictions.
Your child will need to stay on a tyramine-free diet. If he doesn't,
he can develop a hypertensive crisis. Tyramine is found in hard
cheeses, yogurt, fava beans, red wine, soy sauce, and other foods. If
your child has an eating disorder or a drug or alcohol addiction, this
drug is generally not advisable because, under the influence of alcohol or drugs, or under the influence of an intense food craving,
he might forget the dietary restrictions, consume a food high in
tyramine, and suffer a hypertensive crisis. If he is prescribed an
MAOI inhibitor, you should also be given one or two capsules of an
anti-hypertensive agent, such as procardia, to keep on hand in case
your child has a hypertensive attack. These capsules are not necessarily swallowed like a pill. With procardia, for example, the instructions are to chew the tablet for a few minutes, then place it under
the tongue. Your child should have one of these on his person at all
times; so should you.

Possible side effects that do not usually require medical attention include dry mouth, constipation, restlessness, mild headaches, muscle twitching during sleep, lightheadedness, increased appetite with possible weight gain, difficulty urinating, drowsiness, and weakness. Some of these side effects eventually disappear; some may not. Although they do not constitute medical emergencies, contact the psychiatrist if they're a cause for concern.

The following possible side effects, however, should be reported to your doctor: severe lightheadedness, skin rashes, extreme restlessness, yellow eyes or skin, swelling of feet or lower legs, diarrhea, dark urine, extreme weight gain.

The following possible side effects may constitute a medical emergency and require immediate medical attention: unusual or extreme sweating (especially if combined with fever and other symptoms), intense headaches, vomiting, changes in heartbeat (extremely fast or extremely slow), chest pains, enlarged pupils, hypersensitivity to light, inability to concentrate, or a total inability to urinate.

Other possible side effects include sexual dysfunction, low blood pressure, and difficulty falling asleep.

Benzodiazepines

The benzodiazepines include diazepam (*Valium*), lorazepam (*Ativan*), clonazepam (*Klonopin*), alprazolam (*Xanax*), and many others. These drugs have antipanic and anti-anxiety effects. Unlike the tricyclic antidepressants and the MAOIs, the benzodiazepines take effect rapidly and have relatively fewer side effects. However, there can be memory problems and some sexual dysfunction; and these drugs should not be mixed with alcohol or other drugs. In addition, there is a potential for withdrawal symptoms once the drug is discontinued.

Much controversy surrounds these drugs. However, they are neither "addictive poisons" nor miracle drugs. They can help decrease nightmares and improve sleep.

Carbamazepine (*Tegretol*)

This is an antiseizure drug that is also used for manic-depressive illness and panic disorders. Blood testing is required.

Propranolol (*Inderal*)

This is useful for the anxiety symptoms of heart pounding, sweating, and shaking.

Librium and Lithium

These drugs may be of help with depression, mood swings, and impulsivity.

Clonidine
This drug helps decrease startle responses, intrusive recall of trauma, and nightmares. However, there is a risk of developing organic brain syndrome.

Fluoxetine (*Prozac*)[12]
Fluoxetine, more commonly known as *Prozac,* is a relatively new drug, and is being used to treat depression, anxiety, bulimia, addictions, and obsessive-compulsive disorder. It has received media attention lately because of its effectiveness combined with fewer side effects than the MAOI and tricylic drugs. However, since *Prozac* is relatively new, there is no information on its long-term consequences.

Negative side effects reported thus far in a small minority of users are restlessness, insomnia, sexual distinterest, anorgasmia (inability to achieve orgasm), headaches, and upset stomach.

7

When Your Child Is Suicidal

Suicide and Sexual Abuse Survivors

When Emily attempted suicide, her family and friends were shocked. They had read about suicide in the papers and heard about it on television, but they never realized it could touch their own family directly. Yet suicide is the ninth leading cause of death in the U.S. Among adolescents (ages fifteen to twenty-four), it ranks as the second leading cause.[1] Although there are no definitive statistics on suicide among sexual abuse survivors, we do know that suicide attempts and completed suicides are more common among the abused than the nonabused.

As an abuse survivor, your child is at special risk. This is a horrible fact to contemplate, but it's one that you *must* face and deal with appropriately. Because of the trauma your child has endured, she is suffering greatly. And people in pain, even young people in pain, want an end to that pain. One sure way to end pain is death. You may have heard your child say, "I want to die. I'm worthless. There's no hope for me. I don't want to go on living." Listen to what she's saying. Your listening—and acting—may save her life.

Jeb's mother didn't want to hear her son talk about suicide. Her view, shared by many, was that suicide—like sexual abuse—only occurred in "crazy" or "godless" families. Besides, Jeb was in therapy now. He was supposed to be getting better, not worse. Probably he was just acting like a baby, wanting more attention. How infuriating! Wasn't it enough that he banged his head against the wall and pulled out his eyebrows? How much more could one mother take?

"Oh, come on now, Jeb. Don't talk like that. It's bad luck."

"I mean it, Mom."

"You think you mean it, but you don't know what you're talking about. You're too young even to be thinking like that."

"Mom, I'm planning to kill myself next Tuesday. I've got it all planned. Next Tuesday, I'm going to..."

"Hush now! Stop that crazy talk and ask God to forgive you."

Jeb's mother, already strained and anxious, found that she just couldn't cope with the issue of suicide. Emily's mother felt the same way. Perhaps you have similar feelings. But as the parent of a potentially suicidal child, you need to free yourself from the ancient stigmas and taboos surrounding suicide. You must realize that suicide, like depression, is a treatable, preventable problem that can be solved if it is recognized and dealt with openly. Suicide has nothing to do with morality, intellectual competence, or other measures of self-worth. It's simply one possible outcome of prolonged stress or unendurable pain. Even children who are in therapy can become suicidal. In fact, some sexually abused children and teenagers can become suicidal as the direct result of therapy which brings their memories of, and feelings about, the abuse out of repression. (A competent abuse therapist will be alert to this danger.)

According to some researchers,[2] approximately one-tenth of those who threaten suicide follow through to completion. Some thirty-five to forty percent of suicides have been found to have been preceded by unsuccessful suicide attempts. (Some researchers even contend that eighty percent of suicides are preceded by at least one prior attempt.)[3]

All statistics on suicide have to be reviewed with caution, however. If suicide is defined as a self-inflicted act intended to end one's life, suicide statistics may be skewed by the inclusion of self-destructive acts that lead to death but were not necessarily intended to be fatal. On the other hand, some suicides are not reported as such because of the stigma associated with the act, or because there is genuine confusion about whether the death was accidental or suicidal. As Victor Victoroff, a psychiatrist who has studied suicide extensively, notes: "Many suicides are probably buried in sport, industrial and household accidents."[4]

In some instances, the suicide is masked. For example, some car collisions and other vehicular accidents may be suicides. Obviously it's impossible to interview the victim to determine whether the cause of death was an unintentional driving error or a wish to die. The same problem arises regarding certain poisonings and drug overdoses. Were they accidental or deliberate? Alcohol, food, and drug abuse—as well as other forms of self-destructive behavior—can be seen as mini-suicides. For some sex abuse survivors, these behaviors ultimately lead to death, but are typically not included in suicide statistics.

There are several factors that may put the sexually abused child at special risk for suicide:

- Alcohol, food, or drug abuse

- Social isolation

- The hopelessness which she may experience as part of her post-traumatic stress disorder, depression, substance abuse, or other problems

In Jeb's case there was no substance abuse. He did, however, feel that he would be a social outcast and "oddball" forever, and that his feelings of despair would never end.

The risk for suicide is especially high if your child has been diagnosed as having a clinical depression. The suicide rate among patients hospitalized for depression has been found to be twenty-five to thirty times higher than among the general population, with approximately fifteen percent of them committing suicide.

The correlation between alcohol and/or drug abuse and suicide has been verified by many studies. Some studies show alcoholism to be involved in twenty to thirty percent of suicides.₅ Alcohol and drug abuse have also been found to be significant risk factors in teenage suicide. For individuals of all ages, alcohol or drug abuse impairs the ability to control impulses. Since suicide can often be an impulsive act (especially among teens), the individual whose judgment is skewed may easily give in to a momentary feeling of desperation.

The social isolation which characterizes many sexually abused children also increases their risk. Your child may have you and other family members who love her very much. She may even have a network of friends. However, the concern of all of you may not be enough if she begins isolating herself. Her support system will do her no good unless she uses it. Some children, out of self-hatred and low self-esteem, not only do not use their support system, but begin to destroy it by alienating those who love them. Jeb, for instance, started hitting his sister and calling his mother names.

Suicide is often viewed as the opposite of aggression. But it actually is a form of violence. In some cases, it's possible that the suicidal individual is turning her anger toward another person in on herself—especially if that other person is both loved and hated, such as an incestuous abuser. Suicide risk is consequently higher for children who were sexually abused by family members or other trusted adults than for those who were abused by strangers. For both Emily and Jeb—who were abused by adults they admired and trusted and on whom they were dependent—the suicide risk is higher than for children who are victims of a one-time rape or molestation by a stranger.

Tunnel Vision

Sexually abused children still suffering from painful and anxiety-producing symptoms, such as those associated with depression or post-traumatic stress disorder, may say, "If I don't get better, I'm going to kill myself." It was that way for Jeb who, although he was in therapy, did not feel that he was making progress. The child who is hurting, who has made a habit out of certain self-destructive behaviors, or who has been unable to develop a satisfying lifestyle and network of friends, often suffers from tunnel vision. She cannot look forward in time to a positive change—either in herself or her environment.

For example, it's not uncommon for compulsive overeaters or bulimics to view themselves exclusively in terms of their symptoms. Such children may say to themselves, "I'm nothing but a fat slob." Similarly, a depressed child may feel that she will never be able to enjoy a normal night's sleep, concentrate, or maintain a relationship. "I'm lazy and a failure—of no use to anybody."

While the impairments in her concentration, everyday functioning, or relationships are real, they should be recognized as after-effects of the sexual abuse or part of her clinical depression or post-traumatic stress disorder—*not* as permanent personality characteristics. Yet the depressed child, like the depressed adult, may not view these impairments as temporary. Such negative self-labeling only increases an individual's depression and/or other symptoms, as well as increasing her tendency to isolate herself. This isolation, in turn, reinforces her tunnel vision and pessimism, while depriving her of much-needed attention and love. Thus the child becomes even more depressed—and hopeless—and comes to see suicide as a way out of living with the pain of her symptoms.

Emily felt helplessly trapped in the incestuous relationship with her father. For Jeb, being sexually abused reinforced his lifelong feelings of inferiority with respect to his older, taller, and more athletic brother; it reaffirmed his deep-seated feeling that he would forever be the "runt" of the family and an eternal disappointment to his parents. Before Jeb was abused, he tended to be shy—but at least he tried out for school plays, art contests, and other such events. After the abuse, his feelings of inferiority extended even to his special talents, and he began to withdraw even from those activities at which he had once excelled.

Warning Signs

You need to be alert to signals from your child that she may be contemplating suicide. Most suicides do not happen without warning. The suicidal child—like anyone else—often gives clues regarding her intentions. Don't make the dreadful mistake of thinking, "No, it could never happen in my family"—as if suicide were a moral disgrace or a phenomenon limited to the mentally deranged or the lower socioeconomic classes. In the United States suicide is no respecter of persons: it occurs across all levels of our society.

Although there is no one pattern for suicidal children who have been sexually abused, the following characteristics have been found to correlate with suicide:

- A family history of suicide or depression, or the recent suicide of a friend, relative, or close associate

- A prior suicide attempt

- Lack of strong affiliative bonds to another person or group of persons—feelings of not belonging to anyone or to any group

- Social isolation: lack of a support system or inability to use available supports

- Alcohol and/or drug use

- Reckless behavior

- Frequent and severe conflicts with authority

- Depression, possibly combined with irritability and/or agitation

- Feelings of being trapped, stuck, or sinful

- Feelings of hopelessness, helplessness, worthlessness, or humiliation

- Suppressed rage and/or free-floating hostility

- Negative thinking: a negative view of past, present, and future; black-and-white thinking; irrational beliefs[6]

Among teenagers, parental conflict, parental separation or divorce, parental substance abuse, parental absence (or emotional aloofness), and violence in the family (including wife abuse, child abuse, and incest) have also been found to be associated with suicide. Teenagers who have unrealistically high expectations of themselves and who struggle ceaselessly to live up to their perfectionist standards are also at risk.

Be responsive to:

- Announcements of suicidal thoughts or intentions ("I'm going to kill myself if..." "I won't be here for Christmas." "You won't have to worry about me any more." "This might be the last time you see me." "This is the last day I'll ever have to feel so bad.")

- Suicidal writings or drawings; notes written that are intended to be read after your child's death

- Your child giving away prized possessions, writing a will, cleaning up unfinished business, saying goodbye to friends and relatives, shopping for a cemetery, writing a eulogy, purchasing a one-way ticket somewhere

- Noticeable withdrawal from family and/or friends and/or from previously attended therapy

- Any dramatic change in mood or emotional state

- Sudden, significant weight gain or loss

- Changes in sleep habits

- Loss of interest in friends, sex, music, books, sports, and so on

- Difficulties concentrating

- Recent loss of a loved one or rejection by a loved one

- Increased abuse of alcohol, food, or drugs

- Impaired functioning at school

- Preoccupation with fanatical or cultist ideas

- Outbursts of violent or rebellious behavior (particularly if this is out of character)

- Uncharacteristically slumped posture, slow movements, repetitive behavior or statements

- Any evidence of being out of touch with reality

- The expression of excessive or inappropriate guilt[7]

What You Can Do, What You Can't Do

Don't try to evaluate your child's suicidal state on your own. You will have to reach out to the appropriate mental health professional, clergyperson, or other authority—such as the police.

As soon as you hear the word "suicide" from your child, or observe any of the signs listed above, find professional help for her. Even if she's only thinking suicidal thoughts and still doesn't seem to have a definite plan, her thoughts need to be aired. If your child is already in treatment, encourage her to share her thoughts of suicide with her therapist. Left bottled up, thoughts can feed upon themselves and develop into a full-blown suicide crisis.

For example, Jeb's mother could have responded more productively to her son's announcement that he was planning to kill himself by saying, "When you say you want to die, I believe you. Have you discussed this with your therapist? Can you promise me you will do nothing until you talk with your therapist? Do you want to call her right now? Do you want to talk with me? This is serious and we have to deal with it now."

If your family has financial difficulties and your child feels guilty about the cost of her treatment, you can stress that such help is not a luxury but a necessity. Her life is the most important thing in the world to you. Money is only a means toward helping the family survive and prosper. You care more about her survival than you care about money.

Young children are in special danger, because they are not always aware of the lethalness of their actions. Also they, like teenagers, tend to be more impulsive than adults—so even more attention needs to be given to any indication that a young child is contemplating suicide.

Children and teenagers are more likely than adults to view life's problems as permanent rather than temporary. They may also react intensely to events that may seem "trivial" to adults. A teenage boy may want to kill himself because his girlfriend began to date another boy; a teenage girl because she gained two pounds.

Never, never, never dismiss your child's concerns, no matter how silly they sound to you. You must talk them out together. You may want to believe that all this talk about suicide will magically go away, but it won't. You absolutely must face this crisis and deal with it, just as you would deal with it if your spouse or a parent were suicidal. You would believe an adult if she were talking about suicide; you must also believe your child. The reality is that suicide exists as an option for teens and children as well as for adults.

Don't worry about perhaps triggering a suicide attempt by talking with your child about her plans to kill herself. Your inquiry and concern may save her life, particularly if you can get her to talk to someone who is trained to deal with suicide crises. Don't let your fear of not saying or doing the "right thing" prevent you from speaking to your child from your heart. What you say may be just what she needs to hear. If you don't speak, the risk is much greater that she will actually carry through with her plan.

You cannot rely on your child's therapist to detect all the signs of suicide or to provide all the support and action your child needs. There have been instances where concerned parents have notified therapists or school officials about their children's suicide plans and these people did nothing, trivialized the possibility, or indicated that the child's suicidal state was not their responsibility but that of another agency or professional. Ultimately, you may be the one who has to take action on your child's behalf.

How to Assess the Gravity of Suicidal Threats or Behaviors

When you're discussing your child's suicidal plans with her, try to evaluate whether this is a generalized "I-want-to-die" idea or if your child actually has a definite plan. The more specific her plan—including a potentially lethal weapon or means of suicide—as well as your assessment that this plan fits her personality, the greater the possibility that she is truly serious.

All this is quite a tricky judgment call: but it's vital that you err on the side of caution. Use your common sense and your knowledge about your child. If she says that she's going to jump off the nearest bridge, but you know her to be afraid of water and terrified of heights, then it might be that she's speaking more symbolically than revealing a specific suicide plan. If she says that she's planning to kill herself with an overdose of pills, but doesn't know what pills to take or how many, and doesn't have a specific date established for suicide, then she's probably less likely to try to kill herself than a child like Emily, who spent two weeks in the library researching various types of medication, purchased the pills, and picked out and announced a date. Had Emily's mother asked, Emily would have told her that she planned to be dead by her seventeenth birthday. She had confided this information to two friends, who were sworn to secrecy. Similarly Jeb had planned to kill himself "next Tuesday," not on some unspecified date in the hazy future. With a specific date in mind, Jeb is closer to suicide than most children who do not have a timetable. Similarly, a child who plans to shoot herself but does not own a gun and has no idea where or how to purchase one is less likely to kill herself than the child who has easy access to a firearm and has learned how to use it.

This does not mean that a child who talks about suicide but doesn't have a plan is not capable of killing herself. On the contrary, she is; and her suicidal wishes must be acknowledged and talked about in detail.

A sign that a suicide attempt may be imminent is if your child feels that some force stronger than her own will is pushing her toward suicide. Such statements as, "I'm afraid to be alone," or "I don't know if I can stop myself," or "There's a voice in my head that says, 'Do it! Do it!'" or "Hide the rat (or other) poison—I'm afraid I'll take some," warrant an immediate response. Even if your child has several powerful deterrents to killing herself—such as strong family ties, an ongoing romance, or religious beliefs—if she's showing any signs that she is unable to control her impulse to kill herself, then she should *not* be left alone. She may need to be hospitalized or, at the very least, to be in close communication with a trained professional. (If she states that God, voices, or some force outside herself is "ordering" her to kill herself, psychiatric hospitalization is almost always needed.)

Emily, for example, started reading books and poems by Sylvia Plath, a poet and novelist who succeeded in committing suicide after multiple attempts. As part of her English homework assignments, Emily wrote essays and poems about Plath, stating how much she admired this author for killing herself and how she felt "called by destiny" to follow in this author's footsteps by killing herself, too. Had Emily's parents read these essays and poems or had the English teacher been well-informed on teen suicide, Emily and her family might have been spared the anguish of her suicide attempt.

Another important clue that a suicide attempt is imminent is if the child first talks about her plans to die, then suddenly refuses to discuss the subject at all. As long as she is talking, she is maintaining some sort of emotional connection with someone. Once she quits talking, she may be very near to taking action. Don't make the mistake of thinking that because she no longer talks about death, death is no longer a threat. It is.

Try to draw her out. Keep trying to establish contact with her in any way you can. Ask her such questions as:

- Do you still want to kill yourself?

- Do you have a plan? Has it changed since the last time we talked?

- On a scale of one to twenty, what's the probability you'll put your plan into effect?

- How much do you want to live? How much do you want to die?

- Do you have a particular date in mind?

- Do you feel that you *must* kill yourself?
- Do you feel that someone is trying to force you to kill yourself?
- Is there someone or something telling you to kill yourself?
- Will you give me the pills [gun, keys to the car, poison, etc.]?
- Can you promise me that you won't kill yourself until you talk to a trained professional?[8]

Your child's response to such questions can help you identify the possibility of a suicide attempt in terms of its actual potential. If she has a plan and a date, will not give you the tool she plans to use, or will not make a commitment *not* to kill herself during a specified period of time while you try to get her help, then you must act immediately.

Taking Action

Even if the only "fact" you have to go on is your own gut feeling, act! Take away your child's weapon, pills, car keys, and anything else that you consider potentially lethal. Get help immediately. Call a local hospital as well as any local suicide crisis hot line. Try the police and/or a rescue squad. In an emergency situation, your child can be taken to any local hospital that offers psychiatric care.

If you are not sure that a crisis is imminent, but you still feel uneasy, don't leave your child alone. If you must go to work, or leave the house for some other reason, have someone stay with her. Your child may appear angry and yell that she doesn't need "baby-sitters." She may also refuse to cooperate with a therapist or to visit a hospital.

If you meet such resistance, state firmly, "I'm afraid. You've told me that you're thinking about killing yourself. I love you too much to take any chance that you might actually do so. Even if the chances are one in a million, that's too high a risk, as far as I'm concerned. You mean too much to me. I'd rather be safe than spend the rest of my life sorry."

Quite possibly, when you're firm about taking responsible action, she will not only agree to let someone "babysit" for her, but will consent to go for help. However, it's also possible that your firmness may only cause her resistance to escalate. She may become even more hostile and/or verbally abusive. This is not uncommon. Many times the hostility a suicidal person displays toward her helper is a reflection of the anger she harbors toward some other person (such as her abuser).

Jeb started calling his mother names and threatened to beat his younger sister "to a pulp" if Mrs. Jones followed through with her plan to stay home with him until he agreed to go to an "emergency" session with his therapist. Very calmly, Jeb's mother repeated her position that she loved him and was going to do everything she knew how to prevent him from killing himself.

"Go ahead and call me names," she said. "If you think that's going to stop me from loving you and doing my best for you, you don't know me very well. I brought you into this world and I'm going to see to it that you stay in it as long as possible. Mr. R. is the one you really hate. I'm on your side and no matter how nasty you act, you won't stop me from helping you through this."

Try to communicate your love in as many ways as you know how and let your child know that you're behind her one hundred percent—for example, by being available to listen at any time, day or night. Assure her that even more help is available through hospitalization, psychotherapy, medication, crisis hot lines, and so on.

Make it your business to find the local crisis line phone number and give it to her. Post it next to every phone in the house. Keep a list of concerned friends and relatives whom she can call when she feels desperate. And, of course, remove any firearms or dangerous medications from the house.

If your family has financial problems and your child feels guilty about the cost of her therapy, stress that such help is a necessity, not a luxury. "You don't know how sad it makes me to see you so unhappy that you want to die. Your life is worth so much more than any amount of money."

If you find your child in the midst of a suicide attempt, dial 911 and ask for the police, fire department, or a rescue squad to send an ambulance immediately. Your child will need to go to a hospital emergency room as soon as possible, since her medical needs are urgent.

Put aside any other commitments and go with your child to the hospital. Call someone to watch your other children and try to get someone to meet you at the hospital to give you moral support. If you can, remember to take your insurance information with you.

Talking With Your Child

Although it's not usually a good idea to try to handle someone who is suicidal on your own, there may be times when you have no choice. If that happens to you, remember that your main goal is to buy enough time for your child to reconsider her desire to die and give you an opportunity to ensure her safety—through hospitalization, therapy, or whatever.

Some parents believe that if a child is in therapy, there is no risk of suicide. This is not the case. Being in therapy does not magically eliminate a child's negative thinking and sense of hopelessness. While suicidal thoughts and plans are often discussed in therapy, in some cases the child chooses only to reveal her wish to die to a family member—especially if she doesn't feel totally comfortable with the therapist. If this happens, your child must be told that you believe her. Never deny the reality of her feelings by saying such things as "Oh, you can't mean it," or "You'll get over it soon enough. You're young yet." Such statements may give your child one or more of the following messages:

- Suicide is so socially unacceptable and/or morally repugnant to me that I don't want to discuss it.

- There's something wrong with you if you're talking this way.

- You aren't entitled to feel that bad.

- I'm sick and tired of hearing you complain.

- I don't care enough about you to listen.

You do care, deeply; but the subject of suicide may create considerable anxiety for you. You may have a great fear of death, or you may be struggling with your own suicidal thoughts. On top of all this, you may feel inadequate to handle the situation. "I can't cope with any more. All this suicide talk is too much." You may want to wish the reality away. Perhaps you are too emotionally numb or exhausted to feel up to handling this latest emergency. Yet you have to. It's your responsibility to do your best: your child has turned to you in her pain.

Your first step is to talk with her openly about her suicide plans and to contact her therapist or group leader. In cases of *impending* suicide (not vague wishes or thoughts), therapists sometimes decide to break the bonds of confidentiality and inform family members that the client is suicidal. In a parallel manner, if you decide that your child is showing definite signs of suicidal intent, you should not hesitate to call any professional or authority figure who you believe can help. You may also decide to inform other family members, friends, or other people who might be helpful.

Jeb's mother, for instance, informed Jeb's art and drama teachers, to whom Jeb felt particularly close. They all wanted to help and called Jeb, complimenting him and making plans for the future with him.

"Our art shows won't be complete without your work." "You'll be perfect for this part in our next play. I'm so glad we can always count on you to do such a good job and help the school."

Although Jeb acted numb on the phone, his teachers' messages of care and hope for the future did begin to penetrate his defensive shell.

You don't need to hide your actions from your child. In fact it can be helpful to her if you say, "I don't care whether you object or not: I'm letting your therapist [father, teacher, etc.] know. Maybe they can help me keep you safe." Your firmness may help convince your child of your love for her and her worth as a human being.

However, if she's capable of violence or extreme paranoia, the above actions may not be a good idea. It's very important for you to discuss your particular situation with a qualified mental health professional.

In general, people who are suicidal usually welcome intervention and the attention it entails. In many cases, the suicidal person is longing for someone else to take over. If she were one hundred percent sure of her course of action, she would already be dead. Instead, she chose to stay alive and tell you about it. She is sending out a signal, hoping that someone will take care of her, and give her hope.

Discussing Your Child's Reasons

While a suicide crisis may be the result of many factors, not just one incident, there may be a single event or source of stress that triggers a suicide crisis. It's usually not the incident itself, but rather the meaning of the incident which has created overwhelming pain. In talking to a suicidal child, it's important not to mock her reasons for wanting to die, regardless of how trivial they may seem to you. Instead, probe beneath the specific incident to discover the real meaning of the event for your child.

For instance, your child's teacher called her stupid and sneered at her performance in class. Instead of saying, "There you go again, overreacting to everything as usual," or "That's a dumb reason for wanting to kill yourself," empathize with your child. "For someone like you, whose identity is so wrapped up in doing well at school, being called stupid must have been a devastating experience."

Then move your child away from the specific incident to the general issues the incident symbolized. For example, the teacher's remarks may have highlighted the fact that ever since the abuse, your child began to lose confidence in her ability to cope. She has always been afraid of being called stupid; and in fact has secretly called herself that for "allowing" herself to be abused. Now "everyone" (represented by the teacher) believes that she's stupid.

She may feel both stupid and a failure as a daughter. She knows that she's not interacting well with the family, and may feel guilty for causing a drain on the family's emotional and financial resources. "If I wasn't your daughter, you wouldn't love me," she may say. Caught in the negative thinking which is typical of depressed individuals, she may feel that she'll never get better. "I'm crazy, I'm crazy, I don't deserve to live." You can respond, "You're not crazy! You're a victim of trauma. You can't help it that you were abused. And you *will* get better. It will just take time."

Your child may be berating herself for not standing up to her abuser, or for other "mistakes" or "inadequacies." Tell her that the best way to make up for what has happened to her is to go on living and to help other sex abuse survivors. Remind her that if she dies, she will be throwing away her intelligence, insight, and her chance to help someone else. If your child, like Jeb, is a perfectionist, remind her that no one person has everything—strength, talent, looks, brains; there are pluses and minuses for us all.

If your child believes in God, you're lucky. You can then use all the theological arguments against suicide and stress that God's plan for her does not include a self-inflicted death. Do not, however, imply that God will punish her for being so depressed that she wants to die. Talk about God in a positive way, as a life force, not a punishing overseer.

"The reasons for your existence may not be clear to you right now, and they may not be clear for a long time to come—but God does have a purpose for you. A lot has happened to you and you've had a very hard time. It's natural for you to focus on your problems, but you have a lot of good things in your life, too. You have parents who love you, you are [very smart, kind and loving to animals, talented, a great soccer player, or whatever]."

"I'm a mess, Mom, and you'd all be better off without me. My brother wishes I were dead. And so do I."

"Your brother doesn't mean it. Even a messed-up sister is better than no sister at all. If you think you're a bad sister now, if you kill yourself, you really will be a bad sister. No matter what reasons you may have for killing yourself, your brother won't understand. All he'll know is that you didn't care enough about him to stay alive. He'll feel abandoned, betrayed, and guilty. He'll wonder for years if he caused your death."

You can then list your child's strengths and talents again. At first she may not want to listen, because it's hard for her to believe that there's anything good about her. Yet it will do her good (even if she doesn't seem to be listening) to hear you and see that you appreciate so many of her good qualities.

Jeb was certain that his sister Katie would be better off without him. "I hit her all the time. She'll have a party when I'm gone," he told his mother.

"No she won't. She'll be devastated, as will everyone who loves you. Lots of people love you—do you know that? If you feel so bad about hitting your sister, you can apologize and try not to hit her again. You don't have to kill yourself to say you're sorry.

"You're so down on yourself, you feel worthless, but you're important to lots of people besides me." Then list these people one by one and relate some incident when your child touched these people's lives in a positive way. Remind her that she matters to a lot of people and that if she dies, she will be missed. Furthermore she would be teaching her siblings and friends that life is not worth living.

"Well, that's the truth. Life isn't worth living," your child may insist.

Reasons for Living

Before you can discuss the joy of living with your daughter in her present state of mind, you need to empathize with her pain and depression. If you're like Jeb's mother, who preferred to deny or minimize the sad and painful parts of life, this may be difficult for you. It may be helpful to remember the worst moment of your life, when you were afraid or extremely sad. Imagine that moment being multiplied by a hundred, and living that moment for hours and days on end with no relief, all the while trying to hide your true feelings from others, wearing yourself out pretending to feel better than you do and pushing yourself to get through the day. This is what your child feels when she's depressed. Speak to her depression; do not minimize or deny it.

"I know life seems black to you right now, and with good reason. I wish I could say that I truly understand, but I can't. I was never abused, have never struggled with some of the problems you've had that have made you feel so terrible.

"Perhaps if I were you, right now, I'd want to kill myself, too. But I know that feelings aren't facts and that very few situations are entirely hopeless. I agree that what you've been through emotionally was horrible—horrible beyond belief. Some of your suicidal feelings have to do with your rage and sense of powerlessness about the abuse. But some of your sense of hopelessness is also due to the feelings of powerlessness you have about your life today."

Suggest that with the help of a good therapist, your child can make changes in her present life that will make living more fulfilling and bearable. If your child feels, like Jeb, that her first therapist wasn't helpful, tell her that there are many therapists in your area, and that she can think about talking with a new therapist who might be able to help her more. Keep repeating that no situation is hopeless. "You can get more therapy, medication, and other help. You could even go into an inpatient program for a while. There's no reason for you to feel so bad all the time."

"Nothing can help," your child may insist.

"That's your depression talking, not you! How do you know that nothing can help unless you try everything first? Give therapy another try."

"We can't afford any more help for me."

"What's cheaper, therapy bills or funeral expenses?" Tell her that a typical funeral costs at least $4,000—the price of a year's worth of private therapy sessions. Furthermore, if she kills herself, you would be so depressed that you would end up in therapy yourself and so would most of the family—resulting in extraordinary costs. "So you see, it's really cheaper for you to get help."

Point out that right now she's evaluating everything in terms of mistakes made in the past and problems coming up in the future. As part of her depression, she's projecting only the negative things into the future. "How do you know that you won't feel better? You've already made progress. A year from now you might even be happy doing something you enjoy. You can't predict the future."

Despite your arguments, your child may keep insisting that life is hopeless and not worth living. Furthermore, she wants you to keep your Pollyanna logic to yourself. Nothing is going to talk her out of her misery.

"Even the Jews in the Nazi concentration camps and prisoners of war wanted to live," you could say. "Sure, some of them gave up and died, but some of them carried on, hoping against hope that they would survive."

"They were stupid! They should have all committed suicide."

"Life can be hard," you answer. "No one is happy all the time. But there are times when we feel at peace with ourselves, when we see something beautiful, or when we feel close to someone. Some of those prisoners kept on living just to see a bird or the sun in the morning, or to show a small kindness to someone else in pain.

"I'm not bringing up the concentration camp victims to make you feel guilty, or to make you feel that you have no right to feel miserable. But your situation, terrible as it is, isn't as hopeless as theirs."

Mention any friends or relatives who have endured struggle, hardship, or persecution. "They could have given up, many times, but they didn't. We all have the urge to live; you do, too, although right now it's buried under all that depression. A part of you wants to die, but another part wants to live."

Draw examples of friends or relatives who may have a severe handicap or illness. "Would you tell your friend to die because she lost a leg or went blind? No, because you know that even though she's in pain right now, there's a future for her and it can hold happiness as well as sorrow."

"Are you angry at me?" you can ask. "They say that sometimes people kill themselves out of suppressed rage, as a way to get even with other people. If you're angry with me, say so. I would rather have you yell at me and throw things all over the house than have you die."

Yes, your child may be angry at you, but she is even angrier at her abuser. "Maybe you think that if you kill yourself, you'll be punishing the person who abused you. Do you picture him at your funeral, overcome with remorse for how he mistreated you? Maybe he will feel guilty—but I guarantee that a week later, he'll be at a party having a wonderful time and not thinking about you at all."

Basically your child needs to be told that suicide is not a rational solution to her problems. Ask her to think of some reasons to go on living. Remember them and remind her of them over and over again. Ask her to go back in time and remember when she felt safe and loved. This can be tricky, because if she is severely depressed, she may not be able to remember such a time. You'll have to use your own judgment about whether this is an appropriate tool to use.

If your child fears that she is "insane" or "crazy" because she has suicidal thoughts, she needs to be reassured that many "normal" people have felt suicidal at various times in their lives. In time, and with help, these thoughts will diminish and she will feel freer to cope with the problems. And she *will* get better.

She needs to see that her depression and hopelessness are symptoms of her stress disorder and not permanent parts of her personality. Reassure her that she can look forward to a future in which she has a greater sense of mastery over herself and her life is not so painful.

Even if you have successfully weathered this crisis, it's possible that there may be another one in the future. Suicidal thoughts *can* return. If your child's response to pain, frustration, or to life's many dilemmas was suicidal at one point in time, it's possible that she will react that way again. This is a possibility to which you must remain alert as long as your child is in your care.

Being abused is a terrible and powerful experience. But its aftereffects can be overcome. If your child has endured her feeling this long, then she has nothing to lose by waiting a little longer and giving life a chance. And this is what you must make clear to her.

In talking with your child, use only the suggestions given here that you feel would be effective with her. Don't limit yourself to material contained in this chapter. Use any arguments you feel would be encouraging to your child and ask those who know and love her to help, too. Even if she's in treatment, don't hesitate to speak up. In our culture, we tend to rely too much on professionals. Parents often feel inadequate, yet may have as much wisdom to offer as any helping professional. You can support your child on a day-to-day basis with a depth of love and commitment that far exceeds what may be found in a therapist's office.

Even Jeb's mother, who had great difficulty expressing herself on an emotional level and who was intimidated by emotional interactions, proved powerful when she simply stated, "Jeb, I love you. If you kill yourself, I'll never be the same. I'm not a counselor and I don't know the right things to say to you. All I know is that you are my precious child and if you die, I'll feel as if someone sliced me in half.

"Your dad feels the same way. He doesn't show it, but I know that one reason he works so hard is for you. He'd lose his mind if he lost you.

"Please don't do it, Jeb. Please. Hang on just a little longer. It's got to get better. I love you, Jeb. I love you."

Suicidal thoughts are never a joke. You must always take them seriously. Your child's life may depend on it. Be alert and get help when it's appropriate. Do whatever you must to reassure your child that her pain will diminish over time and that there will come a day when she'll actually feel happiness and peace. Offer her a guarantee in writing. Tell her to take a survey among people she respects if the words don't weigh enough coming from you alone. Most importantly, reassure your child over and over again how much you love her, and how much she deserves to live.

Further Reading

Burns, David D., *Feeling Good: The New Mood Therapy.* New York: Signet Books, New American Collection, 1980.

8

Considering Hospitalization

How To Determine What Kind of Care
Your Child Needs

Outpatient care refers to all forms of psychological and medical care
available outside a hospital or psychiatric ward. Your child lives at
home, or at another residence, and commutes to individual, family,
or group counseling; to special focus programs such as Alcoholics
Anonymous or Al-Anon; or to a psychiatrist for consultation on
medication.

In general, outpatient care is sufficient for children who are in
touch with reality and able to function normally most of the time,
but who are unable to function optimally due to fear, anxiety, addiction, or other symptoms.

If your child is receiving outpatient care from a variety of professionals, you will have to make a special effort to coordinate communication between all the people involved (or perhaps to assign
one professional the role of coordinator so that the therapies do not
duplicate themselves or work at cross-purposes).

Inpatient care, on the other hand, means that your child is for-
mally admitted to a hospital or psychiatric facility where he will live
for a specified period of time. He will eat and sleep in this facility
and receive most, if not all, of his mental and physical health care
from doctors and other professionals who are part of the staff. An
inpatient unit assumes responsibility for your child. Although he
may be allowed to leave the unit at specified times, he'll basically
spend most of his time in the hospital.

Emily first revealed her incest secret while on an inpatient psychiatric ward. Perhaps it was living apart from her father that freed her to share her pain. After the incest was revealed, the ward physicians did not allow her to visit home and, for a period of time, restricted her contact with her family. (Of course, she could have left the hospital ward against medical advice at any time or her family could have withdrawn her from the program.)

An inpatient psychiatric ward or program is not a prison. Unless your child is court-ordered to be institutionalized because a psychiatrist has found him to be mentally incompetent or a danger to himself or society, and a court agrees with that diagnosis, you can withdraw your child from the ward or program at any time.

In general, inpatient care may be needed if your child is unable to take care of himself, function "normally" for his age, or is in some way a danger to himself or others. You should consider inpatient care if your child

- Is almost completely unmanageable at home or at school

- Appears so depressed that you are afraid to leave him alone even for short periods of time

- Is abusing alcohol, food, or drugs so severely that his physical health and safety are endangered

- Seems to be losing touch with reality—for example, if he imagines things or people that aren't there or is consistently mistaken about what you or someone else has said or done

- States that he is hearing voices or seeing visions (or responds to these)

- Is mutilating himself (scratching his skin off with his nails or a razorblade, making cuts on his body with sharp objects, pulling out his eyebrows or pubic hairs)

- Indicates that he is afraid of his impulses to hurt himself, another person, or a pet; or talks about suicide or homicide, especially if he has a specific date, plan, and weapon in mind

- Asks for hospitalization because he feels unable to manage on his own

Any child may have short periods when he seems unusually depressed, anxious, or neglectful of himself and his responsibilities. However, if these periods persist over time and if each time your child takes a "dip" he "dips" further and further into his depression, anxiety attacks, or self-destructiveness, it may be time to call a therapist to discuss the possibility of inpatient care. For example, if Jeb's head-banging had not only continued, but increased in frequency and duration after he began seeing a therapist, or if his eyebrow plucking had led to poking himself with pins or nails, inpatient care would probably have been warranted.

Similarly, if a child who rarely, if ever, consumed alcohol or drugs suddenly begins using, if not abusing, these substances, that child is crying out for help. The substance abuse in itself may not be severe enough to warrant hospitalization. But it may well be an indication of a deeper problem developing below the surface, such as a serious depression or panic disorder. Likewise, a sudden gain or loss in weight—perhaps fifteen to twenty pounds, depending on your child's size—may be important if it signals another problem.

On the other hand, it's normal for people recovering from an addiction to sometimes "slip." Inpatient care is not needed just because your child went on two or three eating binges or because he indulged in drugs "just one more time." However, if these slips become more and more frequent, if the amount of the substance consumed increases over time, and if your child seems less interested in getting help for his addiction, then it may be time to consider the possibility that these slips aren't just slips but rather signs of a full-scale relapse. Be especially watchful for any hint that your child may be giving up rather than fighting harder—for example, attending fewer self-help meetings and therapy sessions. If this is the case, intensified outpatient care at the very least will be needed.

If your child is seeing a therapist, or attending group therapy on an outpatient basis, the therapist or group leader may call you when he or she senses that your child needs more help than outpatient therapy can provide. Or perhaps a teacher or family friend will alert you to certain changes in your child's behavior that warrant your concern.

But you can't really rely on others to monitor your child's mental health and frame of mind. You need to trust and rely on your own observations and intuition. In the first place, he may be presenting a "perfect child" front to the outside world and only be revealing his anxiety, fear, or anger at home. In the second place, you need to consider yourself to be the resident expert on your child. You've known him longer and more intimately than anyone else in the world. You've seen him day in and day out in a variety of situations from the day he was born. As his parent, you are in a unique position to detect subtle changes in his behavior and habits which might indicate that he needs more help.

If You Suspect That Your Child Needs Hospitalization

The first step is to observe your child carefully and write down your observations of his troubling behaviors or moods. Carefully note any negative changes in behavior or attitude. Are there areas in which his functioning seems to be decreasing? At home? At school? With friends? Is he slowly but gradually retreating from others, turning down more and more invitations, or having more and more conflicts with others? Is he continually becoming involved with people who abuse him emotionally, physically, or both? Is he becoming abusive towards others? Is he damaging property, injuring pets, abusing others, or making threats to do so?

Does he seem to be sleeping or television-watching his life away? Is he able to take care of his grooming and personal needs, or is his self-care deteriorating?

When he's sick, does he tell you about his symptoms immediately or does he value himself so little that he waits for days until he's really ill?

Is his substance abuse taking over more and more of his life? For example, is he spending more time (and money) on alcohol, drugs, and/or food? Is he beginning to steal or otherwise break the law to support his habit? Is he spending more and more time with his addicted friends and losing touch with his friends who are sober and clean? What about his attitude? Is he becoming increasingly negative, bitter, or hopeless?

The second step is to discuss your concerns with your child. If you don't receive satisfactory explanations from him and you have even the slightest suspicion that he may be getting worse, you need to tell him that you're going to contact a therapist (if he doesn't already have one) or call his present therapist to talk over the issues or behaviors that are worrying you.

At this point, you may want to check out your observations by asking your child's therapist, friends, your neighbors, or members of your family if they've observed any disturbing changes in your child. Tell your child first, however, that you will be talking to these people, not to hurt or spy on him, but to help him. You do not need to obtain your child's permission to take such action, but let him know. As you discuss your concerns with others who know your child, bear in mind that even if their observations do not agree with yours, your hunches as a parent may still be right.

Don't ignore your intuition if you believe that something is "seriously wrong." Share your concern with your child by discussing your observations with him.

Your child may insist that he's "fine" and that you're overreacting or blowing your observations out of proportion. Since you want to believe this, too, you might be tempted to give up your resolve to discuss the situation with a mental health professional. At this point, refer to your written list of disturbing behavior and attitudes. This will help remind you that your observations are real.

You can expect that if your child is a teen or a preteen, he may yell and scream that you're "butting in" on his life or infringing on his privacy. Assure him that you're not going to pump his therapist for information about him; you're simply going to discuss your concerns about what's going on because it frightens you so much.

"I'm not trying to take over your life—I'm trying to save it," one mother told her teenage daughter. "I love you so much I don't want to lose you. I know you don't like me calling your therapist; but when I see you like this, I'm scared that you're so unhappy you're going to hurt yourself.

"You say I'm a busybody, but as your mother it's my responsibility to take action if I suspect that your life may be in danger. I love you too much to take any chances. I hope I'm one hundred percent wrong. Maybe you're fine and don't really need any more help. Maybe calling your therapist is a waste of my time, but I have to do it, for my own peace of mind. If something happens to you because I failed to act, I would never be able to forgive myself."

How To Judge Whether Outpatient Care Is Enough

If your child is receiving outpatient care now, ask yourself, "Is it working? Is my child getting better, staying the same, or getting worse?"

Perhaps the answer is "no"; perhaps you feel that your child is actually getting worse. Before hospitalizing him, you may want to try increasing the amount of outpatient care he's receiving. His therapy sessions could be increased in frequency, or supplemented by a group experience or a self-help program. If these steps still don't help your child, you should consider an inpatient program.

When Amelia, the anorectic teenager who had been sexually abused by her cousin, was released from her first hospital stay, she attended individual therapy twice a week and a hospital support group once a week. Over time she reduced her individual therapy to once a week and dropped the hospital group altogether.

Amelia was able to maintain her weight and function normally until she saw her cousin making sexual overtures to another, younger cousin. This intensified Amelia's memories of, and feelings about, the abuse; her anorexia reappeared and her depression worsened. As her parents saw their daughter wasting away, they increased her individual therapy to twice a week and had her see a nutritionist once a week. They also increased sessions with the psychiatrist for medication from once every two months to once every two weeks. Amelia also rejoined the eating disorders support group at the hospital and met with her former primary physician twice a month there.

Despite all this help, Amelia made several suicide attempts and inflicted severe self-mutilations which took her to the emergency room more than once. At this point, it became obvious that outpatient help, however intensified, wasn't working. Amelia's condition was actually getting worse. She and her parents were exhausting themselves running from one part of town to another to meet doctors or to attend some form of therapy almost every other day—and Amelia still wasn't getting better.

Another problem concerned coordinating the efforts of all the professionals involved in Amelia's case. Her parents were constantly making phone calls to the therapist, the support group leader, the dietician, the physician, and the psychiatrist, trying to keep them advised of what each of the others had recommended and observed regarding Amelia. Finally the parents arranged a meeting of all the professionals involved (which cost a small fortune). The conclusion reached at this meeting was that it was futile to increase or otherwise intensify Amelia's outpatient care: she needed to be rehospitalized.

John, a seventeen-year-old who had been sexually abused by a male relative from the time he was five until he was twelve, began drinking at the age of nine. His drinking did not interfere with his functioning until he was fifteen, when his grades began to drop and he began showing up late to his part-time job. Soon after his sixteenth birthday, he was arrested three times for driving while intoxicated and lost his license.

Court-ordered to attend Alcoholics Anonymous meetings, John became sober immediately. After nine months of sobriety, he was jubilant; he thought his troubles were over. However, after the "pink cloud" of sobriety, so common to newcomers in AA, drifted away, John began drinking again—first only on weekends, then on a daily basis. Ashamed of his drinking, he stopped attending his AA meetings and eventually landed in jail again after starting a bar-room brawl.

Since no one was seriously injured, John was released on bail. He wanted very much to stop drinking and went back to AA on a daily basis—sometimes attending meetings twice a day. Yet he still had the urge to drink and, all too often, gave in to it. At this point, it was obvious that AA was not enough; John needed an inpatient alcohol rehabilitation program.

How To Assess Inpatient Programs

Inpatient psychiatric programs vary in the age and type of patients they accept and in the length of time they will keep them. Some accept only children; others accept only adolescents or adults; still others accept a variety of age groups. Some units are not specialized and accept patients with a variety of diagnoses. Some treat only nonpsychotic patients; others specialize in psychotic patients. Some facilities do not accept suicidal, aggressive, or acting-out patients or patients who have eating disorders or who are addicted to drugs or alcohol. Others have special facilities for such patients. Drug or alcohol rehabilitation units or eating disorders programs accept only patients with those addictions.

When you are assessing an inpatient unit, it's important to ask about the types and ages of patients accepted on the ward—these people will be your child's companions for a prolonged period of time and will influence his attitude about his recovery. You also have to ask how long the facility will keep your child. Some units keep patients for only thirty days; others for sixty or ninety days. Some programs keep patients up to six, nine, or twelve months, while others, such as state hospitals, will keep a patient for several years, or an entire lifetime if necessary.

You'll probably want to try a three-, six-, or nine-month facility first, unless advised otherwise by a mental health professional. Sending your child to a state hospital or to a year-long "home" for emotionally disturbed children should be a last resort. This option should be considered if and only if

- Your child is unmanageable or dysfunctional in a noncontrolled environment

- Different forms of outpatient therapy have been tried, but have proven ineffective

- At least two certified mental health professionals advise this decision

Thirty-Day Units

Thirty-day psychiatric units, usually called short-term units, exist in both general and psychiatric hospitals. They serve primarily to stabilize the patient, usually following some crisis. Some of these hospitals also have longer-term units (for stays of three to six months) to which a patient can be transferred should he need additional care. A thirty-day unit can provide your child with medication (if needed) and care for any medical problems, can keep him safe from self-injury or from injuring others, and provide him with some counseling. However, in-depth exploration of major issues (such as sexual abuse) will require longer-term care. In some cases, the thirty-day unit serves as a "babysitter" for a child until a bed in a longer-term unit or facility becomes available.

After a crisis such as attempted suicide or self-mutilation, you may be advised to hospitalize your child immediately. Begin by making a list of all facilities in your area. Ask your friends, family doctor, clergyman, or any well-respected therapists you know for recommendations; but also look through the phone book and call your local mental health association for additional listings.

In considering thirty-day units, ask the following questions: How many patients are on the ward and what are their diagnoses? What is the staff-to-patient ratio? Will your child receive medication only or will he also receive psychotherapy? If so, what type is provided? How frequent and how long are the sessions? Sometimes a psychiatrist's five-to-ten-minute bed check is called "psychotherapy," but consists primarily of finding out how the patient is responding to medications. Finding the right medication and the proper dosage is extremely important; however, it's also crucial that your child be helped in understanding the roots of his emotional problems. Such insight cannot be achieved in brief sessions.

Ask who on the staff, if anyone, specializes in the particular symptoms troubling your child and/or in the area of sexual abuse. If your child is going to receive some individual or group psychotherapy from this specialist, will he be able to continue with this therapist or group on an outpatient basis?

What precautions are taken on the ward for the suicidal patient? What protection does your child have from violent or aggressive patients?

Regarding finances—before you sign any papers, find out what your insurance covers and what you will have to cover yourself. Hospitalization insurance does not necessarily cover all costs. For example, most plans distinguish between the cost of the hospital room, the physician's fee, the psychiatrist's fee, and the fees for social workers and/or psychologists—you may be responsible for some of these costs on your own. Some plans cover tutoring or schooling which your child may need or use during his hospitalization. Some do not. Find out the maximum coverage on these various components of hospital care. Inquire if there are any grants available if the noninsured portion of the care is too expensive for you. Keep in mind that most insurance plans have a one-time, maximum figure that they'll pay for any mental illness: it's quite possible to use up the entire allotment in just one hospitalization.

Longer-Term Care

At the outset of hospitalization, you don't have any way of knowing how your child will respond. He may respond so well to treatment that within thirty days he can be discharged to an outpatient therapy program and will not require further hospitalization.

If, however, your child needs more than thirty days of hospitalization, you'll need to consider the various longer-term units available in your area. Once again, make a list of available facilities and begin by using the telephone. Eliminate those facilities that seem inappropriate for your child, and visit the rest in person. Don't exclude facilities that are far from home and will require some driving on your part. Finding the right unit is worth the extra burdens the distance may impose. What you spend in time and effort now may save you not only additional time and effort later, but considerable heartache as well. Remember that your goal is to help your child get better as quickly as possible—not to establish a convenient commute.

While you're visiting various facilities, your child should be somewhere safe and protected. If he's in a thirty-day unit and his time is almost over, perhaps the staff could be persuaded to keep him a few more days until you locate a longer-term facility. If advisable, he could accompany you as you tour the various facilities. Very often a child's perceptions can prove invaluable and, once again, it's very important that your child feel that he has some control over decisions affecting his life.

Evaluating the Appropriateness of a Facility

Before you begin phoning or visiting, have a clear diagnosis or list of your child's symptoms in mind. Since there is no psychiatric disorder called "reaction to sexual abuse," your child could have any one of a number of psychiatric diagnoses—from depression to multiple personality to character disorder. He might have a dual diagnosis such as post-traumatic stress disorder with bulimia, alcohol, or drug abuse.

Learn more about your child's diagnosis by going to the library and checking out a basic book on the subject. Since you'll be dealing with mental health professionals, it's important that you understand what they're talking about. On the other hand, don't let them use their professional jargon to keep you at a disadvantage. It's possible for mental health professionals to discuss your child's diagnosis and still keep the conversation mainly in clear, everyday English. You don't have to become a mental health expert yourself, but you do need to know enough so that if your child is misdiagnosed and subsequently given inappropriate or insufficient treatment, you'll be able to speak on his behalf.

Keep a list of *all* your child's symptoms and concerns in front of you as you inquire about the credentials and experience of the hospital staff. The basic question is whether or not there are staff members who can guide your child step-by-step through the healing process. It doesn't matter whether these people are social workers, psychologists, or psychiatrists; what matters is that they have expertise in sexual abuse and in post-traumatic stress disorder, that they understand the nature of trauma, its psychological consequences, and the healing process.

How were the staff trained? How do they keep up with new developments in the field? How many abuse survivors have they treated or seen on the ward? Are they currently teaching or conducting any research on the topic or in their private practice? Do they conduct in-service training for other staff members on sexual abuse?

If there are staff members who have expertise in the area of sexual abuse, will they be assigned to your child's case automatically, or will you have to make a special request for such an assignment? Exactly how much time per week will your child be spending in individual therapy with a professional who has studied sexual abuse? Will the psychiatrist who sees your child for medication also be conducting the individual therapy? If so, how long and how frequent are the sessions?

What about group therapy? What types are offered on the ward? Are there any groups that focus on sexual abuse? If there are no such groups, is the topic of sexual abuse ever brought up in the general group therapy? Are there any other abuse survivors on the ward, or will your child be alone with this problem? If there are others, why doesn't the facility have a group or program especially for them?

There should be at least one staff member, hopefully more, who specializes not only in sexual abuse, but in the other problems your child might be suffering from, such as depression, addiction, or paranoia.

You'll need to ask many of the same questions about a long-term facility that you had to ask about a short-term one: the number and type of patients on the wards, the staff-to-patient ratio, precautions for the suicidal or aggressive patient, the limits of your insurance coverage, and so on. Ask about other wards in the hospital, too. Suppose your child is diagnosed as having, first, a clinical depression and, second, an addiction or an eating disorder. This means that the clinical depression is considered to be primary and needs to be treated first, before the addiction or eating disorder.

If the facility you're considering has an addiction or eating disorders unit as well as a depression unit, this can be an advantage. Once your child's depression begins to lift, the staff could consider transferring him to their addiction or eating disorders ward. The fact that such a ward exists in the same hospital as a depression ward means that the staff on the depression ward have a good chance of being informed about addictions, too. Even if they aren't, at least there are staff members nearby who are available for consultation.

Ask for a schedule of the unit's activities. How much time is allocated for individual or group therapy? For school or tutoring? For exercise or other forms of recreation? Which activities are mandatory and which are optional? Think about this schedule in terms of your child's needs.

Be wary of any program in which most of the day is spent doing schoolwork, arts and crafts, or recreational sports. These activities are all valuable and necessary, but the emphasis should be on healing your child, not simply maintaining him.

Is family therapy offered? Is it mandatory or optional? What kind of access will you have to your child's primary physician, psychiatrist, and/or therapist? Who will keep you informed of your child's progress, and to whom should you direct your questions? Is there a definite schedule of parent-staff conferences, or will you have to request such conferences yourself?

In some cases, a social worker is assigned the task of handling communications with the family and conducting the family therapy sessions. To avoid issues of confidentiality and conflict of interest, your child's therapist or physician may not become involved with you directly. However, the social worker or some other liaison should be meeting regularly with your child's therapists and doctors and be available to answer your questions. Social workers may also be available to provide supportive therapy for you and/or other members of your family.

Be alert to any pressure tactics on the part of admissions personnel. You may be told, "You'd better decide right now whether or not you want your child admitted here. There have already been three people in here this morning and I have four more tours scheduled this afternoon. Unfortunately, there are only two beds left and I can only hold a bed for you six more hours (or twelve more hours, or one more day)." After your tour, phone the admissions office and the nursing station at the unit you are considering to ask about bed availability and double-check this information.

Remember that *you are the consumer and have every right to information about the facility.* Don't cower before admissions personnel or the professional staff. You have nothing to hide or be ashamed of. The fact that your child needs hospitalization does not mean that you are a failure as a parent or that your child is "inferior" or "defective."

Countless children and adults in this country are troubled and need help. The real tragedy is not that your child needs help, but that most abused children in need of help never receive it and live most of their lives crippled by their experiences. Instead of berating yourself for having a child who needs hospitalization, congratulate yourself on having the courage to reach out for help. Also give yourself a pat on the back for having the willingness and unselfishness to shoulder all the many tasks and expenses involved in finding the best possible care for the child you love so much.

Don't be afraid to ask questions. The hospital staff should know that parents are not mental health experts and that families come to their hospital anguished, exhausted, and confused.

The manner in which the hospital staff treats you may give you an indication of how your child will be treated as well. If you are treated with respect, as a person in pain who is acting responsibly, it's to be hoped that your child will be treated with respect, too. The last thing he needs is to be treated like someone who is less worthy than others.

Your child's dignity was trampled on when he was abused. His hospitalization should help rebuild and promote his dignity, not erode it further. If many people on the staff treat you or your child with contempt or condescension, consider going elsewhere.

Assessing Eating Disorders Programs*

Obesity, compulsive overeating, bulimia, and anorexia are psychologically debilitating and life-threatening problems. In some cases the diagnoses of bulimia and anorexia can overlap one another; patients with these problems may also be diagnosed with multiple personality or depression. All of these problems can be addressed in one program for eating disorders.

A solid eating disorders program has two components: symptom management and in-depth or insight therapy. Symptom management means that your child will be prevented (as much as possible) from practicing her eating disorder and encouraged to eat sanely. Insight therapy means that she'll learn to identify and own her feelings, and

---

*Since the majority of children with eating disorders are female, I'm breaking the pattern in this section by using feminine pronouns.

find more constructive ways of coping with stress and her own emotions.

Don't let anyone persuade you that your child's eating disorder is "not that important" or that it will go away once insight therapy has begun. Eating disorders, like drug and alcohol addictions, are self-perpetuating, vicious cycles that only grow worse when left untreated.

More than self-knowledge or insight is required to overcome an eating disorder. The body must be restored to health, not only for physical or medical reasons, but for psychological ones as well. The starved state of the anorectic and the bulimic may not only reflect emotional problems and depression, but may actually create the mood swings, personal insecurities, and despondency that can appear as a psychiatric disorder.

For your child to be accurately diagnosed, her eating disorder first needs to come under some control. Otherwise it's too easy to confuse the effects of the eating disorder with its causes.

Symptom Management

Keep these things in mind as you observe the hospital staff's management of your child's symptoms.

At least initially, all her eating should be strictly supervised, bathrooms should be locked, and she should have no access to her individual binge foods or other foods which might cause her to overeat. She should not be allowed to go to the bathroom alone until she has earned the right. Nurses or trained paraprofessionals should watch and keep track of everything your child eats, make sure that she eats all that she's supposed to be eating, then stay with her for up to an entire hour after the meal to make sure that she keeps the food down. She will usually be asked to rest after each meal with a professional nearby in case she needs to talk.

She may need to talk after eating because, often, the process of ingesting a full-sized meal will cause her considerable anxiety. If she is anorectic, she will probably worry about getting fat. If she is bulimic, she is used to overeating and throwing up. Without self-starvation or purging as coping mechanisms, all the feelings that have been suppressed via the eating disorder will begin to emerge. Your child will need support as she faces her feelings "in the raw."

She will also become anxious, if not panicked, when she begins to gain weight on the ward. She needs to be reassured that even though she may initially gain some weight, she will not get fat. Her ward needs to be set up to handle her panic as she puts on weight.

Dealing with this panic is an important part of therapy, because the road to recovery involves examining the meaning of her intense fear of being fat and her compulsive need to be "thin." Your child needs help in confronting what body size means to her in terms of her self-esteem and her identity as a person and a sexual being.

In some of the better eating disorders units, patients are warned that they might panic when the scale begins to change, but are assured that they will be helped in dealing with these feelings.

Other issues with which the staff should be familiar (or have special groups for) are body imaging, assertiveness training, and women's issues. Usually it's in the women's issues groups that sexual abuse is discussed. In some eating disorders units, it's not uncommon for over half, if not more, of the women to have been sexually assaulted.

Most important of all, the individual or group therapy should address the relationship of the eating disorder to your child's experience of sexual abuse. To what extent is the eating disorder a means of coping with the self-hatred, rage, grief, and other feelings associated with the abuse? To what extent is the eating disorder a means of punishing her sexual self, the abuser, or somebody else? Is the powerlessness with respect to food in any way a reenactment of the powerlessness experienced during the abuse? It's essential that these and other related questions be addressed.

Ask how the therapists on a prospective ward handle weight-gain panic, body image distortions, and the other issues listed above—especially sexual abuse. If they don't know what you're talking about, consider another facility.

Assessing Drug and Alcohol Treatment Units

There are many more drug and alcohol inpatient facilities than eating disorders units. These drug and alcohol rehabilitation programs vary in approach. Some are more confrontational than others. Some work on the theory that alcoholism and drug addiction are diseases. Still others focus more on psychological factors. Some facilities separate alcoholics from drug addicts, and others separate cocaine abusers from other types of drug addicts.

Since many drug addicts also abuse alcohol, and many drug addicts are addicted to more than one drug (possibly including alcohol), it's important to inquire whether the unit you're considering for your child combines dual or poly-addicted patients with singly addicted ones, and whether or not the staff has expertise in dealing with the category of substance abuse that covers your child.

Since cocaine addicts have special needs and are often disruptive when mixed with noncocaine abusers, you many want to eliminate from your consideration programs that have a high number of cocaine abusers (if cocaine abuse is not one of your child's substance problems). See the section below, "The Special Case of Cocaine," for further discussion of this issue.

Whatever the structure and constituency of the unit, it's critical that it be more than a babysitting operation. The rehabilitation program should contain the following components: education about drugs and alcohol, medical back-up, psychiatric assessment and consultation, nutritional education, individual and group therapy as well as family counseling, and recovery coping skills training or relapse prevention. Ideally, an aftercare program should also be available.

Education About Drugs and Alcohol

The unit should offer lectures, as well as written material, about the nature of alcohol and the various drugs, and the medical, psychological, and other consequences of prolonged use. In my opinion, the disease concept should be a part of these lectures, as well as a description of the dynamics of alcoholism and drug addiction. The information should emphasize the progressive nature of addiction and explain how addiction can grow from a small "habit" to an entire way of life.

There should be open discussion, charts, and pamphlets on the unit which clearly show your child the potential effects of the changes in biochemistry, personality, and life-style which attend habitual abuse and how these can establish a vicious, ever-escalating cycle. Your child should be taught to understand potential consequences: not only financial ruin, but physical deterioration, the loss of significant relationships, and even death.

It's also desirable for family members to be involved in the educational component of the program.

Medical Back-up

If your child is chemically dependent, it's highly possible that he suffers from a medical problem as a result of his substance abuse. As has been emphasized in this book, a complete medical examination is a necessity. More and more studies are revealing that psychologically troubled individuals, as well as substance abusers, often suffer from a medical problem which either contributes to, or compounds, the psychological difficulty and/or addiction.

Psychiatric Assessment and Consultation

Do not enroll your child in any unit that lacks a psychiatrist. A complete psychiatric assessment is necessary to determine if your child has a problem in addition to the substance abuse, such as depression or panic disorder. However, people who are actively drinking should not be given a psychiatric diagnosis until they have been sober for a while. It's not a good idea to diagnose a new alcoholic admission and prescribe medication until he has "dried out." Alcohol abuse may simulate psychiatric symptoms that will disappear once the person is sober. However, other individuals may have a diagnosis of both alcoholism and a psychiatric problem. If this is the case for your child, he must get treatment that addresses both components.

Psychiatric assessment and consultation are necessary before the proper medication can be prescribed for your child. Certain psychotropic drugs are now increasingly being used (with great success in some cases) to help reduce the cravings and other painful side effects of withdrawal from drugs. Some of the psychotropic drugs have proven effective in reducing the craving and compulsiveness that form the root of the addiction.

Nutritional Information

Many chemically dependent children are malnourished. Like the eating disordered child, the chemically dependent child needs to learn how to eat, and what to eat.

Sound nutrition is necessary, not only to restore physical health, but mental balance as well. If your child has been feeding himself with drugs and alcohol rather than with healthy foods, then he may be suffering physiologically from some of the same problems as children with severe eating disorders. Alcohol and other drugs are notorious for seriously disturbing electrolyte balance, cell functioning, and certain vitamin supplies. The malnutrition will not only prematurely age your child, but will contribute to his anxiety, depression, mood swings, and inability to concentrate.

If your child is seriously malnourished, he may be given megadoses of vitamins, or even injections of certain B vitamins. Depletion of these vitamins, which is very common in alcoholics, contributes to the "jitters" and nervous tension. A nutritionist or dietician needs to be part of your child's inpatient program.

Individual and Group Counseling

As with eating disorders, simply depriving your child of the abused substance and cleansing his body of toxins is not enough. Counseling is necessary to help him become aware of why he abused drugs or alcohol in the first place, what behaviors can be substituted for the comfort provided by the substance, and what the warning signs are that he might be "slipping" into addiction once again. Counseling may also be necessary to educate family members about addiction, improve communication within the family, and examine any family issues that may be contributing to the substance abuse.

Ideally, AA and/or NA meetings, as well as Al-Anon and/or Nar-a-non meetings, are part of the rehabilitation process. If these meetings are not available on the unit, perhaps transportation to such meetings is available. Look into the options. This is a very helpful part of your child's recovery program.

Warning: Because courts are now increasingly requiring attendance at AA or NA meetings, some meetings are filled with people who are there not because they want to be, but rather because they're being forced to attend. Such meetings may or may not carry the spirit of the program, and may be harmful to your child if he picks up the attitude that the meetings are like unwanted "homework." It's not unheard-of for drugs and alcohol to be passed around after these meetings by resentful court-ordered attendees.

The best AA and NA meetings are those which are dominated by individuals who are sincere about their recovery and who are attending because they want to get better.

Recovery Coping Skills: Preventing Relapse

To prevent relapse, your child needs to learn coping skills such as those described in Chapter 6. In addition, the treatment program should help him plan how he will use his leisure time, how he will cope with former friends who are still drinking or using drugs, how he will develop new friendships, and how he will handle "slippery" times and places.

Aftercare

You need to inquire about the unit's aftercare program. Do they have one, or do they refer your child to another institution for aftercare? Where should your child go if he relapses? Will the same unit readmit him, or will they suggest another unit?

Good aftercare is designed to prevent relapses. It usually includes gradually decreasing attendance in an outpatient group or individual therapy sessions. If the unit has an AA and/or NA meeting as part of its program, it may be suggested that your child continue attending those meetings to maintain a link with the unit. Attending meetings outside the unit should not be discouraged, however.

If there is no aftercare program directly connected with the unit, there should be an aftercare plan which includes provisions for continued individual and/or group therapy, continued psychiatric monitoring of any medications, and continued involvement in developing coping skills. For example, it may be suggested that your child take an assertiveness training course, a course in communication, and so on.

The Special Case of Cocaine

Many drug rehabilitation programs are now recognizing the special needs of cocaine abusers. Whereas in previous times all drug abusers were mixed together, an increasing number of units now exist that specialize in cocaine rehabilitation. If your child abuses cocaine, a specialized unit would be ideal. However, if no such unit exists in your area, you need at least to find a drug rehabilitation program where there is awareness of the special problems faced by cocaine abusers.

Cocaine abuse is extremely serious. Compared to alcohol, the overdose potential is very high. One must drink a lot of alcohol before one dies of it. With cocaine, however, overdosing is an ever-present possibility. In the first place, one never knows what type of cocaine one is buying: how potent it is, or what other drugs are combined with it. Second, compared to other drugs, cocaine is rapidly addictive. Preliminary research shows, for example, that experimental rats will work harder for cocaine than for alcohol or for any other drug. They have been found to keep ingesting increasing doses of cocaine until they die.[1]

Some of the usual psychological effects of cocaine abuse—suspiciousness, paranoia, hallucinations, grandiosity, and arrogance—have important implications for treatment: For example, cocaine abusers often feel that they're "special" and "better" than heroin or alcohol abusers. They tend to dominate and otherwise not function well in groups with other types of substance abusers, and can easily become enmeshed in power struggles with the staff. If the staff is not well-trained in the area of cocaine abuse, they may find a disproportionate amount of their time spent in conflicts with cocaine abusers, to the detriment of the entire ward. Units sensitive to the characteristics of cocaine abuse will organize their programs to counteract these influences.[2]

On such units, the staff doesn't blame the cocaine abuser for acting like a cocaine abuser. Understanding the dynamics of the typical cocaine abuser, the staff avoids contests of will and tries to give the cocaine addict some measure of control over his treatment. The addict may be asked for suggestions for group topics, group structure, and so on.

The staff will also understand that cocaine addicts face enormous hurdles in overcoming their addiction, since cocaine is a highly reinforcing drug and the craving for it is much more intense and prolonged than the craving for alcohol or other drugs. In many cases, recovery is harder because it's very difficult to find activities and relationships that are as reinforcing and pleasurable as cocaine. This is particularly true if the addict comes from a background where cocaine is an acceptable recreational drug.

Recovery is also complicated because of the depression that often accompanies cocaine withdrawal; and because so many cocaine addicts are cross-addicted to alcohol and/or marijuana. The depression needs attention, as does any alcoholism or other drug addiction. Even more than other recovering substance abusers, cocaine addicts need expert psychiatric assessment and diagnosis with a good medication program. They need intensive work in developing coping skills such as relaxation techniques, assertiveness training, and goal setting if they are to sustain their desire to stay in recovery. In addition, the underlying issue of sexual abuse needs to be discussed at least in individual counseling if not in a "special issues" group on the ward.

Keeping Your Options Open

If you decide that your child needs hospitalization, try not to think of it as a setback, but rather as another step forward in the healing process. Indeed, that is what it is. You are taking the very courageous step of admitting that your child needs a "time-out" from the world in order to gather his strength and continue healing.

If your child is coping reasonably well on an outpatient basis, you are both lucky. If things get worse, remember that hospitalization is an option. Knowing this can ease your mind during those long weeks when it seems as if your child's symptoms will never get better. Don't ever give up hope. Recovery will come—either on an outpatient basis, or in a hospital setting if this is what it takes. The important thing is that your child is on the road to recovery and you are helping him along that road in any way you can.

9

When Hospitalization Is Necessary and Afterwards

Think of the words "mental hospital." What image do they conjure up in your mind? Tormented individuals chained to walls? Shabbily dressed people so drugged that they seem to be walking zombies? Such is the heritage of the days when mental illness was misunderstood and when mental institutions were worse than prisons.

While in the past, conditions in psychiatric facilities were certainly deplorable, if not horrendous, today most facilities are caring, humane places where people go to be helped. There may remain some old-fashioned horror hospitals—but you will make sure that your child doesn't go there. Use the guidelines in this book to evaluate hospitals and help you pick the right one for your child.

Preparing Your Child for Hospitalization

You'll probably need to reassure your child that being hospitalized doesn't mean that she's "crazy." Explain over and over that she needs extra care due to the stress she has endured over the sexual abuse. You'll also have to reassure her about the facility you've chosen. Emphasize that it's a place of rest and hope where she can have a "time-out" from the world to get herself together. Give her your word that if the facility proves not to be right for her, you'll find another place for her recovery.

"If you broke your leg, you would have to be in a cast for a few months to let your leg rest and heal, wouldn't you? When you were sexually abused, your abuser broke your spirit. Going to a hospital for a while is like putting your spirit in a safe place so that it can heal

"Just as a broken leg doesn't stay in a cast forever, you won't be in a hospital forever either. But you need to be in one for a while. Just as it's hard for a broken leg to heal if you go on running around on it, it's hard for your emotions to heal from abuse if you're trying to cope with the pressures of regular life.

"Anyone who has gone through what you've gone through deserves a little rest just to focus on herself and get over the trauma. Instead of being ashamed that you're in a hospital, let's be grateful that such places exist and can help you."

If your child is male, he may feel especially humiliated and ashamed of needing to be hospitalized. If Jeb had needed to be hospitalized, for example, most likely he would have interpreted his hospitalization as yet another sign that he was "weak" or "unmanly," since he couldn't cope with his problems on his own.

Your son will need extra assurances and extra explanations regarding the necessity for and nature of hospitalization. He may need to be reminded that hospitalization is temporary and that male sexual abuse is widespread, more widespread than has been previously thought. If you know for a fact that there are other male sexual abuse survivors on your child's ward or somewhere in the facility, or that male victims have been treated there in the past, be sure to mention this to your son so that he doesn't feel so alone with his problem.

If, however, he's the only, or one of the only, male abuse survivors on the unit or in the facility, emphasize that there are many boys who have been abused, but only a few are fortunate enough to get the help they need. Also, it's highly likely that some of the hospitalized males in the facility have been abused but either have repressed the memory or are too ashamed to admit it. Or perhaps they've accepted the erroneous attitude, so prevalent in our society, that sexual activity—regardless of its form—is not abusive to males, only to females.

If your son is going to a therapy group composed predominantly of female abuse survivors, explain that this does not mean that he is "like a girl." As obvious as this might be to you, he needs to hear it put into words.

You could say, "There are more girls than boys in your group because sexual abuse happens even more to girls than it does to boys and because girls, more often than boys, admit to their problems. This doesn't mean that you are a girl, a queer, a weakling, a sissy, or anything like that. It means that you are being very brave—just like all the others in your group—and facing some of the same experiences and feelings...painful feelings like fear, anger, loss, and shame.

"Some of these girls may hate all boys and men right now because of what they have been through. Maybe you can show them that boys have feelings, too, so that these girls will understand that good, strong boys like you exist in this world as well."

To further prepare your child for hospitalization, explain that hospitals have many rules, some of which may seem overly restrictive but which are necessary because the hospital needs to take care of and protect so many different kinds of people. Your child will not have to follow such rules forever, just for a while.

Visitation

Do not be surprised if, when you get home after admitting your child into a hospital or psychiatric ward, you feel so relieved that she is in somebody else's charge, and that you are no longer responsible for her daily, minute-by-minute care, that you want to forget all about her and her problems for a while, maybe even for a long time.

"Thank goodness! I can take a rest," you might think, with a sigh of relief.

If your child was suicidal and suffering terribly as a result of the abuse, it is certainly true that it's easier for you to have her hospitalized than to witness her daily pain and feel so limited in your ability to help. However, your role as your child's caretaker is not over, not even when she is under the care of qualified physicians and therapists. While her hospitalization may grant you a "mini-vacation" from the work, self-sacrifice, and pain involved in having a child who is suffering from the consequences of sexual abuse, there is no true "vacation" or rest from concern, worry, effort (and those endless phone calls!) until your child has begun to heal in substantial ways.

One of your first jobs is to decide when and how often you'll visit your child. With these visits, you show your support. They also afford you the opportunity to listen to her reactions to the facility, to assess her progress, and to communicate with the staff.

Your presence on the ward will tell the staff that your child has a family behind her, which in subtle ways gives her a higher status and more prestige than a child whose family never comes to visit, or rarely shows any concern. Also, the staff may treat your child better because they know that someone is watching out for her and that she has someone to complain to if their services fall short.

Go over visiting hours or telephone regulations with your child. Even if she acts like she doesn't care when or whether or not you write, call, or visit, in truth she does care. Regardless of their ages, children often suffer separation anxiety when they are hospitalized.

As much as they may hate to admit it, even teens and preteens come to miss their families. Be specific with your child about how she can reach you and about when you can or cannot visit.

Assure your child that you will be in touch with her as often as you can be. Even if you can't visit often, tell her that you'll call frequently and keep in touch with the staff so that you know how she's progressing. And make sure you do it! Encourage her to contact you if something happens in the hospital that disturbs her.

You may want to work out a plan for your child to keep in touch with some of her friends. Does she want to telephone them herself or can you help by contacting a few for her? Do her friends have transportation or could you help by bringing some to the hospital when you go to visit? You could work out a time schedule where she can visit first alone with you and then with her friends.

There may be people whom you or your child do not want to know about the hospitalization. Decide, with your child, what you will tell these people should they ask about her. Hopefully the decision can be discussed with your child without her getting the feeling that hospitalization is in any way "shameful."

Schoolwork

The hospital may have a school or tutoring program in which your child can participate. However, your child's main purpose in the hospital is to begin to overcome her sexual trauma, not to make good grades. Keeping up with her schoolwork is secondary to taking advantage of the therapeutic opportunities in the hospital.

Schoolwork can always be made up later. Your child's academic and intellectual prospects and skills will not suffer permanent damage if she misses a semester—or even a year—of schooling. Her abilities will, however, be impaired if she doesn't learn to deal with her traumatic feelings constructively. If she continues to be depressed or engages in self-defeating behaviors because she has not made headway on resolving her problems, her academic and, later, her vocational successes will be significantly lessened, no matter how hard she tries.

Common Complaints of the Hospitalized Child

No matter how agreeable a child is about going to a hospital, once she's there, it's common for her to want to leave within a few days.

After the initial relief of being in a protected and controlled environment, your child may start to feel confined. "Get me out of here, Mom," she may plead. "Please, Mom, please. I hate it here!"

It's extremely difficult to ignore such pleas. Realize, however, that they're often a normal part of the process of a person's initial adjustment to hospitalization. You want to be supportive, but not to the point of taking your child out of the hospital before she's really had time to adjust.

"But you said if I didn't like it, I could leave. And you said if they were mean to me, to tell you. Well, nurse so-and-so did such and such, and Dr. X did this or that. Get me out of here, Mom, please. Please. Please."

Take a notepad and write down all of your child's complaints. Read them back to her so that she knows you've been listening. Then ask if she left anything out. Tell her you'll continue to listen to, and document, all her grievances. Then explain that there's an adjustment period to any change. While it may be hard to be in the hospital, and while nurse so-and-so really did do such and such, it's necessary to give the hospital (and nurse so-and-so) a chance. If the situation doesn't improve, then you'll consider finding a new facility.

Your Role as Case Manager

Understanding the Roles of Different Helping Professionals

Once your child is hospitalized, one of your most important roles will become that of case manager. A case manager is someone who supervises the treatment of a patient, checks schedules, keeps an eye on the daily interactions of the various professionals working with that patient, and also provides feedback from the professionals to the patient and vice versa. That's your job.

Most likely your child is being seen by at least a medical doctor, a psychiatrist, a psychologist, and/or a psychiatric or regular social worker. She is also perhaps being seen by a family therapist, a psychiatric nurse, students of various sorts, and volunteers. She may be confused about the role of each of these people; it may be up to you to explain how they are different and how their jobs overlap.

Don't be surprised if at first you yourself feel unclear about how all these different people function. There is considerable overlap in the functions of various mental health professionals. In addition, the roles of each professional may vary from one setting to another. In some settings social workers conduct therapy; in other settings social workers only make practical arrangements for insurance payments, aftercare, and so on; and in other settings they do both. Sometimes psychiatrists are concerned only with prescribing and monitoring psychiatric medication and are members—not leaders—of the treatment team. Other times, psychiatrists not only handle medication but conduct individual and/or group therapy and serve as leaders of the team.

Quite understandably, you may need to ask a staff member to clarify the functions of the various professionals in the particular facility you've chosen. Also find out how often your child can expect to be visited by each of these professionals, what the system is, and other relevant details. Both of you need to know what to expect from each professional. If interns or nursing, psychology, or social work students are also seeing your child, ask for the names of the students' supervisors and find out how much supervision those supervisors will be giving. If a problem arises, you may need to speak with both the student and the student's supervisor.

Communication Among Different Members of the Hospital Staff

Most well-run psychiatric or recovery units have weekly or even bi-weekly staff meetings during which each case is reviewed and each professional involved shares his or her perceptions of a particular patient's progress and makes recommendations for the patient's treatment. However, staff time is limited, and important points can be overlooked in the staff meeting. Or perhaps a member of the psychiatric care team is out.

There may also be communication problems among the staff. After all, they are human, too. They may not hear everything that is being shared about your child at the staff meeting or they may fail to follow up on some of the recommendations made. This does not necessarily mean that they're incompetent, only that they're fallible. If, for some reason, the facility is short-staffed or under some other pressure, there may not be time to discuss all the relevant points about your child in the meeting, or the staff may be too overworked to do its best job.

For these reasons, it's important that you don't assume that because your child is in a hospital, you don't have to do anything except visit her a few times, say "I love you," and then go home. Once you suspect that one or more of the professionals does not seem to be working in coordination with the others, or if you or your child become confused about how a certain issue is handled, it's time to ask the professionals involved to clarify what is happening.

It may be that your child has gotten mixed up, or perhaps you've misunderstood some ground rules or points of procedure. Or there may be a communication problem between the professionals, in which case you will have to ask them to improve their communication mechanisms and to give special attention to your child's case at their next staff meeting in order to correct the problem.

Your Role as Liaison

In the meantime, you may have to serve as a sort of messenger, asking Dr. X to call Dr. Y and Dr. Y to get back to Ms. L; or call them all yourself so that everybody is informed about a problem, whether it's a change in medication, a new therapeutic activity, or an issue raised in group.

In addition, you need to play an active role in making sure that all the professionals agree on the goals for your child and that they are aware of each other's treatment plans and methods of operation. Get the name of your child's case leader and inquire of that person:

- What are the treatment goals?
- What is the treatment plan?
- How often does the team meet, and when?
- What can I do to help?

Write down the answers to these questions and read them back to the case leader to be certain that you have heard correctly. If you don't understand what you've been told, don't hesitate to ask the questions again. You may need to be bolder than you ever thought possible. Remember, this is your child and you are paying these people to help her. You are entitled to have at least an outline of their treatment purposes and strategies.

Your Input as Part of the Treatment Team

You may also wish to suggest treatment goals or strategies that you feel could help. Even though you may not be a trained mental health professional, you probably have many sound ideas about what will and won't work with your child. Don't be afraid to bring up your ideas or to suggest treatments you've learned about that you think might work. The professionals you're working with should appreciate your involvement.

It's important to talk to the staff about your ideas before your child is discharged. You don't want to wonder afterwards, "Why didn't they try this? Would my child have been better off if they had done such and such? I wonder if they realize that she really hated that and would have responded better if they had done this?"

Bring it up. Talk it over with your child's team; it could be valuable input. For example, your child may be having difficulty remembering the abuse, especially if she was abused violently or when she was very young; and you've just read an article on the use of hypnosis to bring memories to the surface. You may wonder why the hospital staff isn't planning to hypnotise your child to help her remember the abuse. It may be that the staff feels that your child is not yet ready emotionally to handle her memories and that a slower approach is better for her. But it's better to mention your ideas and be advised of the staff's rationales than to think that your child was denied the benefits of a treatment simply because the facility was unaware of it, did not have the necessary tools, or was too stingy to pay for an outside consultant.

Your Role in "Policing" the Staff

Once you're clear about the treatment goals and plans for your child, be on the alert for any discrepancies between what is going on in the hospital and the treatment objectives and methods. For example, some abused children need help in building their defenses toward others and in not making themselves vulnerable. Others need help in letting down the walls they have built to shut others out and to practice sharing openly.

Suppose your child has been a wall-builder and needs help opening up about her feelings. Yet she tells you that the group leader accused her of talking too much and told her that she needed to learn how to restrain herself from taking up too much time in group. Your child tells you that she was sharing something important, which—she thought—was the purpose of group therapy.

Don't jump to conclusions until you gather some more information. Ask your child to explain more fully the nature of the group session, and ask the therapist if he or she recalls this specific incident and the reasons for it. It may be that your child was monopolizing the group when another member was in obvious crisis. Or it may be that the therapist was unaware that self-expression was a treatment objective for your child. If the latter is the case, your role as case manager is to bring the episode to the attention of the team leader.

Just as you need to be aware of the discrepancies between treatment goals and methods and occurrences on the ward, you also need to keep an eye out for staff rivalries. Sometimes, for one reason or another, some staff members may be working at cross purposes or undercutting each other—not from lack of communication, but because of personal hostility or competitiveness. This doesn't happen often, but it does happen and you should be alert to the possibility. If you think this might be a problem, ask if disagreements exist between the team members. Are they honest differences of opinion that can be worked out in a team spirit? If so, fine. If not, then you need to be very clear about what is happening and demand from the team leader that the whole team make an effort to work as a unit for the benefit of your child and other patients on the ward.

Make sure that you are kept up to date on what is going on with your child. What new treatments, medications, or therapies are being tried? What changes in staff or procedures may affect your child? Remember that ultimately the staff—no matter how well-intentioned—is limited in its commitment to your child. Staff members all have other lives, other responsibilities, other patients. You, on the other hand, are concerned only with your child. Involvement and vigilance on your part can significantly contribute to the speed and success of your child's recovery.

Aftercare

Being Supportive

It's not within your power to prevent your child from relapsing after discharge. Relapses do occur. You can, however, be as supportive as possible and be willing to provide your child with the best psychological, psychiatric, or other aftercare you can find. You can support her therapy and progress by preparing her for the realization that adjusting to "normal life" after a period of hospitalization is going to be difficult; and that the process of growth and recovery will be punctuated by inevitable "slips."

Your child has learned new coping skills while hospitalized. As she practices these skills in the real world, she may experience many successes that will thrill her. However, she will undoubtedly regress at times, falling back into her old self-defeating ways. While she may have dreamt that the hospital would fix her forever and that she would never again have to struggle or feel beaten, she needs to know that a few slips are inevitable and will not seriously hold her back from achieving a full and happy life.

You can keep your child from interpreting these slips as indications that the hospitalization and therapy didn't "work." She needs to understand that such slips are normal in the healing process. You can help her keep her periods of backsliding in perspective by using the analogy of a baby who is learning to walk. First the baby crawls, then she stands, then she takes her first step. In the process, she falls over and over again—but that doesn't mean that she's not making good progress toward learning to walk. No one can learn to walk without falling—and failing—many times.

Your child may be trying to learn some new, positive behavior, such as being more assertive and saying "no" to unwanted friendships, activities, or invitations. Just because she sometimes gives in to peer pressure doesn't mean that she has totally regressed to her old, people-pleasing ways. The fact that she has, on other occasions, exercised her freedom to say "no" indicates that she's making progress. She may sometimes find herself doing what her friends want rather than what she feels is best for her. This doesn't take away from the basic fact that, for perhaps the first time in her life, she's actually aware of her choices. With some encouragement and practice, she will be able to make better choices for herself in the future.

Next time she may be able to say "no." Such courage does not develop all at once. It comes slowly, over time. In a parallel manner, body muscles develop slowly over time. Daily exercise is desirable, but missing a day or two of exercise does not mean that the positive effects of the previous exercise have been lost.

Coping With Change

Another issue with which your child will be confronted after discharge is the fact that she has changed. Her interests, personality, and outlook on life may be substantially different as a result of therapy. Perhaps she was depressed and now her depression has lifted somewhat; or she may have more energy and become involved in new activities. Her sleeping and eating habits may also have changed.

At times she may be frightened by these changes, even if they're what she wanted. Reassure her that such changes are positive signs of growth. Warn her that other people may need some time to get used to the "new" her. Even you will need to take time to know your new and developing child. Be prepared to see changes in her schedule, friendships, and patterns of relating to you and other family members. If all this is a bit much for you to get used to, consider talking with a friend or a therapist. Remember—change, even positive change, is stressful; and you have to take care of yourself as well as your child.

10

Handling Feelings

It's perfectly normal for you to experience a variety of strong feelings as a result of your child's victimization: anger at the perpetrator, yourself, and your child; a sense of powerlessness over the abuse itself as well as about your child's recovery and his future safety; guilt and shame; resentment and exhaustion in the face of the financial and emotional strains. All of these reactions swirl around you, threatening your emotional equilibrium. This is all normal. Everyone in similar situations goes through what you are going through and feels what you feel.

There is no way to minimize or avoid the anger, pain, shame, or guilt. These feelings will only get worse if you try to ignore them. You have to acknowledge and cope with them—all of them—as best you can.

Anger at the Perpetrator

Your anger at the perpetuator is normal. In fact, it would be abnormal for you not to harbor a deep resentment toward this individual who violated your child and robbed you all of so much. Even if your religious or spiritual beliefs include forgiveness of one's enemies, you will probably experience more than one bout of deep, abiding rage toward the abuser. This anger may be experienced not only when you are thinking about your child and what happened to him, but at other times of the day—especially when you encounter a person, place, or situation that somehow reminds you of what happened to your child. Jeb's father was an avid church-goer who strongly believed in forgiveness of one's enemies. On Sundays he would say prayers for Mr. R., the cub scout master who had sexually abused his son; but on Wednesday nights—the night when the cub scouts used to meet—Mr. Jones would find himself filled with hate and often prayed that Mr. R. would either die or be castrated.

News stories, magazine articles, or media presentations about sex abuse may also trigger your anger, as will any off-color jokes about incest or other forms of sexual abuse. You may become especially incensed when you read or hear about offenders who receive light sentences or no sentence at all.

But no rage will match the rage you feel when you see your child somehow stunted emotionally, physically, socially, intellectually, or spiritually by his experience. You may even, like Jeb's father, want to kill the offender or wish upon him incredible evil. Such a reaction is normal: you are not an evil person for wanting the offender to hurt just as he hurt your child. But revenge doesn't work. Ultimately, you will only be doing more harm to yourself and your child if you act on your rage and take justice into your own hands.

Your anger at the perpetrator may be with you until the day you die. It will ease somewhat and possibly you will only experience widely spaced moments of intense rage. But be prepared to feel the anger over and over again. It won't last as long and it won't always be so powerful, but there will be times when it pops up. You can make the anger more manageable and take action to prevent your anger from harming you or your child. You can't make it disappear forever, but you can channel it so that you learn to cope with it constructively.

The first step is to realize that, regardless of your religious or spiritual orientation, you have a right to be angry. Then allow yourself to feel that anger when it arises. Since many of us have been taught that anger is "bad," it may be a triumph for you just to be able to recognize how angry you really are and to accept it.

The next step is to release your anger physically. All emotions have a physical component, but especially anger and rage. When you are angry, your adrenaline and blood pressure levels rise. There is an increase in your energy level that needs to be released. You may want to punch pillows with your fists or go to the nearest track and run and run and run. What you need first is constant, sustained physical activity. Then you can ease yourself into step two, which may be a violent spring housecleaning or a six-hour stint of yard work. Turn that energy to a safe channel (and accomplish something positive at the same time). You can use the techniques suggested in Chapter 6.

Jeb's father found that while prayer was essential for his serenity, it was not enough to get rid of his anger. He found that he needed to join an exercise club as well. This helped to dissipate his anger and helped him lose a few extra inches around his waist—inches he had halfheartedly been trying to take off for some time. This gave him a faint sense of accomplishment and put him a little more in control of his life.

When you have tired yourself sufficiently to feel in control of your physical body, try writing about your emotions, or rant and rave into a tape recorder. The important thing about this step is to verbalize your feelings. Be sure to erase the tape later so that your child doesn't come across it. Your anger may be threatening to him.

If you are someone who has tended to suppress anger, you may fear dealing with it: perhaps you're overwhelmed with the prospect of dealing not just with your anger at your child's abuser, but with years of stored-up hurts and resentments about other issues. You don't have to deal with all your anger at once. You can deal with it in smaller, more manageable doses. Acknowledging anger does not mean acting on it. It means learning to channel it. It does not have to control you.

If you're very afraid of all that pent-up anger, you may want to turn to a therapist or a trusted, nonjudgmental friend on whom you can unload.

Powerlessness

Your child's situation has spurred you to action and has probably even increased your feelings of love and protectiveness toward him. Yet on some level you realize that you're powerless. You've tried to provide the best doctors and therapy programs you can find. You've tried as hard as possible to be understanding and supportive; you have put aside much, if not most, of your personal life to deal with this crisis. Yet all your efforts and sacrifices cannot guarantee your child's recovery and future well-being. If he is not responding well to treatment, you may feel particularly frustrated and discouraged.

You may also feel powerless because your child was abused in the first place. However, powerlessness in the past does not necessitate powerlessness in the present. While you were unable to protect your child in the past, in the present you can and must continue to do all you can to help strengthen him and protect him from any further abuse. In a parallel manner, in his therapy he should be learning that while he was powerless to stop the abuse, he is far from powerless in working toward healing and his own personal happiness.

A danger for both you and your child is that the feelings of powerlessness that stem from the abuse may spill over into other situations in which you and he are *not* powerless. Remember, what is past is over with; it cannot be changed. But you can be strong enough to do the best you can for your child and yourself *now*. You are not powerless. Look at all you are accomplishing. You have read this book to learn what to do. You have pondered how best to get help for your child. You have decided to try to control your feelings and help your child in every possible way so that you both can get on with your lives. That is very powerful work you're doing. Give yourself credit for it; draw strength from it.

Shame, Guilt, and Self-Punishment

Rationally, it makes no sense for you to feel ashamed or guilty about the fact that your child was sexually abused. Emotionally, however, you—like your child—may feel ashamed or guilty because of the shame and guilt associated with sexual abuse and sexuality in general in our culture. This is especially the case if you and/or your child are female, because females, more than males, are taught to be ashamed of their sexual organs and their sexual desires.

Just as your child will learn in therapy that his sexual feelings and sexual attractiveness were not the causes of the abuse, it's important for you to remember that your sexual thoughts, fantasies, or behavior in the past did not precipitate the abuse either. The abuse was the result of another person's desires and actions: his motivational system was not connected to your inner or outer life or that of your child. Nothing about your personality, thoughts, or behaviors caused the crime.

Even if you have fantasized about violent sexual acts, sexual acts involving children, or sexual behavior which you consider "abnormal" or "indecent," it was the abuser, not you, who committed the crime. Your fantasies had nothing to do with it. The abuse of your child is not a "punishment" for any of your behavior either. Don't punish yourself because your child has been hurt. The abuser caused this pain, not you.

Some parents punish themselves because they feel guilty about resenting the emotional and financial strains imposed upon them by their child's abuse and any subsequent legal action and mental health expenses. Feeling resentment is normal. This crisis has exacted a terrible toll on all aspects of your life. It has reduced the time and energy you have to devote to your marriage, love life, children, and other relationships, not to mention your career and personal goals. It's only natural to resent the many financial and emotional impositions created by your child's situation and extraordinary needs.

Holding on to the impossible ideal that parents should always be full of unselfish love toward their children and should always be willing to sacrifice their all for their offspring will only make matters worse. Rather than berating yourself for being a normal human being, spend your time and energy figuring out how you can take better care of yourself and how you can minimize the stresses in your life. Try not to vent your anger and resentment on your child or other family members. Remember that your anger and resentment should be directed toward the perpetrator and exercised against the relative lack of social and other support services for abused children.

Taking Care of Yourself

It's always important to take care of your physical health, but it becomes even more critical in times of stress. So often in the flurry of activity and anxiety, the basics of good nutrition, proper rest, and exercise are overlooked. You may feel that you don't have time to eat right, get enough sleep, or take time out to exercise—you may even feel that *not* taking time for your personal well-being is a way of showing your devotion to your child. This is wrong. If you take care of yourself physically, you will ultimately save time, because you will be functioning more effectively and efficiently; and no one else will wind up having to take care of *you.*

Sometimes parents deprive themselves of physical care because they are subconsciously punishing themselves for what happened to their children. Or they feel that by hurting their bodies, or by making other sacrifices, they can somehow "buy" their child's recovery. This can be part of the bargaining stage of the grieving process, where parents make "bargains" with God or with life (see Chapter 2). But such sacrifices are fruitless. Not only will they not further your child's recovery from the trauma, they will provide your child with a poor adult role model for self-care.

So often child sexual abuse survivors punish their bodies because their bodies were involved in the assault. In therapy, they learn to value and take care of their bodies once again. You can help the therapist restore your child's appreciation and respect for his body by respecting and appreciating your own physical needs.

It has been found that psychological stress often undermines the body's immune system and that the individual undergoing psychic stress gets sick more often and develops benign tumors more often than the unstressed person. Consequently, it's necessary that you not only maintain your previous efforts at self-care, but increase them. This may involve improving your nutrition, taking vitamin supplements, participating in a regular exercise program, and setting limits on activities and work commitments so that you get enough rest.

Perhaps you are overdue for a checkup or an X-ray. Or perhaps your teeth need attention. It's surprising how often mothers keep postponing appointments with their gynecologists for pap smears, mammograms, or other necessary preventive medical work in the name of taking care of their families—especially when their children are in pain. Yet what better gift can a parent give a child than a healthy parent?

Emotional Health

Emotional health involves recognizing your emotions and considering them when you make decisions. Although you may not choose to allow your emotions to dominate you, they do exist—and they count. For example, sometimes it's important to take into account the irrational reasons for making a particular decision, as well as the rational ones.

One mother found it necessary to take time off from work to take her daughter, who had just been released from a hospital program, on a short vacation. The decision was financially impractical, but emotionally necessary. Similarly, other parents have found it necessary to spend more time pursuing favorite hobbies, praying, or spending more time with their families and friends than may have seemed "practical." Yet these involvements served an important emotional need during their time of stress.

Emotional health requires a balance between work and play, between meeting your responsibilities and allowing yourself time to do nothing. You can get into as much emotional trouble by neglecting your need for recreation as you can by neglecting to pay your bills.

As a parent under stress, you need to figure out what activities and involvements promote your emotional well-being and to make time for these things in your schedule. The benefits can be enormous.

Stress Management

Many twelve-step meetings begin or close with the serenity prayer. "God, grant me the serenity to accept the things I cannot change, the courage to change the things I can, and the wisdom to know the difference." You cannot change the fact that your child was abused and you cannot change the stressors that fact places on your life. You *can* examine your life and find ways to reduce other stressors.

Because you're dealing with the burdens associated with your child's recovery, you may need to eliminate excess obligations or projects, or to work on them at a slower pace. Don't impose deadlines or burdens upon yourself that are not absolutely necessary.

Jeb's mother gave up preparing elaborate dinners so that she could spend more time with Jeb and catch a short nap when she needed one. She also turned down invitations to volunteer time for charities and (temporarily) reduced her participation in a social club she had been attending.

She could not, however, give up her painting. Yet she did decide not to push herself to produce so many oils a month. The stress of coping with Jeb's pain, her husband's emotional turmoil, and her own emotions was enough. She was kind enough to herself not to pressure herself further by taking on nonessential burdens.

Some of the stress we experience we create ourselves. Bad enough that we're under the real stress of external pressures and demands; but sometimes we create another real stress—the stress of having a critic living inside our heads. This critic, who almost always judges us as lacking or incompetent, berates us for the smallest failing and hardly ever praises us for a job well done or for giving a problem our best effort. This critic sets impossibly high standards, which no human being could fully meet. This critic does not encourage us to take risks, grow, or be gentle with ourselves. Instead, it demoralizes us and hinders us as we try to achieve our goals.

This critic needs to be dethroned, immediately, and replaced with the voice of a compassionate, nurturing parent. Cognitive therapists have long felt that, outside of trauma situations, our moods and emotions are determined not only by external circumstances, but by what we are telling ourselves about ourselves. If you constantly tell yourself that you will fail or that you will—in one way or another—be inadequate to deal with a certain situation, then you will feel depressed and hopeless and be less able to handle the situation. You will also be unable to applaud yourself for partial gains or successes. Complete success or nothing! Yet often a partial gain is an extraordinary accomplishment and should be seen as such.

In cognitive therapy sessions, clients learn to congratulate and reinforce themselves for small victories, as well as large ones, and for every constructive step they have taken toward solving a problem. You can learn to congratulate yourself silently, within your own mind, by replacing that critical voice inside your head with positive self-talk.

When faced with a difficult situation, don't tell yourself "There's no way I can handle this. I've never been successful with such a problem in the past, so I might as well give up right now." Tell yourself instead, "Just because I was not successful in coping with a particular problem in the past does not mean that I can't do it now.

After all, I've grown since I tried it last time and have conquered other problems; I'll have a try at this one."

Allow yourself to feel overwhelmed, frightened, or hopeless, but also tell yourself that feelings aren't facts. "Even though I'm scared, I can take positive action toward resolving the problem. I can make a plan and act responsibly even though my feelings may be out of control."

The first thing to do is to take a piece of paper and list the steps that need to be taken to handle the stressful event. Ask yourself, "What do I need to do first, second, third?" After you complete each step, congratulate yourself. "If I've managed to do this, I can manage to go on to the next right thing, no matter how I feel."

Instead of saying, "I'll never make it. I'll never complete everything I need to do," say "See, I'm making progress. At least I'm willing to look at the problem rather than run from it. I've already taken the first step. Now I can take the second step. If I keep breaking the problem down into small, manageable steps, I can succeed. Just taking the next step is success. I need to keep focusing on what I need to do, rather than on my fear, anxiety, or sense of doom.

"Despite my feelings, I will act as if I'm going to succeed. I will fake it until I make it."

If you hit a hard spot, it may be time to rethink your plan or ask for help. If you do ask for help, don't say to yourself, "You're a weakling!"

Instead, tell yourself, "Congratulations! You know your limits and have sense enough to ask for help instead of trying to figure out everything for yourself. Congratulations on asking for help. This is progress!"

During this stressful period of your life, do not interpret being in emotional pain or turmoil as a sign of failure. Hurting and being confused or conflicted are unavoidable aspects of the human experience. Nobody has it "all together" all the time. If they did, they would never grow or change. They would be stagnant models of emotional control, rigid, closed to new experiences and internal revelations. You need to give yourself a pat on the back for having the courage to face your pain, fears, and ambivalence rather than denying them and leading an emotionally shallow existence.

When you become stressed or depressed, your thinking may become distorted and negative. In *Feeling Good: The New Mood Therapy*, David Burns, a cognitive therapist and an expert on depression, outlines the various forms of distorted thinking that cripple those who are depressed or stressed. Reading this book may help you increase your ability to talk positively to yourself and counter your child's negative thinking with more positive, self-enhancing ways of looking at himself and the world. *Self-Esteem*, by Matthew McKay and Patrick Fanning, is also an excellent resource.

This may be a good time to think about taking a stress management seminar. "I don't have time," you may protest. But you will save time in headaches, inefficiencies, and misery by learning a few practical tips on how to make your life a little more manageable. Often the following five techniques are taught:

1. Relaxation

You can learn relaxation techniques from a therapist or from audio tapes which instruct you on how to contract and relax various muscles so that you can learn how to achieve a state of relaxation. You'll need to practice your relaxation several times a day so that your muscles become accustomed to responding to your command to "relax" or "contract." Eventually you will learn to relax very quickly, almost automatically.

Typically in a stress management seminar you'll be instructed to practice relaxation during routine chores or nonstressful situations first, then during stressful times. See Chapter 6 for specific relaxation exercises and suggestions.

2. Breath Control

Deep breathing exercises usually accompany relaxation techniques. You can learn to use deep breathing along with muscle relaxation when encountering stressful situations. Learning to control your breathing can give you a sense of power over your physical body which you can translate to a sense of power over your circumstances (see Chapter 6 for more detail).

3. Role Playing

Therapy is usually the setting in which stressful situations are role-played. First you will be asked to assume different roles. This will help you "see the other side"; and then you can make decisions based on your increased knowledge. The therapist will encourage you to use your relaxation techniques during this process and will discuss with you alternative ways of handling stressful situations.

4. Visualization

After you're relaxed, close your eyes and visualize yourself being successful in a situation that used to make you feel anxiety and fear.

Picture yourself overcoming your anxiety and triumphing. Practice this exercise at times during the day or night when you're relaxed—before falling asleep, on waking, in the bathtub, and so on. *The Anxiety and Phobia Workbook*, by Edmund J. Bourne, gives detailed step-by-step instructions for such exercises (see especially the chapters on relaxation and visualization).

5. Thought Stoppage

You can learn to interrupt the barrage of fearful or otherwise negative thoughts that flood your mind by substituting positive thoughts. For example, if you hear your inner critic tell you that your child will never heal, tell that voice to shut up and then replace it with a positive affirmation. You can say, "One day at a time, we're both learning to heal," or "I am good and brave for facing this crisis with my child. Healing will come." Write your favorite affirmations on a 3 x 5 card and read them out loud whenever unwanted negative thoughts come into your head.

Think positively. If it's raining and you were planning to run seventeen errands, think about that beautiful sequence in *Singing in the Rain*, or try to picture the lovely spring flowers that will result from the day's weather. Some people have found it comforting to concentrate on the strength they feel building in themselves each time they meet an obstacle and get through it. Just surviving can be positive if you reflect on how easy it would have been to give in and let the hardships overcome you. By surviving you are teaching your child—through your example—that he too can overcome the hardships that he has endured.

Your Feelings Matter

Handling your feelings is just as important a part of the healing process as finding a therapist for your child, helping him through his suicidal thoughts, and anything else you may have had to face. You are important, too. You are the rock your child will cling to as he goes through the long, painful process of recovering from sexual abuse. There is nothing more crucial to his eventual good health than a healthy parent.

Do what you need to in order to heal yourself. It's the single most important element in your child's healing. And you can do it. Ask for help; read books; pray; do whatever you must to get through this. No one knows the future—but it's certain that as you survive this overwhelming crisis in your life, you are becoming a stronger person—better able to face the future and whatever it holds for you.

The chances are great that this will be the worst time of your life. When you look back, you will marvel that you found the strength to endure, to grow, and to help your child do the same.

Further Reading

Bourne, Edmund J. *The Anxiety and Phobia Workbook*. Oakland, CA: New Harbinger Publications, Inc., 1990.

Burns, David D. *Feeling Good: The New Mood Therapy*. New York: Signet Books, New American Collection, 1980.

McKay, Matthew, and Patrick Fanning. *Self-Esteem*. Oakland, CA: New Harbinger Publications, Inc., 1987.

Appendix

Resources for Sexual Abuse Survivors and Their Families

Organizations

Adults Molested as Children United. P.O. Box 952, San Jose, CA 95108 (408) 280-5055. This organization is part of Parents United, a national support group for incestuous families. This organization focuses on "guided self-help" families.

C. Henry Kempe National Center for the Prevention and Treatment of Child Abuse and Neglect. 1205 Oneida Street, Denver, CO 80220 (303) 321-3963.

Forensic Mental Health Associates. A. Nicholas Groth, Ph.D., Director, RR #1, Box 404, Lakeside Beach, Webster, MA 01570 (617) 943-2381. Information and professional training regarding abuse.

Harborview Sexual Assault Center. 325 9th Avenue, Seattle, WA 98104 (206) 223-3047.

Incest Recovery Association. 6200 North Central Expressway, Suite 209, Dallas, TX 75206 (214) 373-6607. Offers a newsletter and brochure, helps train professionals, and provides groups for male and female survivors.

Incest Resources. Incest Survivors, Women's Center, 46 Pleasant Street, Cambridge, MA 02139. Individual and group therapy for incest survivors and family members, educational materials, national networking, and legislative advocacy.

Incest Survivors Anonymous. P.O. Box 5613, Long Beach, CA 90805-0613. A self-help group for incest survivors based on the twelve-step program model of Alcoholics Anonymous and Narcotics Anonymous.

Looking Up. P.O. Box K, Augusta, ME 04330 (207) 626-3402. This organization has a newsletter and provides a variety of public education and political lobbying activities for survivors who are not also offenders. There are also workshops, conferences, wilderness trips, and other forms of experience for survivors.

Mothers Against Abuse. Richmond Mental Health Center, 501 North 9th Street, Richmond, VA 23219.

National Coalition Against Sexual Abuse (NCASA). 8787 State Street, East St. Louis, IL 62203 (618) 618-7764. This organization consists of professionals who provide services to victims of many forms of violence, including sexual abuse.

National Self-Help Clearinghouse, Graduate School, City University of New York, 33 West 42nd Street, Room 1221, New York, NY 11036 (212) 840-1259. Has listings of self-help groups throughout the nation.

Parents Anonymous. 6733 South Sepulveda Boulevard #270, Los Angeles, CA 90045 (213) 4199-9732. National hotline and services for abusive parents or parents who fear they may become abusive.

Parents United. P.O. Box 952, San Jose, CA 95108 (408) 280-5055. A self-help group for incestuous families. The chapters vary greatly in terms of leadership as well as orientation. Some are led by professionals; others are run more on a self-help model. Some stress family reconciliation and forgiveness; others are more tolerant of anger and more confrontational towards the abuser.

P.L.E.A. (Prevention, Leadership, Education, Assistance). Box 59045, Norwalk, CA 90652 (213) 863-4824. An organization of professionals and non-professionals oriented towards male incest survivors. Publishes a quarterly newsletter written by survivors.

The Safer Society Program. Shoreham Depot Road, RR #1, Box 24-B, Orwell, VT 05760 (802) 897-7541. This society provides a national list of agencies, hospitals, clinics, and other organizations which provide assessments and treatment specifically oriented towards sex abuse survivors and offenders.

S.C.A.P. (Survivors of Childhood Abuse Program). 1345 El Centro Avenue, P.O. Box 630, Hollywood, CA 90028. Research, treatment, training, consultation, public education, development of a national network of professional and technical resources and advocacy on behalf of incest survivors and others from unhappy families. They have a National Child Abuse Hotline (1-800-422-4453) which provides crisis intervention, information, and referrals.

Speaking For Our Selves (S4OS) P.O. Box 4830, Long Beach, CA 90804 (213) 438-7467. An organization geared toward individuals with multiple personalities.

Victims Anonymous. 9514-9 Reseda Boulevard, Suite 607, Northridge, CA 91324.

V.O.I.C.E.S in Action, Inc. P.O. Box 148309, Chicago, Il 60614 (312) 327-1500. Victims Of Incest Can Emerge Survivors: national network of male and female survivors; local groups and contacts throughout the U.S. which have free referrals to therapists, agencies, and self-help groups that are endorsed by other survivors. There is also a listing of over one hundred confidential special interest groups where survivors who have survived particular types of abuse can write to each other. They also have a newsletter, an annual meeting, and training for group leaders.

Newsletters

For Crying Out Loud, c/o Cambridge Women's Center, 46 Pleasant Street, Cambridge, MA 02139. Although this newsletter is written by and for women with histories of sexual abuse, the information that it contains is relevant and helpful for male survivors.

Incest Survivors Information Exchange (ISIE). P.O. Box 3399, New Haven, CT 06515. This newsletter provides a forum for female and male survivors of incest to share their thoughts, ideas, information, poetry, writings, and art work. Published by female survivors.

Parents United Newsletter, P.O. Box 952, San Jose, CA 95108 (408) 280-5055.

Survivors Network Newsletter, c/o Crawford, 18653 Ventura Boulevard #143, Tarzana, CA 91356. Information, resource location, and education for adult survivors of childhood abuse and neglect.

The "Looking Up" Times, RFD #1 Box 2620, Mt. Vernon, ME 04352 (207) 293-2750. A newsletter for survivors of sexual abuse.

The Newsletter. Published by VOICES in Action, this newsletter for adult male and female incest survivors is provided as part of the annual $35.00 membership fee. The Newsletter provides information, resources, book reviews, and writings by and for survivors. It is expanding to include more attention to issues of male survivors. (See VOICES listing for address.)

Backnotes

Chapter I

1. National Center on Child Abuse and Neglect (NCCAN).

2. Ibid.

3. Finkelhor, David, *Child Sexual Abuse: New Theory and Research,* Free Press, Collier MacMillan Publishers, 1984.

4. Courtois, Christine, *Healing the Incest Wound: Adult Survivors in Therapy,* New York: W.W. Norton, 1988.

5. NCCAN, Executive Summary: Study of National Incidence and Prevalence of Child Abuse and Neglect, 1988; Finkelhor, David, "How Widespread Is Child Sexual Abuse?" Perspectives on Child Maltreatment in the Mid 80's, Human Development Services, U.S. Dept. of Health and Human Services (DHHS), National Center on Child Abuse and Neglect, DHHS Publication No. (DHDS) 84-3-3338, pp. 18-20; Deisher, Robert W., and Bidwell, Robert J., "Sexual Abuse of Male Adolescents," Seminars in Adolescent Medicine, March 1987, 3(1/47-54); Archer, Shirley, "Research Issues in Child Sexual Abuse." Paper presented at the Association for Women in Psychology, National Conference, Bethesda, MD March 5-7, 1988; Johnson, Robert, and Shirier, Diane, "Sexual Victimization of Boys," *Journal of Adolescent Health Care,* 1985, 6: 372-376); Herman, Judith, *Father-Daughter Incest,* Cambridge, MA: Harvard University Press, 1981, p. 14.

6. Finkelhor, *op. cit.;* Courtois, *op. cit.;* Rubinelli, Jackie, "Incest: It's Time We Face Reality," JPN and Mental Health Services, April 1980, pp. 17-18.

7. NCCAN, Executive Summary, p. 1.

8. Forward, Susan, *Betrayal of Innocence: Incest and Its Devastation,* Los Angeles: Tarcher, 1978, pp. 1-2.

9. Finkelhor, 1984, *op. cit.*

10. Herman, 1981, *op. cit.;* Courtois, *op. cit.*

11. Courtois, *op. cit.,* p. 5.

12. van der Kolk, Bessel, "The Drug Treatment of PTSD," *Journal of Affective Disorders,* 13, 1987, pp. 203-213. *Idem; "The Trauma Spectrum: The Interaction of Biological and Social Events in the Genesis of the*

Trauma Response," *Journal of Traumatic Stress,* Vol. 1:3, 1988, pp. 273-290; Rossi, Ernest Lawrence, "The Psychobiology of Mind-Body Healing: New Concepts of Therapeutic Hypnosis," New York: W.W. Norton, 1986; Giller, Earl, Ph.D., editor, *Biological Assessment and Treatment of PTSD,* Washington, DC: American Psychiatric Press, 1990.

13. Lew, Mike, *Victims No Longer: Men Recovering from Incest and Other Sexual Abuse,* New York: Nevraumont Publishing Co., 1988.

14. Finkelhor, 1984, *op. cit.*

15. Courtois, *op. cit.,* p. 17.

16. Justice, Blair and Justice, Rita, *The Broken Taboo: Sex in the Family,* New York: Human Sciences Press, 1979, pp. 19-20.

17. Klajner-Diamond, Halena; Wehrspann, William; Steinhauer, Paul, "Assessing the Credibility of Young Children's Allegations of Sexual Abuse: Clinical Issues," *Canadian Journal of Psychiatry,* Vol. 32, Oct. 1987, pp. 610-614.

18. Klajner-Diamond, H. *et al., op. cit.,* p. 612.

19. *Ibid.*

20. *Ibid.,* p. 613.

21. NCCAN, *op. cit.*

22. Lowery, Mathe, "Adult Survivors of Childhood Incest," *Journal of Psychosocial Nursing,* Vol. 25:1, 1987, pp. 27-31; Browne, Angela and Finkelhor, David, "Impact of Child Sexual Abuse: A Review of the Research," *Psychological Bulletin,* Vol. 99:1, 1986, pp. 66-77; Herman, Judith; Russell, Diane; Trocki, Karen, "Long Term Effects of Incestuous Abuse in Childhood," *American Journal of Psychiatry,* 143:10; October 1986, pp. 1293-1296; Gorcey, M.; Santiago, J.; McCall-Perez, "Psychological Consequences for Women Sexually Abused in Childhood," *Social Psychiatry,* 1986, 21:129-133; Conte, J.R. and Schuerman, J.R., "Factors Associated with an Increased Impact of Child Sexual Assault," *Child Abuse and Neglect,* Vol. 11, 1987, pp. 201-211.

23. Browne and Finkelhor, *op. cit.*

24. Klajner-Diamond, Halena; Wehrspann, William; Steinhauer, Paul, "Criteria and Methodology for Assessing Credibility of Sexual Abuse Allegation," *Canadian Journal of Psychiatry,* Vol. 32:7, 1987, p. 616.

25. Courtois, *op. cit.,* Finkelhor, *op. cit.*

26. Courtois, *op. cit.*

27. *Ibid.,* p. 94.

28. Browne and Finkelhor, *op. cit.;* Courtois, *op. cit.;* Gorcey, M. et. al., *op. cit.;* Lowery, *op. cit.*

29. Fisher, Kathleen, "Sexual Abuse Survivors Suffer into Adulthood," *APA Monitor,* Vol. 18:6, June 1987, p. 26.

30. Browne and Finkelhor, *op. cit.;* Courtois, *op. cit.;* Gorcey, M. *et al., op. cit.;* Lowery, *op. cit.*

31. *Ibid.*

32. Summit, Roland, "The Child Abuse Accommodation Syndrome," *Child Abuse and Neglect,* 7, 1983, pp. 177-193.

33. *Ibid.*

34. Finkelhor, D.; and Brown, Angela, "The Traumatic Impact of Child Sexual Abuse: A Conceptualization," *American Journal of Orthopsychiatry,* 55:4, October 1985, pp. 530-541.

35. Courtois, *op. cit.;* Lindberg, Frederick; and Distad, Lois, "PTSD in Women Who Experienced Childhood Incest," *Child Abuse and Neglect,* Vol. 9, 1985, pp. 329-334; Gorcey *et al., op. cit.;* Herman *et al., op. cit.;* Goodwin, Jean, "PTSD in Incest Victims," in *PTSD in Children,* edited by Eth S. Pynoos, RS, Washington, DC: American Psychiatric Press, 1985.

36. Matsakis, Aphrodite, *Vietnam Wives: Women and Children Survivors: Life with Veterans with Post-Traumatic Stress Disorder,* Kensington, MD: Woodbine House, 1988.

37. Haley, Sarah, "I Feel a Little Sad: The Application of Object Relations Theory to the Hypnotherapy of Post-Traumatic Stress Disorders in Vietnam Veterans," San Antonio, TX: Society for Clinical and Experimental Hypnosis, Oct. 25, 1984.

38. Freud, Anna, as cited in "Sexual Abuse in Vulnerable and High Risk Children: a Summarized Report," Theodore B. Cohen.

39. Herman, 1981, *op. cit.,* p. 22.

40. *Ibid.,* p. 28.

41. *Ibid.;* Forward, S., *op. cit.*

42. Courtois, *op. cit.;* Finkelhor, David, *op. cit.;* Leidig, Marjorie, "Retrospective Incest Therapy," Unpublished paper, Oct. 1979, available from M. Leidig, 885 Arapahoe Avenue, Boulder, CO 80303.

43. Lew, *op. cit.*

44. Herman, 1981, *op. cit.,* pp. 14, 30.

Chapter II

1. Folkenberg, Judy, "Writing and Art Help Heal Post-Traumatic Stress Disorder," *Anxiety Disorders Association of America Reporter,* Vol. 1:2. July-August 1990, p. 1-2.

2. American Psychiatric Association, *Diagnostic and Statistical Manual of Mental Disorders,* Third Edition, Revised, Washington, DC: American Psychiatric Association, 1987, p. 222.

3. Leidig, Marjorie; "Retrospective Incest Therapy," unpublished paper, October 1979, available from M. Leidig, 885 Arapahoe Avenue, Boulder, CO 80303.

4. *Ibid.,* p. 7.

Chapter III

1. American Psychological Association (APA) Task Force on the Victims of Crime and Violence, Washington, DC: APA, November 30, 1984.

2. Holland, Kathryne Quinna, "Long Term Psychological Consequences of Sexual Assault," unpublished paper, University of Rhode Island, pp. 5-6.

Chapter IV

1. Cavallin, Barbara, in "Treatment of Sexually Abused Adolescents: View of a Psychologist," *Seminar in Adolescent Medicine,* vol. 3:1, March, 1987, p. 41.

Chapter V

1. Caplan, Paula J., Hall-McCorquodale, Ian B., "Mother Blaming in Major Clinical Journals," American Journal of Orthopsychiatry 55: 3, July 1985, pp. 345-353.

2. Courtois, Christine A., *Healing the Incest Wound; Adult Survivors in Therapy,* New York: W.W. Norton & Company, 1988.

Chapter VI

1. Faber, Adele; and Mazlish, Elaine, *How To Talk So Kids Will Listen, and Listen So Kids Will Talk,* New York: Avon Books, 1980.

2. van der Kolk, Bessel, "The Drug-Treatment of PTSD," *Journal of Affective Disorders* 13, 1987, pp. 203-213.

3. Munjac, Dennis J., "Medications in the Treatment of Panic Disorder and Panic Disorder with Agoraphobia: A Consumer's Guide to

Medications," Rockville, MD: Phobia Society of America, 1988; van der Kolk, *op cit.*

4. These relaxation exercises were adapted from theories and practice of Joseph Wolpe as presented in Wolpe, Joseph, *The Practice of Behavior Therapy*, New York: Pergamon Press, 1969; Wolpe, Joseph and Lazarus, A., *Behavior Therapy Techniques*, New York: Pergamon Press, 1966; and Wolpe, Joseph; Reyna, L.; and Salter, A. *The Conditioning Therapies: The Challenge in Psychotherapy.* New York: Pergamon Press, 1964.

5. American Psychiatric Association: *Diagnostic and Statistical Manual of Mental Disorders,* Third Edition, Revised, Washington, DC: American Psychiatric Association, 1987, pp. 241-245.

6. *Ibid.*

7. *Ibid.,* p. 238.

8. Self, Martin, "A Clinician Addresses Concerns about Panic, Suicide," p. 5, and Folkenburg, Judy, "Interview Myrna Weissman," pp. 3-4, in *Anxiety Disorders Association of America Reporter.* Anxiety Disorders Association of America, Vol. 1:1, April-May 1990.

9. "Models of Treatment," Seminar with Williams, L.; Peurifoy, R.; and Kuczmiercyk, 10th National Conference on Phobias and Related Anxiety Disorders, Washington, DC: 1990.

10. Munjac, *op. cit.;* van der Kolk, *op. cit.;* Williams *et. al, op. cit.*

11. *Ibid.*

12. "Prozac: A Breakthrough Drug for Depression," *Newsweek,* March 26, 1990, pp. 39-41.

Chapter VII

1. Matsakis, Aphrodite, "Suicide," in *Vietnam Wives: Women and Children Survivors: Life with Veterans with Post-Traumatic Stress Disorder,* Kensington, MD: Woodbine House, 1988.

2. Berman, Alan, "Suicide," Staff Development Seminar, Counseling Center, University of Maryland, College Park, MD, April 17, 1987.

3. Berman, *op. cit.;* Burns, David D., *Feeling Good: The New Mood Therapy,* New York: Signet Books, 1980; Reynolds, David; and Farberow, Norman, *Suicide Inside and Out,* Berkeley, CA: University of California Press, 1976; Victoroff, Victor M., *The Suicidal Patient: Recognition, Intervention Management,* Oradell, NJ: Medical Economics Books, 1983.

4. Victoroff, *op. cit.,* p. 12.

258   When the Bough Breaks

5. Berman, *op. cit.*; Burns, *op. cit*; Matsakis, *op. cit.*; Reynolds and Faberow, *op. cit.*; and Victoroff, *op. cit.*

6. Ibid.

7. *Ibid.*

Chapter VII

1. Karuna   t Ap-
   plicatio   man,
   Gerald.   eren-
   ces, Tr   4:3,
   Fall 19

2. *Ibid.*